The Castle
in the Wars
of the Roses

The Castle
in the Wars
of the Roses

Dan Spencer

Pen & Sword
MILITARY

AN IMPRINT OF PEN & SWORD BOOKS LTD
YORKSHIRE – PHILADELPHIA

First published in Great Britain in 2020 by
PEN & SWORD MILITARY
An imprint of Pen & Sword Books Ltd
Yorkshire – Philadelphia

ISBN 978-1-52671-869-3

Typeset by Concept, Huddersfield, West Yorkshire, HD4 5JL
Printed and bound in England by TJ Books Limited, Padstow, Cornwall

MIX
Paper from
responsible sources
FSC® C013056

Pen & Sword Books Ltd incorporates the Imprints of Aviation, Atlas, Family
History, Fiction, Maritime, Military, Discovery, Politics, History, Archaeology,
Select, Wharncliffe Local History, Wharncliffe True Crime, Military Classics,
Wharncliffe Transport, Leo Cooper, The Praetorian Press, Remember When,
White Owl, Seaforth Publishing and Frontline Publishing.

For a complete list of Pen & Sword titles please contact
PEN & SWORD BOOKS LTD
47 Church Street, Barnsley, South Yorkshire, S70 2AS, England
E-mail: enquiries@pen-and-sword.co.uk
Website: www.pen-and-sword.co.uk
or
PEN & SWORD BOOKS
1950 Lawrence Rd, Havertown, PA 19083, USA
E-mail: uspen-and-sword@casematepublishers.com
Website: www.penandswordbooks.com

In memory of my grandmother,
Sonja Spencer (1921–2019),
who I called Nan

Contents

List of Plans

List of Plates

Acknowledgements

In 2016, I delivered a paper at the Fifteenth Century Conference, held at Royal Holloway, University of London, on the role of castles in the Wars of the Roses. Rupert Harding from Pen & Sword subsequently contacted me to see whether I would be willing to write a book on the subject. I accepted his proposal, which led to the creation of the present work. This book therefore owes its existence to him. I am also grateful to my fiancée, Hannah Baldwin, and to my mother, Elizabeth Spencer, for reading draft chapters and offering invaluable feedback and suggestions. My thanks to Cadw and the British Library for allowing me to use images from their collections. I also wish to express my gratitude to Anthony Burton, James Wright and Scott Hall for their assistance with the illustrations, and to Alison Flowers for editing the manuscript. This book is dedicated to the memory of my grandmother, Sonja Spencer, who passed away in 2019. She was a very special person who had a remarkable talent for storytelling, as well as a fondness for bingo and Baileys.

Notes on the Text

Prior to decimalisation in 1971, there were 240*d.* (pennies) to £1, as opposed to 100p (pence), and 12*d.* were equivalent to 1*s.* (shilling), with 20*s.* equalling £1. The standard format for denoting these units of money is as follows: £1 1*s.* 1*d.* It is difficult to compare modern and medieval prices, but, for example, a skilled worker, such as a carpenter, would typically be paid 6*d.* per day in the fifteenth century.

The English peerage by the second half of the fifteenth century consisted of five ranks of nobility, which in order of precedence consisted of: barons, viscounts, earls, marquesses and dukes.

Since the Middle Ages, there have been changes to the historic counties of England and Wales. Some of them no longer exist, whereas the boundaries of others have been altered. The names of the counties used in this book correspond to contemporary usage, where possible, in the mid-fifteenth century, including the appendices. For instance, the historic counties of Cumberland and Westmorland are used, as opposed to their modern replacement, Cumbria. However, in some cases modern spellings have been used to avoid confusion, such as Caernarfonshire, instead of the old spelling of Caernarvonshire.

Quotations from documents written in Middle English have been converted into modern English for the sake of clarity. The original text can be found in the end notes section of the book.

Maps

Royal Castles in England and Wales
c.1460

Berwick-upon-Tweed
Bamburgh
Dunstanburgh
Newcastle-on-Tyne

Carlisle

Scarborough

Lancaster

Knaresborough
York
Pontefract

Beaumaris
Conwy
Caernarfon
Harlech
Chester

Lincoln

Aberystwyth
Shrewsbury
Nottingham

Norwich

Leicester
Kenilworth
Carmarthen
Worcester
Kidwelly
Monmouth
Northampton
Gloucester
Bristol
Berkhamstead
Oxford
Wallingford
Queenborough
Canterbury
Southampton
Exeter
Launceton
Portchester
Dover
Carisbrooke

Drawn by Hannah Baldwin, based on a map by Anthony Burton, © Dan Spencer.

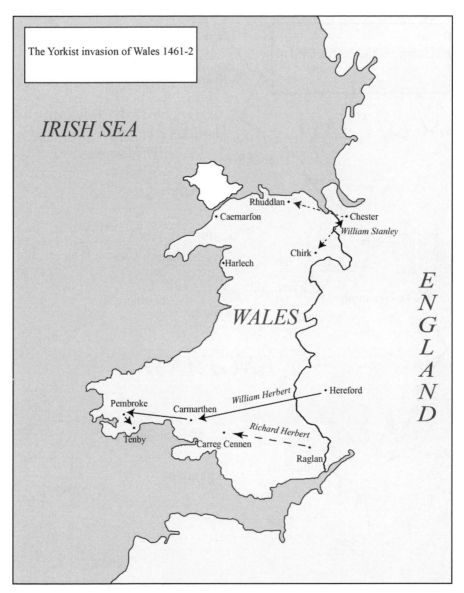

The Yorkist invasion of Wales 1461-2

IRISH SEA

Rhuddlan
• Caernarfon
Chester •
William Stanley
Chirk •
•Harlech

WALES

ENGLAND

William Herbert
Hereford •
Pembroke
Carmarthen
Richard Herbert
Tenby
Carreg Cennen
Raglan

Drawn by Hannah Baldwin, based on a map by Anthony Burton, © Dan Spencer.

The War in the North 1461-4

SCOTLAND

ENGLAND

Berwick Upon Tweed

Norham

Bamburgh

Dunstanburgh

Alnwick

Warkworth

Harbottle

Bothal

Tynemouth

Hexham

Newcastle Upon Tyne

Carlisle

Durham

Kirkoswald

Cockermouth

Penrith

Brancepeth

Middleham

Lancaster

Skipton

York

Sandal

Drawn by Hannah Baldwin, based on a map by Anthony Burton, © Dan Spencer.

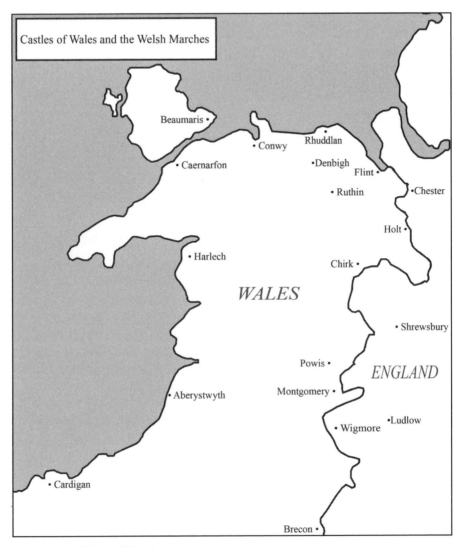

Castles of Wales and the Welsh Marches

Beaumaris •

• Conwy

Rhuddlan •

•Denbigh

Flint •

• Caernarfon

• Ruthin

•Chester

Holt •

• Harlech

Chirk •

WALES

• Shrewsbury

Powis •

ENGLAND

Montgomery •

• Aberystwyth

•Ludlow

• Wigmore

• Cardigan

Brecon •

Drawn by Hannah Baldwin, © Dan Spencer.

Introduction

Richard Neville, earl of Warwick, arrived outside of Bamburgh Castle in Northumberland on 25 June 1464. As he surveyed the castle from afar, he no doubt admired its impressive appearance. Situated dramatically on an outcrop of volcanic rock by the sea, its imposing masonry defences towered over the surrounding area. Warwick came as the king's lieutenant in the north of England, with full authority to act in the name of Edward IV. Yet he met with a hostile response from the occupants of the castle. The gates were firmly barred against his entry and the walls were manned by soldiers. However, Warwick was not alone. At his back was a large army thousands of men strong, made up of heavily armoured men-at-arms encased in suits of plate armour, footmen armed with long vicious-looking hooked polearms called bills and archers wielding the mighty longbow. Recently victorious in battle, these Yorkist soldiers were prepared to deliver the final blow against their Lancastrian enemies, who had taken refuge behind its walls. To breach their defences, they had brought with them a formidable siege train of gunpowder artillery. Guns of all sizes had been carefully moved into position around the perimeter of the fortress ready to pound the fortifications into ruin.

Nevertheless, the conventions of war were observed. Two heralds bearing offers of pardon were sent to demand the surrender of the garrison. Their entreaties were rebuffed by the castellan, Sir Ralph Grey, who resolved 'to live or die' within the castle. Warwick responded by ordering his gunners to open fire on the fortress. A furious bombardment was unleashed, with the stone projectiles fired from the guns smashing into the fortifications and causing fragments of masonry to fly into the sea below. Under cover of this withering firepower, the besiegers launched a full-scale assault. The Yorkist soldiers clambered up the slope towards the castle, and finding gaps in the defences they overwhelmed the beleaguered defenders and took the castle by assault. Grey was taken alive, albeit badly wounded, and brought before the king at Doncaster, some 150 miles to the south, where he was put on trial for treason. Found guilty by the constable of England, John Tiptoft, earl of Worcester, he was ritually degraded and humiliated with his spurs cut off and his coat of arms reversed. Yet, the king was merciful in sparing him the full horrors of a traitor's death. Instead of suffering the grim fate of being hanged, drawn and quartered, he met his end by having his head chopped off with an axe by an executioner before a crowd at the town's scaffold.[1]

*   *   *

The fall of Bamburgh marked the end of a four-year-long struggle for control of Northumberland. This was part of a wider dynastic conflict between the Yorkist and Lancastrian factions for control of the kingdom of England. For much of the second half of the fifteenth century these two rival houses fought a series of wars to win the English throne, which since the nineteenth century has been commonly called the Wars of the Roses. This era is without a doubt one of the most popular topics in medieval English history. Numerous books, articles, plays and films have been produced over the centuries. Looking at all sorts of aspects ranging from the dynamic personalities of key figures, such as Richard III, the causes of the conflict, its long-term legacy and the military campaigns, particularly the major battles. Given this vast output on the subject, it may be pertinent to ask why it is necessary for yet another book to be written. The answer is that one important area has been almost wholly neglected: the role of the castle in the Wars of the Roses.[2]

Why has this been the case? One explanation is the perception that the campaigns of the Wars of the Roses were dominated by decisive battles, in which castles played a very minor role. This argument does have some substance. The era was unusual for the frequency with which significant battles took place. Nevertheless, this does not tell the whole story. As we will see, there were many campaigns in which castles were used in a significant way. Similarly, the late Middle Ages has been characterised as a period in which castles were in a state of transition and decline, in which their traditional role as fortresses was increasingly no longer necessary due to changes in warfare and society. Instead, castles primarily became residences and status symbols, with their design reflecting architectural tastes as opposed to military considerations. This assessment has some validity, as changes did gradually take place over time, which eventually culminated in a separation of the military and residential roles that were formerly combined together in castles. The latter being replaced by forts and the former by country houses in the Early Modern period. Yet, this view is only partly relevant in the context of the Wars of the Roses.

Castles continued to be used in warfare into the sixteenth century and beyond.[3]

Another reason for this neglect is due to the sources. These are far from straightforward for the study of castles in the Wars of the Roses. The main narrative accounts are provided by chroniclers, such as monastic and urban writers. For previous centuries, chronicles of the former type are often of enormous value as historical sources, with famous authors including Orderic Vitalis, Matthew Paris and Thomas Walsingham. By the mid-fifteenth century, the tradition of monastic chronicle writing was in decline, with few of these chronicles still being written. Those accounts we do have, notably the continuations of the *Crowland Chronicle*, are valuable but are outnumbered by the urban chronicles. The latter were mostly compiled by members of the London civic elite. These are useful as their authors were typically well-informed but are unsurprisingly London-centric in their focus. Other chronicles include ones written by clerical writers, such as the chronicle formerly attributed to John Warkworth, those produced at the behest of the government, including the *Historie of the Arrivall of Edward IV*, and continental chroniclers, such as Jean de Wavrin. These are important accounts but are inconsistent in their chronological scope and level of detail. All the above-mentioned chronicles also tend to focus on particular episodes, notably major battles, as opposed to other aspects of the Wars of the Roses. This means that some campaigns are almost entirely overlooked by the narrative accounts.[4]

The uneven coverage of these sources can be partly rectified through using other types of evidence, for instance collections of surviving letters. The most notable example of these is the *Paston Letters*. They were written by different members of an ambitious Norfolk gentry family, who provide a unique insight into the period but were often concerned with events in East Anglia. The letters of foreign ambassadors, particularly those of the republics of Milan and Venice, offer interesting observations, albeit in an intermittent manner. Another major source of information is the records of the medieval English government. These include administrative documents produced by the office of the Chancery, which contain invaluable details of grants, appointments and orders issued by the king. Financial accounts are also of great importance. Most of the surviving records were created by clerks working for the Exchequer, the principal royal treasury of the English Crown, or in royal lordships, such as the County Palatine of Chester. These documents record items of expenditure, such as the wages of soldiers and purchases of military equipment. In some cases, financial records provide the only information on certain campaigns and episodes concerning castles, such as sieges and garrisons. Yet, the ravages of time have led to the loss of a substantial proportion of these documents.[5]

Researching this topic has therefore involved consulting a wide range of different types of sources. Many of the chronicles, collections of letters and administrative records have been published and are readily available in print. By contrast, most of the surviving financial documents only exist in their original manuscript forms and are held in different archives across the country. Examining these sources necessitated the carrying out of extensive archival research, particularly at The National Archives in Kew. This was a time-consuming but rewarding process that has brought new, interesting discoveries to light, including previously unknown sieges. Taken all together, this body of evidence makes it possible to explore the subject in detail.

This book tells the untold story of the castle in the Wars of the Roses. It discusses the ways in which these buildings were used during the military campaigns of the period. This includes their role as fortresses, mustering points and as secure headquarters for planning and conducting operations. The sieges of the conflict are explored in detail, with notable examples including the Tower of London, Bamburgh and Denbigh. These are placed within the context of the wider course of military and political events of these years. Attention is also paid to the non-military functions of castles in late medieval English society, as centres of manorial estates, local administration, residences, prisons, status symbols and as sources of legitimacy for the landowning elite. Changes in the ownership of castles are discussed, as well as the activities of castle builders.

A chronological framework is used to trace the course of military and political events, with the role of the castle at the centre of the narrative. Chapter 1 starts with a brief overview of the history of castles, their forms and functions up to 1450. This is followed by the second chapter, which discusses the events that led to the outbreak of hostilities at the First Battle of St Albans in 1455 and its aftermath. Chapter 3 explores the civil war of 1459 to 1461, which culminated in the victory of Edward IV at the Battle of Towton. The fourth chapter examines the Lancastrian rebellions against Yorkist rule in the north of England and Wales up until the fall of Harlech Castle in 1468. Chapter 5 looks at the turbulent years of 1469–71, which saw Edward IV first lose and then regain his throne. The sixth chapter examines the period of Yorkist supremacy during Edward's second reign and the Anglo-Scottish war of 1480–2. Chapter 7 discusses the final struggle between the two factions, with the narrative finishing with Henry VII's triumph at the Battle of Stoke in 1487. The conclusion analyses the role of castles in warfare in the period. This is followed by three appendices: Appendix A provides brief biographies of the key figures associated with the Wars of the Roses, Appendix B lists all recorded and possible sieges that took place between 1455 and 1487 and Appendix C lists recorded castle garrisons during the same period.

Chapter One

The History of the Castle

On 22 May 1455, the first engagement of the Wars of the Roses took place at the Hertfordshire city of St Albans. For the next thirty or so years, the rival houses of Lancaster and York were locked together in a dynastic struggle for the English throne. This conflict involved numerous battles and skirmishes, which finally culminated at the Battle of Stoke in 1487. Yet this was not the only form of military activity that took place in these years. Both sides were also actively engaged in gaining control of fortified buildings known as castles. These fortifications were a long-established part of the kingdom of England. They were large, visually imposing structures that dominated the landscape. In an era when the only other buildings of a comparable size were large churches or cathedrals, they served as a potent visual symbol of the wealth and power of their owners. Yet, not all castles were alike. Some were ancient structures that incorporated old and new architectural elements and which had been adapted over time. Whereas others had been recently built by upwardly mobile and ambitious members of the gentry or minor nobility. Similarly, their designs and functions varied markedly. Nevertheless, castles had a common identity as fortified structures, which belonged to the landed ruling elites of medieval society. To understand why this was the case, we need to go back 400 years in time.

The History and Development of the Castle

The story of the castle in the British Isles begins with the Norman Conquest of England in the eleventh century. In 1066, the most famous date in English history, Duke William of Normandy defeated and killed King Harold at the Battle of Hastings. This was not the first, or the last time, that England would be invaded by a foreign army, but this invasion was to be responsible for bringing about fundamental changes in English society, culture and governance. Rebellions against his rule prompted William to enact severe punishments against the rebels, including the infamous 'harrying of the north', which saw the widespread devastation of large parts of northern England. These measures included the systematic dispossession of most of the old English nobility who were replaced by incomers from northern France. The extent of this transformation can be seen in the great survey that was carried out and compiled by the king's officials in 1086 called Domesday Book. Another change was the introduction of the castle, a new type of fortification, whose name derives from the Latin words *castra* or *castellum*, meaning fortress. Fortifications of this type were not entirely unknown in England. A small number of castles had been erected during the reign of Edward the Confessor (1042–66) by Norman and French settlers who had been encouraged to come and live in the kingdom. The Anglo-Saxon nobility also had a tradition of constructing fortified residences called burhs, which often incorporated towers, walls and ditches.[1]

Yet, the new buildings were used in a very different way to earlier structures. This can be seen from the writings of monastic chroniclers who identified castles as being instruments of Norman oppression. The horrified author of the Anglo-Saxon Chronicle remarked that the new king 'Had castles built and wretched men oppressed'. Most pre-Conquest fortifications had been intended to protect urban centres and were communal in nature. By contrast, castles were fortified residences built for royal or aristocratic owners and their immediate followers. These buildings had multiple functions, serving as administrative and judicial centres, both for royal officials in the counties and for manorial lordships. They also were used as fortresses that could be held against enemy attacks and as bases for offensive operations. Large numbers of castles were built following the Norman Conquest, which was often accompanied by the destruction of existing structures, particularly in towns. This development coincided with the extensive rebuilding of churches and cathedrals across the land in the northern French Romanesque architectural style. The English landscape was therefore transformed by the Normans, with castles continuing to play an essential role in medieval society over the following centuries.[2]

The Conquest also had a profound effect on England's neighbours. This was particularly felt in Wales, where the Normans soon made inroads against the warring Welsh kingdoms. To counter raids into England, William founded border earldoms at Chester, Shrewsbury and Herefordshire, but his followers soon went onto the offensive. For a time, it looked as though all of Wales would be conquered by the invaders but a major Welsh rebellion in the 1090s stemmed the Norman advance. Thereafter, until the reign of Edward I in the late thirteenth century, the country would be divided between the Normans and the native Welsh. Castles were used as a key instrument of conquest by the invaders to secure captured territory. This was essential as Norman control over large parts of the country was often tenuous. At first, the Welsh destroyed any castles that they managed to capture, but over time they also made use of these fortifications. The border region with Wales, known as the Welsh Marches, has a very high concentration of castles. This was because it was a frontier zone often marked by conflict, with the Marcher lords and native Welsh competing for power and authority over the area. Castles were later introduced to Ireland by the Normans, during their invasion of the country, as well as to Scotland by French and Flemish settlers, who were invited to the kingdom in the twelfth century.[3]

The form of the castle was not static but changed markedly over the centuries. In the eleventh century most of these structures consisted of an enclosure or courtyard of wooden buildings, called a bailey, that was encircled by a ditch. These were by far the most common type of castle in England and Wales and are called ringworks. Some of these fortresses also incorporated mounds, often man-made, known as mottes, where high-status buildings were located, which are known as motte and baileys. Comparatively few castles were built of stone in the Norman period. The most famous example is the Tower of London, memorably described by the Anglo-French chronicler Orderic Vitalis as being built by order of William the Conqueror as 'a defence against the numerous and hostile inhabitants' of London. This castle takes its name from its most notable structure the White Tower, an impressive tower 90ft tall that was entered at first-floor level via a forebuilding. Not merely was this building designed as a palace that was used for ceremonial events, but it also served as a powerful visual demonstration of the power of the new king. Structures of this type were referred to by contemporaries as being great towers or *donjons*, but in the modern era are more commonly called keeps. Castles made of stone were at first comparatively rare due to the cost of their construction but became more common from the reign of Henry II onwards. The latter was responsible for the construction or rebuilding of many eminent castles, including Dover, Scarborough and Orford, each of which had impressive keeps. It was not until the thirteenth century that the dominance of the keep in castle design began to be challenged.[4]

From the latter part of the reign of Henry III onwards, an increased emphasis was placed on the importance of grand and elaborate gatehouses. The earliest surviving example is at Tonbridge Castle in Kent, where extensive works were carried out by order of its owner Richard de Clare in the 1250s. This included the construction of a grand twin-towered gatehouse made of fine cut ashlar stone, with two outer and two inner towers. It was a form that came to be used extensively in castle construction over the next fifty years.[5] The most notable examples of these gatehouses can be seen with the royal castles built in Wales in the late thirteenth century. These buildings were constructed following the wars fought with Llywelyn ap Gruffydd, prince of Wales, in 1277 and 1282–3. The latter conflict saw the final conquest of Wales with Llywelyn killed in battle. To cement his control over his newly conquered territory, Edward I ordered the construction of castles to overawe the Welsh. These structures are some of the finest buildings to have been constructed in the British Isles during the Middle Ages. This can be seen with Harlech Castle, which has a splendid twin-towered gatehouse, closely modelled on the style of Tonbridge. Similar examples can also be seen at Rhuddlan and Aberystwyth. The style was also used in baronial castles, such as at Denbigh, which has a magnificent triple-towered gatehouse, and at Dunstanburgh in Northumberland, where the gatehouse was originally five storeys high.[6]

The increased prominence of the gatehouse coincided with a change in the layout of castles, which were now designed in the shape of regularised courtyards. This architectural style had its origins in the design of monasteries, with buildings set around the edges of a rectangle with a courtyard in the middle. In many cases these castles had two wards, with service buildings concentrated in one and higher status structures situated in the other. At Conwy in Caernarfonshire the outer ward contained the great hall, kitchen, stables and chapel, whereas the principal residential chambers, including the royal apartments, were in the inner ward. Mural towers often contained multiple suites of rooms across different floors. For example, the upper two floors of the North-West Tower at Caerphilly in Glamorganshire contained chambers for high-status guests furnished with glazed windows, hooded fireplaces and latrines.[7] Other towers had service functions, such as the Garderobe Tower at Goodrich, which served as a communal latrine for the use of the household. The trend for building large gatehouses also meant that these structures had far more space for rooms. This can be seen at Kidwelly in south Wales, where a new gatehouse was completed in 1422, which contained the lodgings of the castle's constable. The building contained twenty rooms, many of which were served with fireplaces and chimneys for the comfort of the residents.[8] Great towers, although no longer the focus of castle design, continued to be constructed in the late Middle Ages. Unlike their predecessors, these structures were more directed towards providing residential accommodation as opposed to grand ceremonial rooms. Old Wardour in Wiltshire, constructed in the late fourteenth century, is an example of one of these tower-keeps. This hexagonal two-storeyed building is arranged around a small courtyard, the entrance of which is flanked by two towers. It contained rooms such as a great hall and kitchen, but also many chambers for residents and guests.[9] A similar structure can be seen at Tattershall in Lincolnshire, which was built in the 1440s. However, unlike Old Wardour, it was primarily constructed using bricks as opposed to masonry. This was a building material that was first adopted for the construction of high-status structures in the fifteenth century and gradually increased in popularity over time.[10]

These alterations in castle design were due to a change in how these sites were used by their owners. Medieval kings and nobles rarely spent much time in any one place but would frequently travel between their estates accompanied by their households. For the former, it was a necessary part of kingship to impose their authority with their presence throughout the kingdom, to receive petitions, administer justice and to impress their subjects with their power and splendour. It was also important for aristocrats to visit their often far-flung lordships in person, and to cultivate their relationships with their dependents in the localities. In practice, this meant that the greatest landowners needed to maintain numerous castles and manors where they could stay and entertain guests. These places were generally left only partially furnished and with only a small staff permanently resident to maintain them during the absence of their lord. Instead, many items of furniture were designed to be portable and were transported between sites. However, over the course of the late Middle Ages, kings and nobles gradually became less itinerant and spent progressively longer lengths of times in a smaller number of places. It was therefore no longer essential to maintain as many castles and manors as previously, as a result of which some fell into decay. Instead, greater resources were allocated towards improving and maintaining those buildings that were still regularly used as long-term residences. Accordingly, there was a requirement for more rooms, which were now increasingly allocated to individual residents. This coincided with a greater emphasis on privacy, as opposed to communal living, and on providing more luxurious accommodation in castles. Improvements were often carried out to existing sites, as only a comparatively small number of castles were built in entirely new locations. Therefore, by the mid-fifteenth century many castles incorporated both old and new structures.[11]

War and Peace

When castles were first introduced in the eleventh century warfare was a frequent occurrence. William the Conqueror used these fortifications to secure his control over the kingdom of England, and these were garrisoned with contingents of knights and other soldiers to protect them from attack and as bases from which to crush rebellions. One of the methods used to provide garrisons for these fortresses was a form of land tenure called castle-guard. In return for being granted land by the lord, the tenant was expected to provide military service at the castle at their own expense for an agreed length of time. Yet, this service could be commuted in return for monetary payments and it was rarely used from the mid-twelfth century onwards.[12] Instead, the onus was on castle owners and their officials to provide for their safe keeping. This task was primarily the responsibility of constables who were accountable for the defence of their castles. These men were accompanied by the servants and retainers in their households who would ordinarily be expected to provide security. On occasion, particularly during wartime, they were supplemented with continents of paid soldiers. The Angevin kings regularly maintained small garrisons in key castles, such as Dover, although this practice became less common over time.[13]

This was because the late Middle Ages saw the gradual demilitarisation of many castles in England and, to a lesser extent, in Wales. From the late thirteenth century onwards, rebellions against the Crown became less commonplace, with the last major siege of a castle in southern England, prior to the fifteenth century, taking place during the Despenser War of 1321–2 at Leeds Castle in Kent.[14] This was partly because the penalties for rebelling against the king became more severe due to the adoption of the treason laws in the late Middle Ages.[15] Such castles still had the potential to be employed as fortresses but were rarely used in this way, and instead there was an increased emphasis on providing comfortable accommodation. It was only in the frontier regions of England and Wales that garrisons were still routinely maintained in key castles. This was particularly the case with the far north of England where the threat of attack from the Scots meant that significant resource had to be allocated for its defence. Anglo-Scottish relations since the reign of Edward I had been marked by hostilities and frequent cross-border conflict.[16] The defence of the region was entrusted to wardens, one for the western march and another for the eastern march. These men were allocated specified wages from the Exchequer to resist Scottish incursions and to pay for garrisons at strategic places, such as Berwick-upon-Tweed and Carlisle. For instance, Henry Percy, eldest son of the second earl of Northumberland, indented to serve as warden of the east march on 1 April 1440 in return for an annual payment of £2,500 during peacetime, which would be doubled during outbreaks of war.[17] Another key border castle was Roxburgh, which was administered as part of the east march, but whose keepers received payments directly from the Exchequer. Its garrison fluctuated over time, consisting of fifty-two knights and men-at-arms and eighty archers in 1401.[18] Nevertheless, the financial problems of the Exchequer meant that the condition of these fortresses were often neglected. In 1451, the inhabitants of Berwick-upon-Tweed petitioned the king for assistance as the walls of the town and the castle were said to be in a ruinous state.[19]

By contrast, greater sums were expended on providing for the security of the Pale of Calais. This was a small enclave of English-occupied terri-tory in north France that had been conquered in 1347 by Edward III, who had expelled the native population and replaced them with settlers from England. The Pale principally consisted of the town and castle of Calais, the town and castle of Guînes and Hammes Castle. It was of strategic importance due to its location at the narrowest part of the English Channel, which meant that armies could be easily transported between England and the continent. This was a great advantage during the Hundred Years War as it allowed the English to invade northern France with ease. Successive French rulers were keen to regain control of the region and Calais had been besieged on multiple occasions, notably in 1349 and 1436. It was for this reason that a large permanent garrison was maintained at the territory, hundreds of men strong, with substantial quantities of weaponry including ordnance stockpiled there. The post of captain of Calais was therefore not merely prestigious but also gave control over the only professional military force in the kingdom. This was crucial as England, unlike some of her continental rivals, lacked a standing army prior to the seventeenth century. The town was also important as it was the location of the wool staple, the official designated trading post for this product, which was England's most important export in the Middle Ages. Nevertheless, despite the strategic advantages of Calais, it placed a heavy burden on the Exchequer.[20]

Wales was another area where it was necessary to keep castles in a state of defence. Despite the Edwardian conquest of the late thirteenth century, English control over the country was not entirely secure. In the early fifteenth century, a major rebellion broke out led by Owain Glyn Dŵr. The rebels succeeded in seizing large parts of the country, including major castles such as Aberystwyth and Harlech. For a time, it looked as though the English would be driven out of Wales entirely, with the rebellion only being suppressed after years of conflict. The threat of further uprisings prompted the installation of small permanent garrisons in key royal castles and towns. In the early 1450s, this included a force of one man-at-arms and twelve archers at Aberstwyth, whereas twenty-four soldiers were present at Harlech.[21] Elsewhere, it was rare for castles to be garrisoned except during times of crisis, such as in 1386, when the threat of a French invasion prompted the government of Richard II to install as many as 720 men in castles and towns in southern England.[22] It was expensive to keep castles in a defensible state on a long-term basis, to supply them with provisions and to pay the wages of soldiers. Instead, the peace-time establishments of most castles were small. At Portchester in Hampshire, the only staff to receive specified wages from the Exchequer were the constable at 12*d*. per day, a porter at 3*d*. per day, a groom at 1½*d*. a day, an artilleryman (responsible for looking after the weaponry kept at the castle) at 6*d*. per day and a watchman at 3*d*. per day.[23]

Castles were also frequently allocated to absentee constables. Members of the nobility and gentry often received grants of constableships from the king, but it was rare for them to be personally involved on a regular basis in the governance of these places. Instead, this responsibility was almost always delegated to a deputy who acted on their behalf. In July 1450, Humphrey Stafford, duke of Buckingham, was given the combined offices of constable of Dover Castle and Warden of the Cinque Ports.[24] This was a potentially lucrative and important grant due to the strategic importance of the castle. Since the reign of Henry II, it had been a major royal fortress and palace, which overlooked the town from its striking position on the cliffs above. Dover's location at the nearest geographical point to the continent meant that it had played an important role in national events, particularly during the civil wars of the thirteenth century.[25] Yet, the duke was an important figure on the national stage, therefore he employed a lieutenant to run the castle for him. The man chosen for this role in 1456 was Sir Thomas Kyriell, a prominent member of the gentry of Kent and a veteran of the wars in France. An agreement known as an indenture was drawn up between the two individuals, with Thomas receiving £40 per year for his wages. In return he was expected to serve at the castle in person with his household. The accounts rendered by Thomas Hexstall, the duke's financial officer, known as a receiver, show that a further twenty-eight men received wages. These included the principal officers for the administration of the castle estates, such as the steward, clerk, warenner and marshal, as well as a rector and chaplain for the church of St Mary in Castro. A further six men were responsible for running the keep, namely Thomas Cook the keeper, assisted by an artilleryman and four janitors. The rest of the staff consisted of a plumber, carpenter and twelve watchmen, supervised by two chief watchmen.[26]

Castles also played an important role as estate centres. Medieval England was primarily a rural agricultural society, the economy of which was based on the manorial system. Manors were administrative units of land held as fiefs from the Crown by a lord that often included a residence or manor house. Land managed directly by the lord's officials was known as the demesne and was farmed by unfree serfs or, as was increasingly common following the Black Death, by paid labourers. Other parts of the estate were held by sub-tenants, such as copyholders in return for services rendered, or freeholders. A manor's income was typically drawn from the profits of the demesne, rents, service commuted for money, fines imposed by the manorial court and various customary rights. Other economic resources were gathered from adjacent deer parks, fishponds, forests, rabbit warrens and mining. Some manors were grouped together to form great lordships called honours, such as the Honour of Richmond, which could comprise as many as 100 or more individual manors. Most castles, particularly in the countryside, were the administrative centres of manors or honours, which were maintained by the revenues generated from their estates. This money was used to pay the wages of officials and their expenses, the costs of repairing and constructing new buildings, and any exceptional expenditure, such as garrisons during wartime. Any remaining surpluses were then sent to the receiver-general. Yet, by the mid-fifteenth century a change in manorial administration meant that most estates were farmed out to tenants, who leased them in return for an annual fee. Many lords therefore effectively became absentee rent collectors. It was not uncommon for many lordships to be visited very infrequently, if at all, by their owners, who were instead represented by their officials.[27]

The security features of castles meant that they were natural places to hold prisoners. High walls, ditches, moats, towers, portcullises and strong doors were not only good at keeping attackers out but also inmates securely inside. Inventories reveal that fetters, manacles, collars and shackles were often used for restraining prisoners. Yet, negligence by warders and badly maintained fortifications meant that escapes by inmates from some prisons were relatively commonplace. On 15 June 1455, the keeper of the gaol of Cambridge Castle, William Bury, received a royal pardon for the escape of a prisoner called William Bowre. According to Bury's account, the felon pretended to be mortally ill and requested a confessor. A chaplain was brought to the garden of the castle, with both men left alone during confession. Taking advantage of the jailor's absence, the felon then escaped over a wall and into a place of sanctuary, most likely a church, where he remained at large.[28] One of the most prominent castles to be used as a prison was the Tower of London. High-profile prisoners were frequently kept there, including troublesome nobles and prisoners of war, such as Charles, duke of Orléans, who was captured at the Battle of Agincourt in 1415. The Tower was unusual in that it also housed the mint, a menagerie with wild animals including lions and an arsenal, where guns and other equipment was produced and stored.[29]

Other places served as comfortable residences for their owners. This can be seen with the household of Sir John Luttrell at Dunster in Somerset. In the early fifteenth century, the residents of the castle generally consisted of a steward, a chamberlain, a cook and fifteen other men in addition to a laundress, with Lady Luttrell attended by a damsel. In 1405–6 the foodstuffs purchased for the household and their guests included a rich variety of goods including wheat, pigs, goats, mutton, eggs, turbot, salmon, oysters, mussels, olive oil, figs, raisins and saffron, together with wine and beer. Oats, halters and shoes were also acquired for the horses kept at the castle.[30] Surviving inventories for Caister in Norfolk reveal the high standard of living enjoyed by its residents. It was founded by Sir John Fastolf, a veteran of the wars in France, from 1438 to 1446, who richly furnished his new castle. The walls were lavishly decorated with tapestries of Arras, which mostly depicted scenes from domestic life. These included images of a gentlewoman playing a harp by a castle, archers shooting a duck in the water with crossbows, and a man drawing water from a well. In the chapel there were vestments, chalices, candlesticks, carpets and pillows, with the kitchen stocked with a variety of pots, pans, spits and hooks. The chambers for the household and guests were amply provided with feather beds, bolsters, blankets, sheets and curtains. Fastolf also had a small library with twenty-five books written in French kept in the stewhouse, including the Bible, the chronicles of France, a book of Julius Caesar and the *Romance of the Rose*.[31]

Royal Castles

Many of the largest and most important castles in the kingdom belonged to the Crown. This was particularly the case with royal urban castles, almost all of which dated from the eleventh century. These were mostly located in major cities and towns such as London, York, Bristol, Norwich, Carlisle, Winchester, Gloucester, Newcastle upon Tyne, Rochester, Salisbury (Old Sarum) and Nottingham. Responsibility for their management and safekeeping was entrusted to officials called constables. These were men from the landowning elite and included the greatest lords in the land, such as dukes and earls, as well as gentlemen of lesser rank. For example, in 1453, a man called Bewes Hampton, who held the distinction of being described as a king's esquire, was granted the constableship of Shrewsbury Castle by Henry VI with an annual fee of £10.[32] This payment was not merely given to cover his expenses for managing the castle, but would also have been expected, ordinarily, to have given him a tidy profit. Most probably he employed a deputy to serve on his behalf, who would have been given a smaller portion of the total amount. In some instances, the constables of royal urban castles also held the office of sheriff, such as with Sir William Pecche, the sheriff of Kent, who was granted the constableship of Canterbury Castle in 1462.[33] Sheriffs were the most important royal officials in the counties and were responsible for a variety of administrative and judicial duties. These urban castles were often also used as prisons for their counties, generally for prisoners who were awaiting trial. Responsibility for safeguarding and caring for the inmates was often entrusted to keepers of gaols or porters. For instance, John Clerk, a king's serjeant, was entrusted with keeping the gaol of Northampton Castle in 1455.[34] Other royal castles had more rural settings such as Ludgershall in Wiltshire and Portchester in Hampshire. Some of these places had adjoining forests and parks such as Windsor in Berkshire, where Sir John Bourchier was appointed as constable of the castle and keeper of the forests, parks and warrens in 1458.[35]

The number of castles in the custody of the king's officials varied markedly over time. It was incumbent upon medieval rulers to reward their followers with grants of lands and money, therefore castles were frequently granted to royal favourites. For instance, the lordship and castle of Corfe in Dorset were granted to John Beaufort, earl of Somerset in 1407.[36] Periodically the king would also acquire possession of other castles on either a temporary or permanent basis. Upon the news of the death of a landowner who held lands directly from the king, known as a tenant in chief, royal officials called escheators would take possession of their lands. If their heir was an adult then they would have to pay a fee, called a relief, to enter into their inheritance, or alternatively if they were a minor, they would be taken into wardship. During their minority their estates would be held by a custodian appointed by the king who supervised their upbringing. This was an important source of patronage for kings, as it allowed them to reward loyal supporters at no cost to themselves, who received the profits of the lands they held in wardship. Castles were also gained through the confiscation of the estates forfeited by traitors. For example, Scarborough was seized by Henry I in 1155, having previously belonged to William le Gros, earl of Aumale, and thereafter it remained a royal castle until the reign of James I.[37] In other cases, forfeited castles were later regained by their ancestral families. The estates of John Montagu, earl of Salisbury, were confiscated due to his participation in the Epiphany Rising of 1400 against Henry IV, but were later regained by his son, the fourth earl.[38]

The biggest acquisition of lands by the Crown in the late Middle Ages occurred as result of the accession to the throne of Henry Bolingbroke in 1399. Following the overthrow of his cousin Richard II and his coronation as Henry IV, he decided to retain the lands he had inherited from his father, John of Gaunt, duke of Lancaster. The duchy of Lancaster was subsequently held as a possession of all subsequent monarchs but was administered separately to other royal estates. These lands were substantial and at their greatest extent brought in a net income of approximately £10,000. They also included major castles situated throughout England and Wales including Kenilworth in Warwickshire, Lancaster in Lancashire, Pevensey in East Sussex, Melbourne in Derbyshire, Tutbury in Staffordshire, Knaresborough, Tickhill, Pickering and Pontefract in Yorkshire, Dunstanburgh in Northumberland, Carreg Cennen, Kidwelly, Monmouth, Ogmore and the Three Castles of Grosmont, White Castle and Skenfrith in south Wales. Therefore, by the mid-fifteenth century a sizeable proportion of the realm's castles were in royal hands.[39]

The heir to the throne also held extensive estates and lordships. In 1301 Edward I bestowed the title of prince of Wales and earl of Chester onto his eldest son Edward of Caernarfon (the future Edward II).[40] A practice that was followed for subsequent heirs apparent to the English throne. The Principality of Wales comprised all the royal-held lands in the country, consisting of the shires of Merioneth, Caernarfonshire and Anglesey in the north, Cardiganshire in the west and Carmarthenshire in the south; whereas Flintshire in the north-east was attached to the earldom of Chester. The prince's officials were therefore responsible for managing many of the most important castles in Wales including Beaumaris, Caernarfon, Conwy, Harlech, Rhuddlan, Flint, Aberystwyth, Cardigan and Carmarthen, as well as Chester in Cheshire. The duchy of Cornwall was another title held by heirs to the throne since 1337, starting with Edward of Woodstock, the eldest son of Edward III. Castles administered by the duke's officials were principally located in Cornwall, such as Restormel, Launceston and Tintagel, but also included other places such as Lydford in Devonshire, Castle Rising in Norfolk and Wallingford in

Berkshire. For most of the first half of the fifteenth century, following the accession of Henry V to the throne in 1413, these lands were administered by the king's officials. This situation arose because the position of prince of Wales was vacant, until the birth of Henry VI's son, Edward of Westminster, in 1453.[41] Queen consorts were also important castle owners. Margaret of Anjou, who married Henry VI in 1445, was in the following year granted a generous endowment, which included the castles of Tutbury in Staffordshire, Pleshey in Essex and Hertford in Hertfordshire. She subsequently acquired other castles including Devizes and Marlborough in Wiltshire, Berkhamsted in Hertfordshire, Rockingham in Northamptonshire and Odiham in Hampshire.[42]

Private Castles

The next most significant group of castle owners was the nobility. These were the landholding elite of medieval society who held numerous estates across the kingdom. They generally held their lands directly from the king as tenants in chief, with peers of the realm having the distinction of receiving personal writs of summons to Parliament from the monarch where they sat in the House of Lords.[43] Their support was crucial to the Crown for the effective governance of the kingdom and in providing financial and military assistance during times of crisis. The wealthiest of the magnates in the mid-fifteenth century was Richard, duke of York (he assumed the surname of Plantagenet in 1460).[44] It has been estimated that the net annual income he derived from his lands was approximately £4,000 in the mid-1430s, with annuities paid from the Exchequer worth another £600 per year. He had inherited substantial estates from his parents, Richard of Conisbrough, earl of Cambridge, and Anne, daughter and heir of Edward Mortimer, earl of March. Richard's ancestry also meant that he had a strong claim to the English throne due to his descent from Edward III through both his parents. Through these lordships he owned multiple castles throughout England, Wales and Ireland. In the Welsh Marches this included Wigmore, Clifford, New Radnor, Montgomery, Hay-on-Wye and Knighton, as well as Ludlow, his favourite residence. This was in addition to castles in England, such as Sandal and Conisbrough in Yorkshire and Fotheringay in Northamptonshire, as well as in Wales, notably Denbigh in the north-east.[45]

The duke of York was related by marriage to another important noble family, the Nevilles. This union dated from the 1420s, when Richard was married to Cecily, daughter of Ralph Neville, earl of Westmorland, when he was a minor. The earl was an important magnate in the north of

England who had been richly rewarded for his loyalty to Henry IV earlier in the century. Following Ralph's death in 1425, most of his lands passed to his children from his second marriage, principally to the eldest son, Richard. The latter inherited the main Neville estates, including the lordships and castles of Sheriff Hutton and Middleham in Yorkshire, Raby in the Palatinate of Durham and Penrith in Cumberland. This was at the expense of the children from his first marriage who were largely dis-inherited by the terms of their father's will. Richard, who became earl of Salisbury following his father-in-law's death in 1428, was forced to contend with legal challenges from his relatives.[46] His half-nephew, Ralph Neville, earl of Westmorland, was largely unsuccessful in this venture, although he did manage to acquire the lordship of Raby. Ralph instead had to be content with inheriting a small share of his father's estates, which included the castles of Brancepeth in the Palatinate of Durham and Bywell in Northumberland.[47] Richard's eldest son, also called Richard, was the beneficiary of an advantageous marriage to Anne Beauchamp, daughter and heir of the earl of Warwick. Upon the latter's death in 1449 he succeeded to the title, thus making him the premier earl in the kingdom with an annual income of over £5,000. Through his wife he also acquired a joint share of both the Despenser estates and the lordship of Abergavenny. This inheritance was shared with her young nephew, George Neville. Yet, the latter was largely deprived of his share by the actions of his uncle-in-law, who quickly managed to secure control of the principal lordships in Wales, including the castles of Abergavenny and Cardiff. The two Neville earls, father and son, were therefore powerful supporters of their relative the duke of York. Their position was further strengthened through hold-ing the wardenship of the west march of Scotland, which included the city and castle of Carlisle.[48]

The main northern rivals to the Nevilles were the Percies. They were a powerful family that had been dominant in the north-east of England since the fourteenth century. This was reflected in the creation of the earldom of Northumberland for Henry, Lord Percy, by Richard II in 1377. The first earl was attainted for treason in 1405, but the title was sub-sequently regained by his son, also called Henry, in 1416. Their power-base was in Northumberland where they could draw upon strong military support from their retainers. This was a militarised region due to its proximity with the Scottish border, with numerous castles that were kept in a defensible condition. They owned major castles including Alnwick, Warkworth, Prudhoe, Langley and Spofforth in the county, as well as Cockermouth in Cumberland. This was in addition to the office of warden of the east march of Scotland, which was regularly granted to members of the Percy family, with responsibility for the defence of Berwick-upon-Tweed. Yet, the payment of his wages as warden were frequently in serious arrears from the cash-strapped government of Henry VI. This placed a strain on his finances as he lacked the resources of some of his richer peers, with the gross annual income of his estates having been estimated at over £3,100 in the mid-1450s. Furthermore, his focus on building up a strong military support base meant a significant portion of his revenues were spent on retaining fees. The earl had also experienced difficulties in securing the return of some of his ancestral estates, such as the lordship and castle of Wressle in Yorkshire. Following his father's forfeiture, it had been granted to Henry IV's second wife, Joan, and after her death to Ralph, Lord Cromwell, in 1438.[49] In their rivalry with the Nevilles they had the support of another noble family that was prominent in the north, the Cliffords. The latter had a strong presence in Westmorland and held the castles of Appleby, Pendragon, Brougham and Brough, together with Skipton in Yorkshire.[50]

Another notable magnate was Humphrey Stafford, duke of Buckingham, who had an income of approximately £5,000 per annum. He held multiple castles including Kimbolton in Huntingdonshire, Maxstoke in Warwickshire, Tonbridge in Kent, Oakham in Rutland, Stafford in Staffordshire and Brecon in Wales.[51] In other parts of the kingdom, notably in southern England and the Midlands, the nobility tended to own fewer castles. The most prominent magnate in the south-west of England was the earl of Devon, who held the castles of Tiverton, Plympton and Okehampton. Yet, the thirteenth earl, Thomas Courtenay, had a fairly limited net income of £1,500 and faced competition from regional rivals, such William, Lord Bonville.[52] This competition even included his relative from a junior line of the family, Sir Philip Courtenay, the owner of Powderham Castle. In East Anglia, an area conspicuous for having a low density of castles, few magnates were castle owners. The main exceptions being the duke of Norfolk, who held Framlingham in Suffolk, and the earl of Oxford, the owner of Hedingham in Essex.[53]

Lower down the social spectrum the castle-owning community included lesser landowners such as knights and members of the gentry. Only the wealthiest amongst their number could afford the great expense of maintaining a castle by the late Middle Ages. The possession of one of these buildings was therefore an important status symbol that attested to the wealth and prestige of its owner. This can be seen with two castles that date from the late fourteenth century, Nunney in Somerset and Bodiam in

East Sussex. They were commissioned by ambitious members of the gentry who had profited from their military service in France during the Hundred Years War, namely Sir John Delamare for the former and Sir Edward Dallingridge for the latter. Members of the clergy were also castle owners. Bishops were important landowners in medieval society who were expected to contribute to the security of the realm. Ecclesiastical castles included Farnham in Hampshire and Taunton in Somerset, held by the bishop of Winchester, Saltwater in Kent by the archbishop of Canterbury, and Amberley in Sussex by the bishop of Chichester. The special status of the bishop-prince of Durham, ruler of the Palatinate of Durham in the north-east of England, meant that he had an important part to play in the defence of the region. His castles included Durham and Auckland, where he had residences, as well as the strategic fortress of Norham on the Scottish border. Ownership of these fortifications even extended to some monastic foundations with the priory of Tynemouth in the Palatinate of Durham enclosed within the walls of a castle that dated from the late eleventh century.[54]

Chapter Two

Lancaster and York

The End of the Hundred Years War

On 1 May 1450, an English ship on a voyage from East Anglia to the Low Countries was intercepted by another vessel in the English Channel. On board the first ship was an illustrious passenger, William de la Pole, duke of Suffolk, who had recently been banished from the realm. Suffolk was invited by the crew of the second ship, *The Nicholas of the Tower*, to speak with their captain. His decision to accept this invitation proved to be a grave mistake. The sailors seized him as soon as he came on board and after a show trial he was beheaded on the following day. Their hostility towards Suffolk stemmed from the prominent role he had played in the government of Henry VI. He had exerted a strong influence over the king since the mid-1430s and as a royal favourite had benefited from substantial patronage. These grants included the offices of chamberlain of England and justiciar of Chester and north Wales. Yet, this prominence meant that he was personally blamed for the failures of the king's government. By early 1450, a succession of problems meant that the realm was in a crisis. Military defeats in France, the threat of invasion and economic difficulties had caused widespread discontent across the kingdom. Suffolk was accused of treason by the Commons in Parliament, with the charges against him including the ludicrous accusation that he intended to surrender the inland castle of Wallingford in Berkshire to the French. The anger of the Members of Parliament towards Suffolk prompted the king to agree to his imprisonment in the Tower of London and afterwards his banishment, thus leading to the circumstances of his demise.[1]

Yet, this outcome did nothing to resolve the problems faced by the English state. Suffolk took the blame for the failures of the government, but ultimately many of these problems derived from the shortcomings of the king himself as a ruler. One of his principal faults was his lack of martial prowess and ineffectiveness in military affairs, which was a major factor in the final defeat of the English at the end of the Hundred Years War. Henry VI had become king at a very young age, when he was only 9 months old, upon the death of his father, Henry V, in 1422. The latter bequeathed to his infant son not merely the English throne but also a claim to the kingdom of France and substantial territories in the north and south-west of the country. The exercise of power was therefore vested in the new king's relatives during his long minority, principally his uncles. Responsibility for the governance of England was given to Humphrey, duke of Gloucester, with the title of defender of the realm and chief councillor of the king. His older uncle, John, duke of Bedford, was entrusted with ruling the English-occupied lands in France, with the title of regent, and responsibility for conducting military operations against the supporters of the Dauphin (the future Charles VII).[2]

At first the war went well for the English, but the turning point came in 1429 when Joan of Arc lifted the siege of Orléans. Thereafter, they were primarily on the defensive and it became increasingly clear that that the English had little prospect of winning an outright victory in the conflict. This was a view shared by Henry VI who was keen to negotiate a settlement with Charles VII to end hostilities. By 1437, the king had entered into his majority and began to pursue a policy of seeking peace with France. A truce was eventually concluded in 1444, with Henry marrying Charles's niece, Margaret of Anjou, in the following year. However, this match was far from universally popular in England, as the new queen was only provided with a modest dowry. Further opposition was caused by the king's ill-judged decision to surrender the strategic county of Maine to the French in an unsuccessful attempt to secure a lasting peace. Gloucester's vocal opposition to these concessions led to his arrest at his nephew's command in 1447. He died soon afterwards whilst still in custody.[3]

Two years later there was a resumption of war. Remarkably, this was due to an act of English aggression against the semi-autonomous duchy of Brittany, with the town of Fougères seized in a surprise attack. This prompted a French invasion of Normandy in July 1449. The invaders rapidly overran the duchy, whose defence had been neglected during the time of truce, with Edmund Beaufort, duke of Somerset, the lieutenant of France, surrendering Rouen the capital in October. On 15 April 1450, an expeditionary force led by Sir Thomas Kyriell was vanquished at the Battle of Formigny. This defeat led to the capitulation of the remaining English garrisons in Normandy. In the following year, the French invaded and conquered the duchy of Gascony in the south-west of France. Gascony was briefly recovered due to a pro-English uprising two years later but was finally lost for good after an English army led by John Talbot, earl of Shrewsbury, was routed at the Battle of Castillon on 17 July 1453. Thus within a few short years all of England's territorial possessions in France, except for Calais, were lost. This was a major blow to the prestige of the king and his government. Not merely were all the hard-won gains of Henry V lost, but so was Gascony, which had belonged to the English monarchy since the reign of Henry II in the twelfth century. The sudden nature of this defeat sparked accusations of treachery, with English commanders, such as Somerset, said to have accepted bribes from the enemy.[4]

The loss of Normandy and its ports also exposed England to attack from the resurgent French as the English no longer controlled both sides of the Channel. Coastal towns were now vulnerable to raids from enemy fleets and there were fears of an imminent invasion. This prompted concern about the condition of the fortifications of the southern and eastern coasts, which had long been neglected. On 8 May 1450, the constable of Portchester Castle in Hampshire, Robert Fienys, wrote to the king to advise him of the ruinous state of the castle. Many of the structures were said to be damaged or had collapsed including the drawbridge, the inner and outer gates, the towers and walls. He urgently requested that the Clerk of the Works should be sent to survey the castle so that repairs could be carried out. Similar complaints were also made about Carisbrooke Castle on the Isle of Wight. In a petition to the king, the local inhabitants complained that they were in great jeopardy as the castle, the main fortress on the island, was badly maintained and lacked weapons for its defence. These appeals prompted piecemeal measures to improve vulnerable fortifications through carrying out minor repairs. Orders were also issued for commissioners to arrest merchant ships and their crews to serve in fleets to patrol the coastline. However, a more robust response was constrained by the near insolvency of the Exchequer.[5]

The long years of warfare had placed a severe strain on the Crown's finances. As early as 1433, the treasurer of England, Ralph, Lord Cromwell, had presented a detailed report to Parliament outlining the stark shortfall between income and expenditure. Ordinary revenues from the royal estates and custom duties were flatlining or in decline. At the same time, military commitments and the need to provide adequately for the royal household meant that costs were increasing. Despite this discrepancy, successive parliaments were loath to grant adequate taxation to decrease the deficit. They instead claimed that the king's financial problems were due to the mismanagement of royal revenues by his ministers. This forced the government to bridge the shortfall by borrowing large sums of money. However, even this was inadequate to meet the Crown's needs, which meant that the payment of wages for royal officials and soldiers fell increasingly in arrears. The situation was further aggravated by the country's economic problems. From the 1440s a shortage of coinage, due to a Europe-wide deficiency in the supply of silver bullion, caused the economy to contract sharply. This fuelled popular discontent, with foreign merchants blamed for many of the country's woes. In response, the government adopted populalist measures against foreign traders. This only made matters worse as it sparked a trade war with the Burgundian Low Countries, the principal buyer of English wool, the country's main export. Economic hardship was felt across all sectors of society, with popular unrest further aggravated by public anger at the defeats in France and the perceived failures of the king's ministers. This finally culminated in the outbreak of a major rebellion in the summer of 1450.[6]

The Year of Crisis

The rising began in late May in Kent and spread throughout south-east England to Essex, Middlesex, Sussex and Surrey. This was a region prone to rebellions, as was seen mostly notably in 1381 with the Peasant's Revolt. In the petitions they sent to the king they complained of the misgovernance of the realm by the king's councillors, who were described as false traitors. They soon acquired a leader, a man of obscure origins called Jack Cade, who gave himself the title of 'Captain of Kent'. In early June the main rebel host moved westwards to Blackheath, just outside of London, where they established a fortified camp. They refused demands conveyed by royal messengers to disperse, but upon the approach of the king's army the rebels abandoned their camp and began to return to their homes. They were pursued into Kent by a small force of royalists led by Sir Humphrey Stafford and William Stafford. However, the king's men were ambushed and their leaders were slain. This victory greatly encouraged the rebels who now resolved to use force to achieve their objectives. In the meanwhile, their opponents were thrown into disarray by unrest amongst the retainers of the king and his attendant magnates, who threatened to join the insurgents unless certain officials, who they deemed to be traitors, were imprisoned. This development alarmed the king sufficiently to order that the unpopular treasurer, James Fiennes, Lord Saye, should be incarcerated in the Tower. He then withdrew to the safety of Kenilworth Castle in Warwickshire, despite the pleading of the mayor of London for him to remain.[7]

The rebels then advanced on the capital and were admitted into the city on 3 July, after they had cut the ropes of the drawbridge of London Bridge to prevent it being raised against them.[8] Initially the Londoners, whether through sympathy with their grievances or through fear, did little to check their excesses, with unpopular royal officials subjected to show trials and executions. One of their victims was Lord Saye who was handed over by the custodians of the Tower. Cade attempted to win the goodwill of the inhabitants of the city by issuing proclamations that acts of theft would be punished by death, but law and order soon broke down. The rebels ran amok committing acts of murder, robbery and arson. These crimes outraged the Londoners who took up arms to expel the rebels, with the support of soldiers led by Thomas, Lord Scales. On the evening of 5 July, they barred the passage of Cade and his men into the city by holding London Bridge against them. After a fierce struggle that lasted throughout the night and into the following morning they succeeded in blocking their entry, with the rebels agreeing to disperse the following day after receiving royal pardons given by a delegation of churchmen including the archbishops of Canterbury and York and the bishop of Winchester. Cade with a now greatly reduced band of followers fled to the Isle of Sheppey in north Kent. He tried to gain access to the castle of Queenborough, but it was held against him by a garrison led by Sir Roger Chamberlain. This setback prompted Cade to flee southwards to Sussex, where he was mortally wounded in a skirmish fought with a company of men led by the sheriff of the county, Alexander Iden. His body was then taken to Newgate where it was beheaded and quartered, with his head placed on London Bridge and his limbs sent to Blackheath, Salisbury, Norwich and Gloucester for public display.[9]

Cade's demise marked the effective end of the rebellion. Yet, it had demonstrated the weakness of royal authority and the scale of popular discontent with the governance of the realm. Furthermore, in their petitions to the Crown the rebels had identified Richard Plantagenet, duke of York, as a champion of reform. York's decision to return to the realm from Ireland without authorisation later that year therefore posed a direct challenge to the government. He had previously served as the king's lieutenant of France at various times in the 1430s and 1440s, but in 1447 was appointed as lieutenant of Ireland, where he was a major landholder, taking up his post two years later. News of his unexpected landing in north Wales at Beaumaris in Anglesey at the beginning of September in 1450 was therefore a cause of concern for the king and his ministers. In response they ordered the castellans of the region to block his passage eastwards. They could rely upon the loyalty of these men as the office holders of the royal castles of north Wales were members of the king's household. However, York evaded their efforts and made his way safely to his castle at Ludlow. He subsequently complained to the king that certain royal servants had conspired to arrest and imprison him in Conwy Castle. His return from Ireland was justified on the grounds that he wished to declare his loyalty to the Crown, to disprove false rumours, and to draw the king's attention to abuses of power by corrupt officials.[10]

Afterwards York went to East Anglia to gather further supporters, before heading to Westminster to attend Parliament. The situation was tense in the capital due to the presence of large numbers of soldiers who had recently returned from France following the loss of Normandy. These men were angry at their sudden defeat and lack of payment for outstanding wages. They posed a serious danger to law and order, particularly as they had looted weapons from the armoury at the Tower. It was for this reason that the king and the lords brought substantial entourages with them to the capital. Parliament had been summoned by the government to enact measures against the rebels of Cade and to grant subsidies for the defence of the remaining English-held lands in France. Yet, the Commons were eager to punish royal favourites, with a bill introduced demanding the dismissal of the duke of Somerset, who had recently been appointed as constable of England by the king. Their cause was championed by York whose chamberlain, Sir William Oldhall, had been elected as speaker. The former blamed Somerset for the English defeat in France, with his capitulation at Rouen characterised as an act of treachery, which he contended should be severely punished. York's stance had considerable popular support but the king and lords refused to countenance this measure. Frustrated by their refusal to act, a large mob broke into Westminster Hall to demand the punishment of alleged traitors on 30 November, with Somerset attacked in his lodgings on the following day. Concerned about his safety, the king agreed to his confinement at the Tower. However, his imprisonment was brief, as the authorities soon regained control of the situation. Commissions were set up to try rebels, with the king undertaking a personal tour of south-east England over the following months. Yet the crises of 1450 had damaged the prestige and authority of the Crown. As a result, the government found it increasingly difficult to restrain violent disputes between members of the aristocratic elites. This first manifested itself in the outbreak of a private war in the south-west of England.[11]

The Siege of Taunton Castle

The conflict was between two important landowners, Thomas Courtenay, earl of Devon, and William, Lord Bonville. The Courtenay earls of Devon had formerly been the preeminent magnates in the region, but their hegemony was challenged by rivals in the early fifteenth century. Chief amongst them was Bonville, whose military service in France during the reign of Henry V had been rewarded by being granted important administrative offices in the 1420s and 1430s. His appointment as royal steward of Cornwall for life in 1437, however, led to a rift with Courtenay. Tensions gradually escalated, with their followers staging armed displays in public by 1440, with violence only narrowly averted by both men being summoned to account for their behaviour at court later that year. The quarrel subsequently went into abeyance, with Bonville going overseas to Gascony in March 1443, where he took up the post as seneschal of the duchy. After his return to England, he benefitted from the patronage of the powerful duke of Suffolk, which culminated in his elevation to the peerage in 1449. Yet, the upheavals of the following year persuaded Courtenay that he had an opportunity to strike a blow against his rival. He allied himself with the duke of York and with another prominent landowner in the south-west, Edward Brook, Lord Cobham. In August 1451, Courtenay and Cobham were said to have raised a force of between 5,000 and 6,000 men with which to attack Bonville, who had in turn aligned himself with James Butler, earl of Wiltshire and earl of Ormond. They forced Butler to flee from his manor at Lackham before laying siege to Taunton Castle in late September, which was held by Bonville and his forces. The sudden arrival of York three days later led to a cessation of hostilities, with the castle handed over to him for safe keeping. Most of the principal participants were subsequently arrested by royal command and were temporarily imprisoned. Bonville and Butler were held at Berkhamsted Castle and Cobham in Wallingford Castle, although York's support for Courtenay allowed him to avoid punishment. Serious violence had been avoided, yet the episode demonstrated the increasingly factionalism of the English nobility.[12]

The Challenge of York

In the following year, York attempted to use force to gain control of the government. The campaign was planned from his castle of Ludlow, from where he issued a public statement affirming his loyalty to the king but also his concerns as to the supposed machinations of his enemies on 9 January. He had already begun to gather his supporters from his estates in the Welsh Marches and from eastern England. There were also plans for risings throughout England, with his allies, Courtenay and Cobham, raising their forces in the south-west of England. In a letter dated 3 February, he wrote to the town of Shrewsbury, in which he claimed that the malevolent influence of Somerset was responsible for the loss of English territories in France and threatened the safety of the realm. Therefore, he explained, it was his intention to act against him. News of these activities prompted the king to summon a meeting of the council in Coventry, with Bonville given a commission to suppress the rebellion in the south-west on 14 February. York refused to attend the council and instead proceeded with his army towards London. The civic authorities, acting on royal instructions, refused to grant him entry to the city. Thwarted in this endeavour, he instead crossed the Thames at Kingston before heading eastwards to Dartford in Kent, where his forces constructed a fortified camp. Soon afterwards a larger royal army led in person by the king and many of the magnates arrived at Blackheath, only a short distance away. Bloodshed was prevented through negotiations with York submitting to royal authority. He swore an oath never to rebel against his sovereign again on 10 March in St Paul's Cathedral and was pardoned. His associates were treated more harshly, with Courtenay imprisoned in Wallingford Castle and Cobham in Berkhamsted Castle, whereas some of his supporters of lesser rank were subjected to trials and executions.[13]

Illness and Recovery

York escaped the consequences of his treasonous actions but had been humbled. He had failed to gain the support of his peers, or the common people in significant numbers, and was left isolated and discredited. By contrast, the authority of the king and his government was enhanced. Somerset remained in favour and on 6 September was granted the lordship of the Isle of Wight and Carisbrooke Castle. Henry moved to strengthen the royal family through the ennoblement of his two half-brothers, Edmund and Jasper Tudor, who were made earls of Richmond and Pembroke respectively on 23 November. Less than two months later they were knighted in a ceremony at the Tower. The outbreak of a pro-English rebellion in Gascony also provided the prospect of the recovery of the duchy, with John Talbot, earl of Shrewsbury, sent with an army to assist the rebels. Shrewsbury at first enjoyed great success with Bordeaux and other towns quickly recovered. However, he was killed, and his army was defeated at the Battle of Castillon on 17 July. News of this setback appears to have made a serious impression on Henry, who fell ill in early August. This was a grave affliction that left the king incapacitated and incapable of doing anything for himself. He was even said to have failed to respond to the sight of his son, Prince Edward, who was born on

13 October. The personal nature of medieval kingship meant that his government was quickly paralysed, with the resulting crisis providing York with an opportunity to take control of the government, with the support of the two Neville earls, Salisbury and Warwick. At a great council held on 21 November, Somerset was appealed of treason by John Mowbray, duke of Norfolk, for his role in the loss of Normandy. Two days later, he was incarcerated in the Tower, with Courtenay released from Wallingford Castle at around this time. York was subsequently appointed as Lord Protector on 27 March 1454 by Parliament, to serve during the incapacity of the king.[14]

One of the main challenges facing the Protector was the situation in the north of England, where disputes between the nobility had contributed to the breakdown of law and order. Tensions between the rival Percy and Neville families had escalated and resulted in acts of violence being committed throughout Yorkshire and the city of York. The cause of the feud was the marriage of Sir Thomas Neville, the second son of Salisbury, to Maud Stanhope, a niece and heiress of Ralph, Lord Cromwell. This was a contentious match as the latter held estates that had formerly belonged to the Percy earls of Northumberland, including Wressle Castle. The possibility of these lands falling into the possession of their Neville rivals was therefore regarded by the Percies as a provocation. They went so far as to ambush the wedding party whilst it was returning to Yorkshire from Cromwell's castle of Tattershall in Lincolnshire. However, they were repulsed at Heworth Moor a short distance from York, with the Nevilles making their way safely to Sheriff Hutton Castle. Instructions sent in the name of the king for both parties to keep the peace were ignored, with mutual acts of aggression occurring over the subsequent months.[15]

The following year saw further disturbances in the north, due to the machinations of Henry Holland, duke of Exeter, in alliance with Thomas Percy, Lord Egremont. They mustered a large force at Spofford in Yorkshire in late May, where Exeter was said to have asserted his claim to the governance of the kingdom, based upon his royal blood. The rebels used intimidation to gain entry to York but were rebuffed at Kingston upon Hull. Risings took place throughout Lancashire with an attempt made by 'persons of riotous and evil dispositions' to seize control of Lancaster Castle, who were said to have assembled in great numbers. This was an important centre of local administration and justice within the county, the safety of which was therefore vital. Sir Thomas Harrington was sent to secure the castle against the rebels, which he successfully accomplished. Later he was paid almost £40 in recompense for money he had spent on food and drink for the garrison. In the meanwhile, Exeter's attempts to seize control of Lancashire were rebuffed by Sir Thomas Stanley, with the approach of York and his forces prompting him to flee all the way south to Westminster Abbey to seek sanctuary in June. Later, he was unceremoniously dragged out from sanctuary and was imprisoned in Pontefract Castle, where Salisbury held the constableship. Egremont remained at large until the end of the year when he was captured by the Nevilles following a skirmish at Stamford Bridge. Afterwards, he was sent to the capital for incarceration in Newgate prison.[16]

The First Battle of St Albans

Henry recovered from his illness around Christmas. This removed the need for the protectorate, with York soon afterwards relinquishing his office and the king once again assuming control of government. Somerset was released from the Tower on 26 January 1455, although he was bound under sureties to answer the accusations made against him at a later meeting of the great council. Yet, Henry subsequently decided to absolve him of these charges and to remove the conditions placed upon his release on 4 March. He instead determined that the dispute between York and Somerset was to be decided by arbitration by a panel of lords in the summer, with both men entering into a recognisance of 20,000 marks to keep the peace. On 13 March, the king wrote to Salisbury to order the release of Exeter from Pontefract Castle, who was escorted by Humphrey Stafford, duke of Buckingham, to his presence. York was therefore once again in the political wilderness and excluded from the exercise of power. He decided to resort to force of arms to seize control of the government and to destroy his enemies. In contrast to his two previous attempts, in 1450 and 1452, no attempt was made to enlist the support of the commons of southern England. York instead relied on the forces that he and his Neville allies could raise themselves. Ignoring royal instructions to attend a council that was due to meet in Leicester on 21 May, they secretly gathered a sizeable army, mostly made up of their northern supporters, and quickly moved southwards towards London. News of their rapid approach took the king and the court by surprise. The decision was taken to leave the capital and to move northwards to St Albans to await reinforcements that had been urgently summoned to join the royal host. However, they were confronted by the Yorkists before these additional contingents could arrive.[17]

After reaching the vicinity of the town, York sent envoys to negotiate with the king. His principal demand was that Somerset should be handed over to his custody. This was completely unacceptable to the king, who was said to have angrily refused, which led to a Yorkist attack on the royal host. The royalists had deployed in the centre of the unwalled town and had manned the barriers at the entrances. At first, they had some success in repelling the attackers, but were outflanked by Warwick's force who gained an entry through gardens on the south side. This led to the out-numbered royalists being quickly overwhelmed. Contemporary accounts of the battle reporting that between 25 and 400 men were killed. These losses were primarily suffered by the royalists, with Somerset, the earl of Northumberland and Thomas, Lord Clifford slain, with other magnates, such as Buckingham and Courtenay, wounded. Henry, who had been injured by an arrow in the neck, was escorted by the Yorkists with rever-ence to the abbey of St Albans, before being taken the next day to London. Yet, he was now a prisoner of the Yorkists. Therefore, through a flagrant act of violence York had destroyed Somerset and gained control of the king's person.[18]

The Siege of Powderham Castle

York and his supporters had committed an act of treason by attacking the royal host with the king's banner unfurled. They had also incurred the enmity of the heirs of the slain men and the Lancastrian court. It was therefore imperative for York to obtain acceptance for their actions and to secure his position as de facto ruler of the kingdom. Henry was escorted with honour by the Yorkist lords to London, where a public demon-stration of reconciliation was staged. A crown-wearing ceremony took place in St Paul's Cathedral on 25 May, with the king receiving his crown from York. On the following day, Parliament was summoned to meet at Westminster in July. Fears of a royalist counterattack meant that instruc-tions were given to the lords to attend with only small retinues. By con-trast, York, Warwick and Salisbury were reported as being accompanied by armed retainers. Despite these measures, the parliament of 1455 was a fractious affair. Warwick was said to have angrily accused Lord Cromwell of having been responsible for the clash at St Albans. John Sutton, Lord Dudley's vocal complaints about the actions of the Yorkists led to his imprisonment in the Tower, with Exeter having already been sent to Wallingford Castle for safekeeping. Nevertheless, a parliamentary act of 18 July provided a full pardon for all those who had fought with York and immunity from prosecution. The blame for the engagement was squarely placed on the deceased Somerset and two other men, Thomas Thorp and

William Joseph. Meanwhile, trouble was brewing once again in the south-west of England due to the revival of the Courtenay-Bonville feud.[19]

Courtenay's participation in York's Dartford campaign of 1452 had resulted in his imprisonment for eighteen months. During this time, his authority in the south-west was further undermined by his rival, Lord Bonville. The latter's influence in the region had been enhanced through royal grants, including his appointment as steward of the duchy of Cornwall, to the constableships of Exeter and Lydford castles, and to various commissions. However, despite the king's largesse, Bonville sought to ingratiate himself with the Yorkists following the First Battle of St Albans through arranging the marriage of his grandson and heir, William, to Katherine Neville, a daughter of Salisbury. This new alliance provoked Courtenay and his affinity into committing fresh acts of violence against his adversary. Operations were organised from the earl's seat at Tiverton Castle, some 15 miles north of Exeter, where he had his own stock of artillery. It was also here that Courtenay gathered together his supporters for the campaign. Their first foray took place in October, when an armed force led by the sons of the earl entered the city of Exeter and through intimidation disturbed the sessions of the peace. This was followed later in the month by the shocking murder of Nicholas Radford, an associate of Bonville, in his own house. On 1 November, the earl was said to have assembled an army of 1,000 men with which he occupied Exeter. Afterwards he headed southwards to Powderham Castle, where he arrived two days later.[20]

Powderham was owned by his cousin Sir Philip Courtenay. Despite their familial relationship, the earl loathed his relative as he felt that the castle by right belonged to him, rather than to a junior branch of the family, and for his alliance with Bonville. It was subsequently alleged that Courtenay's men came in a warlike array to 'threaten, assault, beat, wound, ill-treat & slay' the occupants.[21] Powderham was more a fortified manor than a fortress, consisting of a small courtyard castle entered via a gatehouse, therefore they may have expected little resistance. If so, they were disappointed, as they found the castle to be resolutely defended by Sir Philip and his men. They were thus forced to lay siege to the place. Their first move was to surround the castle and fix their guns into the ground. By the fifteenth day of the month, they were ready to carry out a major assault. According to a later indictment, it was stated that from 8 o'clock in the morning until 4 o'clock in the afternoon, a constant bombardment was maintained by the attackers. They employed large guns firing heavy projectiles, known as bombards, as well as long-barrelled guns called serpentines, and shot many arrows from longbows. Despite this onslaught, the defenders were able to resist the attackers. This setback prompted Courtenay to withdraw to Exeter, leaving his son Henry behind to oversee the siege with 500 men. Three days later, Bonville with a small force attempted to go to the aid of his neighbour but was forced to withdraw by the besiegers. Soon afterwards, Courtenay attempted to solicit the assistance of the citizens of Exeter but was firmly rebuffed by the mayor. Instead, he returned to the siege of Powderham with most of his men.[22]

Bonville had withdrawn to gather reinforcements and a month later felt ready to confront Courtenay in the field, to whom he issued a formal challenge. On 15 December, the two armies encountered each other at Clyst Heath, a few miles to the east of Exeter. Bonville's forces were quickly routed and his main residence at Shute was pillaged four days later, with Courtenay returning in triumph to Exeter. The fighting of a pitched battle prompted a response from York, who had recently been appointed as Lord Protector for second time by Parliament. He travelled toward the West Country accompanied by ten lords and other men of high rank to bring Courtenay to obedience. The latter met him at Shaftesbury in Dorset, where he submitted and was escorted to London. By Christmas he had been committed to the Tower, to await trial by his peers. However, this did not take place due to political developments. York's attempt to enact a radical programme of reform in Parliament met with sustained opposition from the Lords. This principally consisted of proposals to significantly reduce expenditure on the king's household and a widespread resumption of royal grants. These measures were justified as a means of improving the royal finances, which were in a perilous state. However, his failure to garner support from his fellow peers and resistance from the king led to him resigning his office on 25 February 1456. The short-lived second protectorate of York was therefore at an end. Now restored to power, the king and the court sought to bolster their prestige and to quell unrest in the more remote regions of the realm.[23]

The Struggle for South Wales

By the end of November 1455, the king's half-brother Edmund Tudor, earl of Richmond, had travelled to Pembrokeshire in the south-west of Wales, where he spent the winter. Yet, his arrival soon provoked opposition from a prominent local gentleman, Gruffydd ap Nicholas. This was because Richmond had been tasked with restoring royal authority in an area that had long been neglected by the king and his officials. The most important offices in Wales were held by members of the peerage. Yet, these men were frequently absentee office-holders, with their duties instead performed by members of the local gentry. By the 1440s, the most important of their number in south Wales was Gruffydd, who had achieved a position of pre-eminence in the region by using violent and unscrupulous methods. According to a later account he was stated to have been a 'man of a hot, fiery and choleric spirit', who was also 'crafty (and) ambitious beyond measure'.[24] In a petition sent to Parliament in late 1455, it was claimed that Gruffydd had committed many outrages in south Wales. His misdeeds included seizing control of the castles of Carmarthen, Aberstwyth, Carreg Cennen, Kidwelly and Cardigan, which he had fortified and garrisoned. He was ordered to transfer custody of Carmarthen and Aberstwyth to York, who had been appointed as constable of those places in June 1455, but had refused to comply. Richmond's intrusion into his sphere of influence was therefore perceived as a threat by Gruffydd who moved against him. On 7 June 1456, it was reported that both men were 'at war greatly in Wales'.[25] Richmond eventually gained the upper hand in the struggle and had taken control of Carmarthen by August. Yet, this outcome prompted a fierce reaction from the supporters of the duke of York in the region.[26]

The two main adherents of the latter were Sir William Herbert and Sir Walter Devereux, who were both notable members of the gentry in Herefordshire and south-east Wales. They held offices from the duke, with Herbert serving as York's steward in his lordships of Usk and Caerleon, and Devereux as steward in his lordship of Radnor. Both men were connected to each other by marriage, through Herbert's union with Devereux's daughter, Anne, in 1449. Devereux had even vouched for the loyalty of his son-in-law in 1454, when he wrote to the duke to assure him that Herbert had said that 'he is no man's man but only yours'.[27] They were therefore acting on York's instructions, or at the very least with his blessing, when they decided to move against Richmond in the summer of 1456. It was later claimed that they raised a force of 2,000 men from Herefordshire on 10 August. Proceeding westwards, they headed for Carmarthen, the largest settlement and centre of royal government in south Wales. The town was fortified by a circuit of walls and was adjoined by a substantial castle on its southern edge. The latter contained a shell keep as well as an outer and inner ward, with sizeable sums regularly spent on its upkeep and maintenance. Yet, the attackers appear to have had little difficulty in capturing the place, with Richmond subsequently imprisoned in the castle.[28]

Afterwards they advanced to Aberystwyth in the far west of Wales. This was one of the settlements that had been founded in the late thirteenth century during the reign of Edward I. The castle was concentric and diamond-shaped, with two wards and a dry moat. It was situated on the seashore on the west side of the town and was routinely garrisoned by a small force of one man-at-arms and twelve archers. This fortress also fell to the forces of Herbert and Devereux. Having seized the chamberlain's seal from Carmarthen Castle, they then used it to illegally grant themselves the authority to hold judicial sessions and seized administrative records. Richmond was soon released from captivity, but he died of the plague a short time later. News of Herbert's and Devereux's activities led to them being summoned to attend the council being held at Coventry in late September, with both men submitting to the king. Devereux was held at Windsor Castle but Herbert, after securing bail from the Tower, fled to Wales. On 25 October, he allegedly was at Abergavenny, where he attempted to incite the men of the surrounding lordships to join him in arms. Herbert eventually surrendered to the king at Leicester on 7 June 1457 and was pardoned, with Devereux remaining in custody until the following year. The restoration of peace to south Wales coincided with Henry's decision to remove the constableships of Carmarthen and Aberstwyth castles from York, who was granted an annuity of £40 in recompense, and to grant them to his surviving half-brother Jasper Tudor, earl of Pembroke. Thereafter, the latter was tasked with maintaining the interests of the Lancastrian dynasty in the region.[29]

The Defence of the Realm and the Calais Garrison

Yet, regional disturbances were not the only threat to the peace of the realm. On 24 August 1457, a French fleet led by Pierre de Brézé, seneschal of Normandy, attacked Sandwich in Kent. The raiders succeeded in gaining entry to the town, where they caused significant damage, with the mayor killed during the fighting. Eventually they were expelled after a counterattack was launched by Sir Thomas Kyriell, the lieutenant of Dover Castle, with forces drawn from the local area. This raid caused considerable alarm across the kingdom and revived fears of a French invasion. Measures were therefore taken to array men in the coastal regions and to safeguard key fortifications. On 29 August, Sir John Fastolf was instructed to attend to the defence of Great Yarmouth in Norfolk. Four days later, Sir John Lisle was ordered to array men for the defence of Portchester Castle. A commission was also given to Thomas Hexstall, the receiver of Dover Castle and two other men, John Roger and William Armurer, to procure gunpowder, bows, arrows and other equipment for the defence of the castle and the nearby ports on 28 September. Efforts were also made to ensure that strategic castles in the south-east of England were placed into the custody of reliable men who could be trusted by the royal court. On 14 October, Henry Beaufort, duke of Somerset (whose father had been killed at the First Battle of St Albans) was appointed as lieutenant and keeper of the lordship and castle of Carisbrooke with a garrison of ten men-at-arms and thirty archers. This was followed by the appointment of Nicholas Carew, a member of the royal household, as constable of Southampton Castle in Hampshire on November, and Richard Woodville, Lord Rivers, as constable of Rochester in Kent ten days later. Sir John Cheyne was subsequently appointed as constable of Queenborough Castle on the Isle of Sheppey in Kent. The terms of his appointment implied that he was expected to reside at the fortress for its safeguard, as it specified that he was to be given lodgings of his own choice.[30]

Instructions were also issued for a force of 13,000 archers to be assembled for coastal defence at the end of 1457. This was funded by a grant of taxation that had been originally granted by the parliament held at Reading four years earlier. Yet, the great expense of paying for the wages of such a large army meant that it could only be maintained for a short period of time. Another method to safeguard the realm was through the raising of naval forces. The king's father, Henry V, had spent large sums on building up a small fleet of royal ships, but by the 1450s these vessels had long since been sold off as a cost-saving measure. This meant that shipping for naval service had to be obtained through the impressment of merchant ships and their crews, who would be obliged to serve the Crown in return for the payment of wages. On 26 November 1457, Warwick was appointed to keep the sea by the 'advice and assent of the council' for a period of three years by indenture. He was authorised to assemble a fleet of ships to wage war on the king's enemies and to suppress piracy. Warwick made good use of the naval forces he gathered, attacking both hostile and friendly shipping alike, and amassing large amounts of booty in the process. In part his success was because he already held another important military command as captain of the Calais garrison, which gave him access to significant resources in manpower.[31]

This office had been conferred on him in 1455, during the second protectorate of York, and he kept the post even after the resumption of power by the king. Warwick had experienced some initial difficulties in taking up his command, as the soldiers of the garrison were mutinous due to long-standing arrears in their pay. This standoff was only resolved through a settlement whereby the merchants of the staple of Calais paid the out-standing balance, in return for a loan which was to be repaid by assignments from the custom duties. Thereafter, Warwick succeeded in retaining the loyalty of the soldiers through brazen acts of piracy to fund their wages, with his exploits including the capture of a large Hanseatic fleet in 1458 and a Castilian fleet the following year. These actions helped to secure the safety of the Pale of Calais and the English Channel, although they were responsible for straining relations with foreign powers. The embarrassment caused to the government by attacks on ships of countries that had treaties with England, and concerns about the military resources available to Warwick, also contributed to growing tensions between the Lancastrian and Yorkist factions.[32]

Chapter Three

Civil War

Ludford Bridge

After his restoration to power in February 1456, the king sought to reconcile the Yorkist and Lancastrian lords. This was no easy task as relations between the two factions remained fraught. The relatives of the men killed at St Albans, namely the duke of Somerset, the earl of Northumberland and Lord Clifford, were eager for revenge against the Yorkists. However, the king's efforts finally bore fruit at a great council held at Westminster in March 1458, with discussions resulting in an agreement to end the feud. The Yorkist lords agreed to pay financial compensation to the heirs of the killed Lancastrian lords and to endow a chantry at the abbey of St Albans to pray for their souls. This culminated in a public ceremony of reconciliation known as a Loveday, where the magnates swore oaths of friendship to each other at St Paul's Cathedral on 25 March. Nevertheless, tensions remained high, with visits to the capital by the Yorkist lords often resulting in violence. In November 1458, a scuffle between one of Warwick's retainers and a member of the king's household escalated into a full-scale brawl, with Warwick said to have almost been killed by the royal cooks. This situation encouraged the Yorkist lords to spend most of their time away from court. Warwick resided almost continuously at Calais, Salisbury in his northern estates and York in his strongholds in the west of England and Yorkshire. Yet, the uneasy truce between the two sides was soon to be broken.[1]

By the end of 1458 the Yorkist lords had decided to take up arms against the king once again. Salisbury was said to have convened a meeting of his council at his castle of Middleham in Yorkshire, which took place in November. Middleham was his chief residence and was from where he organised the forthcoming campaign. The castle consists of a large rectangular keep, dating from the twelfth century, encircled by a curtain wall and entered through a three-storey gatehouse. It was almost certainly in the great hall or great chamber of the keep, that the meeting took place, where he pledged to 'take full part with the full noble prince, the Duke of York'.[2] The Yorkists could draw upon considerable military and financial resources for this enterprise. In addition to the tenants they could assemble from their own estates, they also held most of the military commands in the kingdom. Warwick was captain of Calais and keeper of the sea, whereas Salisbury was warden of the west march of Scotland and York was lieutenant of Ireland. Yet, it took them almost a year to mobilise their forces. In the meanwhile, their adversaries learnt of these preparations and undertook countermeasures. On 29 April, orders were issued for the gentry of Norfolk to assemble men in defensible array with enough money to cover their expenses for two months to meet the king at Leicester eleven days later. The failure of the Yorkist lords to attend a subsequent meeting of the great council held in Coventry in June led to indictments being made against them. Both sides were therefore prepared for a confrontation, with the Yorkists finally making their move in September. It was subsequently alleged by their enemies that their plan was to make a sudden attack on Kenilworth Castle to take the king and the court by surprise.[3]

Salisbury was said to have marched southwards from Middleham accompanied by a force of 5,000 men. However, forewarned of his movements, the king took to the field with his army and advanced from Coventry to Nottingham to intercept him. This compelled Salisbury to take a different route, as he wished to avoid engaging the main royalist force without the assistance of his allies. Whilst travelling through Staffordshire he was confronted by a Lancastrian army led by James Tuchet, Lord Audley, at Blore Heath on 23 September. Audley's army was said to have comprised a greater part of the knights and gentry of Cheshire, which had been assembled by the command of Queen Margaret, who chose to reside with her son Prince Edward in nearby Eccleshall Castle. The Yorkists were victorious in the engagement against the queen's 'gallants', with the latter suffering significant losses. This outcome was due in part to the failure of Thomas, Lord Stanley, to intervene in the battle on the royalist side with the men he had raised. Nevertheless, with the main royal army closing in rapidly, the Yorkists only barely made their escape. According to *Gregory's Chronicle*, this was because a friar was left behind to shoot their guns all through the night, thereby masking their flight. Yet, Salisbury's sons, John and Thomas, together with Sir Thomas Harrington and some other men, were less fortunate than their companions. On the following day they were defeated in a skirmish at Acton Bridge and imprisoned at Chester Castle.[4]

Despite this setback, the bulk of his army was subsequently able to join forces with York at Ludlow Castle in Shropshire. This was York's favourite residence and an impressive stronghold in the Welsh Marches.

The castle has a large outer bailey, with a smaller inner one incorporating a keep and other high-status buildings. Meanwhile, Warwick had landed in Kent with a contingent from the Calais garrison and was admitted into London where he spent one night. From there he travelled westwards to Warwick Castle before reaching his allies at Ludlow. The combined Yorkist army then moved eastwards to Worcester, where their leaders pledged their allegiance to the king in the cathedral. A royal herald was sent to offer them pardons for their actions, but those men who had fought at Blore Heath were specifically excluded. These terms were deemed unacceptable by the Yorkists. Instead, the rapid approach of the royal host prompted them to flee southwards to Tewkesbury, where they crossed the River Severn before making their return to Ludlow. They took up a defensive position to the south of the castle at Ludford Bridge and deployed guns in carts in front of their army. On 12 October, the king's army arrived in the vicinity and prepared to meet their adversaries in battle the following day. Yet, morale in the Yorkist ranks was low, with many of their men, including the soldiers from the Calais garrison, unwilling to fight against the king in the field. This prompted their commanders to abandon the army in the night and to take flight. Forsaken by their leaders the Yorkist soldiers submitted to the king and were pardoned. The royalists then proceeded to loot Ludlow, with one account claiming that it was robbed to the 'bare walls'. Afterwards a garrison was installed in the castle, with Edmund Delamere, entrusted with its safeguard.[5]

Denbigh Castle and the Welsh Marches

York with his son Edmund, earl of Rutland, fled through Wales, destroying bridges as they went to impede their pursuers. Eventually they reached the coast and travelled by ship to Ireland, where they were well received. At the same time, Warwick, Salisbury and York's eldest son, Edward, earl of March, fled southwards to Devon. There they hired a ship and sailed to Calais, which they reached on 2 November, having stopped at Guernsey on the way. They arrived just in time at the town, as Somerset had been tasked with reclaiming the territory for the king with a force of 1,000 men. He tried to gain entry to Calais a short time later but was repulsed by the garrison. However, Somerset succeeded in taking control of the two other main fortifications in the Pale, the castles of Guînes and Hammes. The territory was therefore divided between the Yorkists and Lancastrians, with both sides engaging in frequent skirmishes over the following months. Attempts were also made by the Crown to compel the king's subjects in Ireland to act against York, but the latter's authority in the country was such that these commands were ignored. The inability of the Lancastrians to dislodge the exiled Yorkists from their overseas strongholds was a major setback, which was to have serious consequences. Yet, the latter still suffered the forfeiture of their estates in England and Wales.[6]

The day after the confrontation at Ludford Bridge, orders had been sent out for royal officials to seize control of the lands belonging to the duke of York and the Neville earls. Seven days later, instructions were issued for a parliament to meet at Coventry on 20 November. The parliament was subsequently known as the 'Parliament of Devils' by the Yorkists. This was because its main purpose was to condemn the duke of York and his adherents for their treacherous deeds. During the parliament it was stated that for their crime of having traitorously waged war against the king they should be 'attainted of high treason, as false traitors and enemies'.[7] Thirty-seven individuals, including York, Warwick and Salisbury, were attainted, thereby forfeiting their lands and titles for themselves and their heirs. Nevertheless, the king exercised his prerogative of mercy. Prominent Yorkists, such as Herbert, were pardoned, as was Stanley, who was widely blamed for the debacle at Blore Heath, and none of the rebels were executed.[8]

The confiscation of the estates of the Yorkist lords presented the Crown with a rich windfall, as they were the wealthiest magnates in the kingdom. Rather than granting ownership of these newly acquired lands to reward loyal supporters, the decision was taken to retain most of them in the hands of royal officials. The intention was to use the revenues from the seized manors to improve the finances of the Crown. Nonetheless, the appointment of office holders in these lordships allowed the king to exercise patronage such as with the allocation of castle constableships. The beneficiaries of these grants included Henry Holland, duke of Exeter, for Fotheringay Castle, Thomas Percy, Lord Egremond, for Conisbrough Castle, John, Lord Clifford, for Penrith Castle, and John, Lord Neville, for the castles of Middleham and Sheriff Hutton. However, the suppression of the rebellion had contributed to a breakdown of law and order. This can be seen from a commission directed to the earls of Northumberland and Westmorland and other notable landowners in Yorkshire to survey and take into their hands the estates of the Yorkists in the county. It refers to 'certain evildoers and disturbers of the peace', who through pretending that the possessions of the king's traitors should be divided amongst his faithful lieges had plundered their castles, manors and other lands. Furthermore, royal officials were met with armed resistance in the Welsh Marches from the supporters of the duke of York.[9]

Responsibility for taking control of rebel lands in the region was officially assigned to the king's son, Edward of Westminster, prince of Wales. On 1 February 1460, he was instructed to seize these estates and to allocate a suitable number of men-at-arms and other soldiers for their safeguard. Yet in practice, as he was only 6 years old, the task was carried out on his behalf by his uncle, Jasper Tudor. Three days later, they were commissioned to investigate acts of treason and rebellion that had taken place in the west of England and Wales, along with notable landowners in the area, such as Sir Walter Skull and Sir John Stanley. However, by the following day, it had been reported to the king that they had been prevented from taking possession of these lordships and their revenues. This was due to the outbreak of a rebellion by adherents of the Yorkist lords. Jasper was therefore allocated the sum of £333 from the revenues of the lordships of Usk, Caerleon and Glamorgan in south-east Wales for retaining knights and men-at-arms for crushing the rebels. Yet, the scale of the uprising meant that within the space of eleven days, by 16 February, he had written to the king to request artillery and money. This was required for the siege of the castle of Denbigh in the north-east of Wales.[10]

Denbigh had been founded in the late thirteenth century following the Edwardian conquest of Wales. It was a large and impressive fortress that served as the seat of one of the wealthiest baronies in Wales. The castle takes the form of an oval enclosure that is situated on the south-west corner of the adjoining town on a hilltop. Its main entrance was via the town through a remarkable triple-towered gatehouse, whereas the external facing postern gate to the south was defended by a barbican.[11] On 5 January 1460, the constableship of Denbigh was granted to Jasper by the king, yet he was prevented from taking possession of the castle by its garrison who held it for the duke of York.[12] Therefore, to capture the place, Jasper required large guns to bombard the defenders. Fortunately for him, the Crown had been steadily augmenting its stockpile of ordnance throughout the 1450s. This included huge pieces, such as the three bombards that were forged between 1453 and 1456, called *Goodgrace* (22,400lb), *Henry* (19,040lb) and *Crown* (7,840lb). In addition, there were three large serpentines under construction in December 1459, which were designed to be 'of power … to subdue any castle or place that will rebel'.[13]

At least some of the royal guns were allocated to crushing the rebellion. By 16 February, Henry had written a letter to the treasurer, James Butler, earl of Ormond and Wiltshire, ordering the despatch of artillery for the subjugation of Denbigh. Instructions were also sent to two men, William Bungey and John Wheler, to procure workers and materials for the

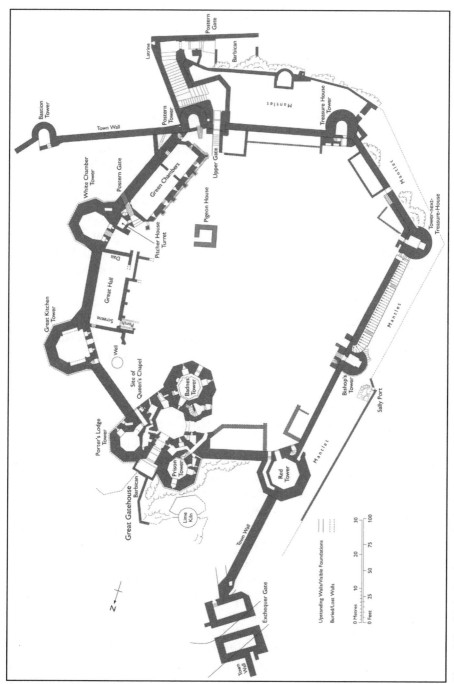

Plan of Denbigh Castle, Denbighshire. (©*Crown copyright (2019) Cadw*)

construction of carts to transport guns to Wales. On the following day, a commission of array was granted to Jasper to assemble men from Wales and the counties of west England to resist the rebels. By 22 February the siege of the castle had already begun, as evidenced by a grant to seize the removable goods of the defenders for his good service in carrying out this task. These were to be distributed at his pleasure in rewarding the king's faithful subjects in his army. Jasper was also empowered to receive into the king's grace any of the rebels in the castle who were willing to submit themselves to his authority. However, this grant specifically excluded any Englishmen or Irishmen in the garrison, who were to be imprisoned by royal command. Furthermore, any Welshmen who were attainted or outlawed were to be kept in prison until they had provided sureties for their future good behaviour. In addition to this, Jasper was given the right to put on trial and execute any of the rebels in the region. At the same time, orders were sent to prominent loyalist members of the gentry throughout western and southern Wales to take musters of the men being assembled for service at the siege. In Pembrokeshire, this task was directed to Sir Robert Veer, Sir William Vernon, Sir Henry Wogan, Thomas Wyryot, esquire, Thomas Wogan, esquire and Thomas Perot, esquire. The same instructions were also sent to gentlemen in Carmarthenshire, Cardiganshire and the lordships of Kidwelly and Gower.[14]

Despite these measures, the defenders of Denbigh were still holding out a month later. Prosecuting the siege proved to be an expensive business for Jasper, who was allocated a total of £1,666 to cover some of his costs on 13 March, which was to be drawn from the revenues of confiscated Yorkist estates. On the same day, he was authorised to arrest and punish their adherents who were said to be wandering throughout Wales. A short time later, the garrison of the castle surrendered, with Jasper travelling to Pembrokeshire to organise its defence in May. Yet, Denbigh was not the only fortress being held by the rebels. Further to the south, in the Marcher lordships of Ewile, Radnor, Clifford, Wigmore and others in east Wales, royal officials had also met with opposition. It was for this reason that Sir John Barre, Sir John Skydmore and other members of the gentry were ordered to seize control of them on 16 April.[15] They had succeeded in quelling all resistance within the space of a month and a half. This was reported to the king in a letter dated 1 June, which was written on behalf of Prince Edward. It was explained that they had occupied the castles of Wigmore, Pencelli, Radnor and Clifford, and garrisoned them with footmen receiving 4*d.* per day. This was ostensibly to ensure 'the safeguard of them and for the defence of robberies and for the tracking of thieves'.

Furthermore, they had extracted oaths of allegiance from the inhabitants of these areas who had sworn to faithfully serve the king as his true liege-men. Therefore, by the summer of 1460 the Lancastrians had succeeded in pacifying Wales. However, this success was overshadowed by events elsewhere. Not merely had the Yorkists fended off royalist attempts to dislodge them from their strongholds in Calais and Ireland, but they were now readying themselves to invade the kingdom.[16]

The War at Sea and Coastal Defence

In the winter of 1459, measures had been enacted by the government to raise naval forces with which to attack the Yorkists and to send rein-forcements to Somerset in the Pale of Calais. This task was initially allocated to Richard Woodville, Lord Rivers, who was also entrusted with organising the defence of south-east England. On 30 October, he was commissioned to array the men of Kent against the Yorkists, who were said to be inciting gatherings and insurrections against the king. Rivers was also instructed to seize the ships belonging to Warwick that could be found in the county. By 10 December, his preparations were sufficiently advanced for him to receive further instructions to muster the men-at-arms and archers that had gathered in and around Sandwich. However, before the expeditionary force could embark, their opponents moved against them. A Yorkist fleet from Calais descended on Sandwich on 15 January catching their opponents completely off-guard. The raiders succeeded in capturing the assembled ships and the leaders of the expe-dition, who were carried off as prisoners. Once in Calais, the unfortunate Rivers was said to have been berated by the Yorkist Lords who called him a 'knave's son' for having dared to call them traitors. Instead, they claimed to be the king's true liegemen and that it 'was not his part to have such language of lords, being of the king's blood'.[17]

This setback prompted the government to redouble its efforts to assemble naval forces capable of countering the Yorkists at sea. Sir Baldwin Fulford, the sheriff of Devon, entered into a contract with the Crown to keep the sea with 1,000 men serving in a fleet for a quarter of a year on 3 February. Later, on 19 March, the duke of Exeter indented to serve for three years with a force of 3,500 men. His appointment was undoubtedly a response to the news that Warwick had landed in Waterford in Ireland only three days earlier. The latter had made the journey so that he could confer with York, so that they could plan their forthcoming invasion of England. This was to be a two-pronged attack, with Warwick landing in the south-east, where they had many supporters for their cause, and York in the north. The royalists, who had some inkling of what their enemies were plotting, attempted to foil these plans. On 25 May, Exeter set sail from Sandwich with a fleet that was said to number 14 ships and had 1,500 men on board. A week later, they caught sight of Warwick's ships off the coast of Cornwall. Yet no engagement took place. It was claimed that this failure was either due to the cowardice of Exeter or because his ships lacked supplies, which forced him to put in to Dartmouth where the fleet was disbanded. Regardless of the reason, Exeter had let slip a golden opportunity to strike a decisive blow against the Yorkists. This was especially unfortunate, as a lack of funds meant that another fleet could not be put to sea by the government. To compound the situation further, Somerset's forces had been routed in a skirmish at Newnham Bridge on 23 April. His losses in manpower and the failure of the government to send significant reinforcements hampered his ability to pressure the Yorkists in Calais. As a result of these reverses, the Lancastrians were now firmly on the defensive.[18]

Fears of a Yorkist invasion meant that the government had frequently issued orders concerning the defence of the realm over the preceding months. Uncertainty about where their enemies would strike meant that commissions were sent to magnates, gentlemen and burgesses throughout the kingdom to array men on 21 December 1459. However, the focus of defence soon shifted to southern England, due to the danger posed by the Yorkists at Calais and their powerful fleet. In January, orders were sent to William FitzAlan, earl of Arundel, and others to organise the defence of Hampshire and Canterbury. This was followed by further instructions regarding the protection of Bristol, Kent and Surrey over the next three months. Yet, concerns about the safety of even inland settlements prompted the government to order Sir Walter Skull and Thomas Throgmarton to oversee the defence of Worcester on 27 March. They were tasked with ensuring that the inhabitants would guard the walls, gates and bridge of the city. This was because the intention of the Yorkist lords was said to be to 'subjugate cities, castles, fortified towns and fortalices and hold them against the king'. It was for this reason that John Judde, the master of the king's ordnance, was tasked with surveying fortifications throughout the realm and to supply them with artillery. This was furnished from both the royal arsenal and from ordnance confiscated from the estates of the Yorkists. In the meanwhile, the king and the court had withdrawn to Kenilworth Castle in the West Midlands.[19]

Kenilworth had several advantages that made it an attractive place as a royalist base. It was in close proximity to regions where the Crown could command considerable support, notably Wales and Cheshire, and had a more central geographical location than London. Kenilworth had also been a favoured royal residence since the reign of Henry IV. The latter's father, John of Gaunt, duke of Lancaster, had spent large sums on transforming it into a lavish and impressive palatial castle. His improvements included the construction of a grand great hall and luxurious apartments, with further works carried out by his successors. Nevertheless, Kenilworth still had powerful defences that meant that it could be used as a place of refuge if required. Since the thirteenth century, the castle had been encircled by a series of water features, including a huge artificial lake, which made it difficult to besiege. Throughout the 1450s it had also been used by the Crown for coordinating operations against rebels, such as Herbert and Devereux, and as a storage area for the royal field artillery. Measures to improve the castle's defences further were carried out in response to the Yorkist threat in 1460. The chronicler John Benet records that the king held a council at Coventry in late May or June, where it was decided to fortify Kenilworth. Orders were also sent for guns to be sent there from the Tower of London, with forty cartloads of ordnance said to have been transported to the castle. Therefore, having strengthened their stronghold, the king and court awaited the Yorkist invasion from the relative safety of Kenilworth.[20]

The Yorkist Invasion and the Siege of the Tower of London

The Yorkist onslaught began in late June with another attack on Sandwich, where reinforcements for Somerset's army were awaiting transportation. Taken unawares, the latter were overwhelmed by their adversaries, with their commander, Osbert Mundford, executed after being taken prisoner. However, unlike with their previous raid, this time the Yorkists decided to retain Sandwich as a base, with William Neville, Lord Fauconberg, left in charge. Having secured this foothold, the Yorkist lords, Warwick, Salisbury and March, landed at the town on 26 June. From there they proceeded inland towards Canterbury. They faced little to no resistance during their journey and the gates of the city were thrown open to them. The defence of the region had ostensibly been entrusted to the duke of Buckingham. Yet, he was with the king in the Midlands. In his absence, the local gentry, including men in service to the duke, such as Sir Thomas Kyriell, constable of Dover Castle, assumed responsibility. However, upon the approach of the Yorkist host, many of them switched sides and joined their erstwhile opponents. This change of heart was partly motivated by the pro-Yorkist sympathies of the commons of the county. The Yorkist lords cunningly adopted some of the demands of Cade's rebels to solicit support from the south-east in a manifesto they disseminated. This scheme succeeded in winning widespread support from the people of the county, who thereafter were prominent in supporting the Yorkist cause. The defection of both the elites and commons of Kent had important consequences. It resulted in the Yorkists gaining control of a strategic county, with its settlements and castles, which allowed them to reinforce their army. Furthermore, it left the way clear for a march on the capital.[21]

The inhabitants of the London were not taken unawares by this development. Since February, measures had been undertaken to ensure the safeguard of the city. The citizens were placed on high alert and the guilds were prevailed upon to make a financial contribution towards the purchase of artillery. News of the Yorkist landing in June prompted the civic authorities to redouble their efforts to prepare the defences of the city. At a common council meeting held on 27 June, the attendees agreed to support the mayor and aldermen in resisting the rebels of the king, with instructions issued for the gates to be guarded. On the following day, the council decided that the gate on the drawbridge of London Bridge should be kept shut, with a garrison of men-at-arms installed in the tower on the bridge, on standby to drop the portcullis against attackers if required. Furthermore, a deputation was sent to the Yorkist lords in an attempt to dissuade them from marching on the city. Yet they also made the curious decision to deny the royalist commanders of the Tower of London, Thomas, Lord Scales, and Robert, Lord Hungerford, any role in the defence of the city. It was subsequently alleged that they had adopted this policy because Scales sought to become the captain of the city and thereby have its 'rule and governance', to which they strongly objected.[22] A more probable explanation is that the citizens were already wavering in their loyalty to the Lancastrian cause. On 1 July, the delegation returned to London, having been unsuccessful in their mission to divert the Yorkist lords. This failure appears to have been the final straw for the citizens, who no doubt feared the consequences of being attacked by a hostile army. A day later the Yorkist army entered the city without opposition.[23]

Their leaders first made their way to St Paul's Cathedral. There they were greeted by the archbishop of Canterbury, Thomas Bourchier, and other bishops, as well as the mayor and aldermen of the city. The next day they attended the convocation of ecclesiastics held at Greyfriars, where they received the support of the clergymen present. Afterwards they moved to quell any opposition to their control of the city. On the following day, at a meeting held at the Guildhall, supporters of the king were indicted and thrown into prison. The bulk of the Yorkist army, led by Warwick and March, then left the city to confront the forces of Henry VI, having been provided with carts, horses and a substantial loan of £1,000 by the civic authorities. However, the earl of Salisbury, Thomas, Lord Cobham and Sir John Wenlock, with some of their forces, were left behind in the city. This was because the Yorkists still had to deal with the remaining supporters of Henry VI, who had taken refuge in the Tower.[24]

The defection of the Londoners must have come as a great shock to Scales, Hungerford and the other royal councillors. They were now isolated and cut off from outside support in the Tower. Nevertheless, they were determined to resist the Yorkists, despite their grave situation. They were experienced veterans of the wars in France and were accompanied by an array of other lords and knights. These included Henry Bromflete, Lord Vessy, John, Lord Lovell, Richard West, Lord de la Warr, John de Foix, earl of Kendal, Sir Edmund Hampden, Sir Thomas Tyrell of Heron, Sir Gervase Clifton, treasurer of the king's household, and many others of lower rank, including thirty-five Italian galley men. They could also utilise the weaponry kept at the castle. Despite the despatch of substantial quantities of armaments to Kenilworth Castle, the armoury was still well-stocked with many guns and crossbows. The Tower was also a formidable fortress, where they could potentially withstand a lengthy siege. It had served as a major royal castle and palace since the reign of William the Conqueror, who was responsible for ordering the construction of its famed White Tower. Substantial works were carried out to the site over the course of the thirteenth and fourteenth centuries, greatly expanding its extent to 12 acres. By the mid-fifteenth century, it was a large concentric castle with outer and inner walls, surrounded by a moat. Its location on the south-eastern edge of the city meant that it could also be supplied by boat. Entry to the fortress by land was via an elaborate entrance that posed a daunting challenge to potential attackers. An outer drawbridge led to a D-shaped barbican known as the Lion's Tower (so-called because lions were kept there). This was followed by a 90-degree turn towards the Middle Tower, which then led to the gatehouse of the outer wall called the Byward Tower. Intruders would then need to make their way through to the gate at the Garden Tower (later known as the Bloody Tower) before they could gain access to the White Tower at the centre of the fortress.[25]

The siege started with the Yorkists and Londoners setting up a blockade of the Tower by both land and water to cut off the supply of provisions and military equipment to the defenders. This action appears to have prompted the garrison to respond by opening fire from the walls at the citizens. It was subsequently alleged by the London chroniclers that the royalists began hostilities even before the Yorkists entered the city. This was said to have been in response to the refusal of the civic authorities to allow Lord Scales to take over the governance of the city. Scales and his companions supposedly retired to the Tower in a state of 'indignation' to make war on the inhabitants. A more plausible explanation is that clashes occurred after the Yorkists entered the city and set up the blockade. Yet, the civic authorities were evidently keen to achieve a peaceful resolution to the situation, with doctors of divinity sent to negotiate with the defenders, to no avail. The latter were in no mood to surrender and seem to have been emboldened by the departure of much of the Yorkist army on 4 July. According to the author of *An English Chronicle*, after this occurred, they fired indiscriminately into the city with their guns. The bombardment was said to have caused considerable damage with men, women and children killed and injured in the streets. This action encouraged the civic authorities to employ more direct methods against the defenders.[26]

To prosecute the siege more effectively the besiegers divided their forces into two. Cobham and the sheriffs oversaw operations from the side of the city facing the Tower, whereas their counterparts on the eastern side of the castle, outside the walls of the city by the hospital of St Katharine's by the Tower, were Wenlock and a merchant called John Harow. To inflict damage on the fortifications and the garrison they required suitable quantities of siege weapons. Fortunately for them, they were more than adequately equipped with large bombards and other guns. The Londoners could draw upon their own substantial stockpile of artillery, as well as the royal guns that had been kept at Whitechapel, which they appropriated for their own use. The gunfire of these weapons succeeded in damaging the outer walls of the Tower, which were said to have been broken in multiple places. Yet, the defences were still too strong to risk a direct assault. What was more the defenders, despite their increasingly desperate situation, still put up a determined resistance and frequently engaged in skirmishes with the besiegers. On one occasion they ventured forth from the castle to seize a boat transporting wine and fish from a ship, the *Nicholas of Spain*, to St Katharine's Wharf.[27]

There were also tensions amongst the ranks of the besiegers. The sailors and boatmen responsible for blockading the Tower by water were vocal in demanding their wages, which forced the common council to hurriedly raise funds to meet their demands. Furthermore, the sympathies of the Londoners were not universally pro-Yorkist. Even after the arrests that had been made of royalist supporters, a small number remained loyal to the cause of Henry VI. It was for this reason that 'in all places of London was great watch for fear of treason'. Despite this precaution, a daring attempt by a small group of men was made to relieve the beleaguered defenders of the Tower. They were led by a man called William Barton and came from the parishes of St Botolph, St Dunstan in the East and All Saints Barking. Remarkably, they succeeded in gaining entry to the castle on 10 July, from where they were said to have shot wildfire and other projectiles into the city. Nevertheless, regardless of how welcome these reinforcements must have been, their presence further aggravated the shortage of provisions within the fortress. This consideration may have prompted Scales and the other lords within the Tower to write to the civic authorities. In their letter they demanded to know why war had been waged against them and why their adherents had been taken prisoner. They also wanted to know how their opponents could reconcile their words and deeds together, given that the citizens continued to profess their allegiance to Henry VI. In response, the Londoners reaffirmed their loyalty to the king and placed the blame for the violence squarely on the lords. The latter were said to have shed first blood through the shooting of their guns, which had caused deaths and injuries. They also claimed that prisoners had been taken in response to breaches of the king's peace and the seizure of goods without payment. Clearly neither side was willing to back down. The advantage lay with the besiegers, but their opponents were said to have lived in daily hope of being rescued by their allies. Yet, the course of events elsewhere meant that their efforts were all to be in vain.[28]

Henry VI had moved eastwards to Northampton after receiving news of the Yorkist landing in England. He was accompanied by the duke of Buckingham, Lord Egremont, John Talbot, earl of Shrewsbury, and John, Viscount Beaumont, together with their retinues. They took up a defensive position to the south of the town, where they constructed a fortified camp. Urgent summons were also sent out across the kingdom for men to join the royal host. Yet, the rapid approach of their opponents meant that many of these reinforcements did not arrive in time. After leaving London on 4 July, the Yorkist army quickly marched northwards to confront the royal army, which they encountered six days later. The battle was preceded by attempts at negotiations, but these were said to have been rebuffed by the Lancastrians. According to the testimony of *An English Chronicle*, Buckingham stated 'the Earl of Warwick shall not come to the king's presence, and if he come he shall die'. The royalists were apparently outnumbered by their opponents but had a strong defensive position and a large quantity of field artillery. Yet, when the Yorkists attacked later that afternoon they rapidly defeated their opponents. Heavy rain rendered the royal guns ineffectual and the treachery of Edmund, Lord Grey of Ruthin, meant that their camp was compromised. Henry was captured in his tent, with Buckingham, Egremont, Shrewsbury and Beaumont slain. The triumphant Yorkists then returned to the capital with the king in tow.[29]

This outcome effectively sealed the fate of the defenders of the Tower, who were low on provisions. On 16 July, the same day the Yorkists returned to London, articles of surrender were drawn up between the civic authorities and the garrison. Three days later, Wenlock and Harow took possession of the castle by appointment. Scales attempted to flee from the Tower that very same night but was intercepted whilst trying to make his way to the sanctuary of Westminster Abbey. According to the testimony of *An English Chronicle*, he was spotted by a woman who recognised him, whilst he was rowing in a boat with three companions. Scales was then killed by boatsmen who left his corpse in the churchyard of the church of St Mary Overy. The author of *Gregory's Chronicle* adds that he was left 'despoiled naked as a worm', but that his demise was regretted by the Yorkist lords. On the following day, Warwick rode to the Tower where he issued a proclamation against theft and murder on pain of death. Two days later, the prisoners were taken from the Tower to the Guildhall where they were put on trial for treason before Warwick, Salisbury, the mayor and others. Six men, including Thomas Brown, the sheriff of Kent, were convicted and sentenced to death. On 29 July, they were taken from their prison at Newgate to the gallows at Tyburn where they were hanged, drawn and quartered. However, their companions were more fortunate. The lords only endured brief terms of imprisonment, whereas others of lower rank, including the Italian galley men, were pardoned.[30]

The Adventures of Queen Margaret and the Siege of Roxburgh Castle

The Yorkist lords now sought to take control of the kingdom. They commanded widespread popular support in the populous counties of south-east England and had the financial backing of the city of London.

Furthermore, as the king was in their custody, they could issue instructions and commands in his name. This allowed them to grant the principal offices of state to themselves and their supporters. However, much of the country was still outside of their reach and in the hands of their opponents. What was more, neither Queen Margaret nor her young son, Prince Edward, had been present at the Battle of Northampton. Instead, they had been residing at Eccleshall Castle in Staffordshire from where they fled westwards after receiving news of the capture of the king. Margaret decided to head for the relative safety of north-west Wales, a region dominated by Lancastrian loyalists, with a small group of companions. However, this was a long and dangerous journey across land. Whilst passing by the castle of Malpas in Cheshire she was said to have been robbed and despoiled by one of her servants, whom she had previously made both a yeoman and gentleman. Whereas according to another account, the perpetrator was John Cleger, a servant of Lord Stanley. The value of goods stolen from her was said to amount to the huge sum of 10,000 marks (£6,666 13s. 4d.). After this no doubt terrifying encounter, that supposedly left both her and her son in fear of their lives, the fugitives eventually made their way to Harlech Castle in Merionethshire. Once there they were all but safe from any potential pursuers, due to the mighty defences of the fortress and its isolated location on the north-west coast of Wales. Moreover, the castle was held by a garrison of soldiers loyal to the cause of Henry VI. There Margaret was greatly consoled and was provided with many fine gifts. She subsequently went in secret to meet with her half-brother-in-law Jasper Tudor. Undoubtedly the purpose of this meeting was to plan a military campaign against her opponents. Afterwards she took ship to Scotland with her son to seek assistance from that quarter.[31]

Margaret's decision was a bold move as the Scots were traditional enemies of the English. Obtaining their assistance thereby risked alienating support for the Lancastrian cause. This was particularly the case as the Scots had already sought to take advantage of England's domestic strife by attacking border castles and settlements. Relations between the two kingdoms had been fraught for many years, often marked by periods of hostilities and uneasy truces. In 1448, warfare had broken out with the English defeated at the Battle of Sark. Later in 1455, the Scots laid siege to Berwick-upon-Tweed, which was only resisted due to the exertions of the earl of Northumberland. Five years later, following the turmoil of the Battle of Northampton, James II, king of Scots, advanced southward with his army to attack Roxburgh Castle. This was one of the principal border fortresses held by the English and had frequently been the target of

Scottish armies in the past. The castle had a sizeable permanent garrison and was well-stocked with armaments including gunpowder weapons. The strategic importance of Roxburgh also meant that efforts had been made to ensure that the fortifications were kept in a good state of repair. For instance, only three years earlier, urgent works had been carried out at a cost of some £258, following the collapse of a tower called the 'King's Tower' and part of the adjoining wall. Yet, the defenders were dependent upon outside relief, due to the size of the Scottish army, which was well-equipped with a powerful siege train. It was for this reason that the Yorkist lords issued commissions for an army to be gathered to rescue Roxburgh. The besiegers suffered a setback when James was killed by the rupturing of one of his Flemish guns on 3 August. Nevertheless, his widow, Mary of Gueldres, carried on the siege. Eventually the garrison was forced to surrender, and its fortifications were demolished by the Scots, who then went on to take Wark Castle in Northumberland. Afterwards they withdrew across the border. This outcome prompted the Yorkist lords to abandon their plans to raise an army against the Scots. Instead, they focused their energies on countering their domestic opponents.[32]

The Realm Divided

The realm was now divided between the two opposing sides. Southern and eastern England was under the control of the Yorkists, whereas the Lancastrians dominated most of Wales and northern England. This territorial division arose because although the Yorkists had the king in their custody, they had failed to capture either Queen Margaret or her son Prince Edward, who now served as figureheads for opposition to the new regime. This meant that many people, particularly in the more remote provinces of the kingdom, refused to accept instructions issued in the name of the king by the Yorkists. Furthermore, many royalist supporters, including the earl of Northumberland, Jasper Tudor and the earl of Westmorland, had not been present at the Battle of Northampton. They had not been defeated in the field and still commanded considerable military resources. This included many of the strongest castles in the country. In south Wales, Jasper Tudor held the castles of Pembroke and Tenby in his own right, as well as the constableships of Aberystwyth and Carmarthen. He had also installed garrisons in the castles of Carreg Cennen and Kidwelly in the lordships of Is Cennen and Kidwelly. In addition to this, his forces had recently taken control of Denbigh Castle in the north-east of the country. Elsewhere, the castles of the north-west were mostly in the hands of loyalists, such as Ralph Boteler, Lord Sudeley, constable of Conwy Castle. It was only in the south-east of Wales that Yorkist supporters, such as Herbert and Walter Devereux, were in the ascendant. The latter being the son and heir of the man of the same name who had died in 1459. A similar situation prevailed in the north of England, with many castles held by the Lancastrians in the counties of Northumberland, Cumberland, Westmorland and Yorkshire.[33]

Yet, the Yorkist lords refrained from leading an army against their opponents, who were anyway geographically dispersed. Instead, they focused their energies on regaining control of these castles, by means of commands issued in the name of the king. On 9 August, the keeper of the privy seal, Robert Stillington, bishop of Bath and Wells, was instructed by a council that included Salisbury, March and Sir John Wenlock, to issue a letter authenticated by his seal to Roger Puleston, who had been appointed as keeper of Denbigh Castle by Jasper Tudor. Puleston was to be informed that the duke of York was not a traitor but a true subject and faithful friend. Therefore, he was commanded to hand over Denbigh to representatives of the duke. A similar instruction was also directed to Richard Grey, Lord Powis, who was told to surrender Montgomery Castle, which belonged to the duke of York, to Devereux. In addition to this, Stillington was ordered to send letters to the keepers of Beaumaris, Conwy, Flint, Harwarden, Holt and Ruthin. These men were commanded to ensure that their castles were kept securely and should not be delivered to anyone else upon the faith and allegiance that their owed to the king. However, these instructions appear to have had little effect.[34]

Only eight days later, a letter in the name of the king was written to Sir William Herbert, Walter Devereux and Roger Vaughan. It was explained that creditable reports had been received of diverse people who had illicitly fortified and provisioned castles in Wales. They were also said to have been responsible for assembling large numbers of people in a riotous fashion, which endangered the keeping of the peace. Unless the situation was soon resolved it would be responsible for causing 'great hurt and inconvenience'. They were therefore given full authority and power to repress and subdue all perpetrators of these acts. It was also stated that the 'principle doers and stirrers' should be kept in secure custody until they received further orders. Furthermore, they were to seize control of the castles held against them and to ensure their safeguard. Support was to be provided from constables and other officials throughout both Wales and England, who would receive instructions directing them to give assistance. Nevertheless, they were constrained by the strength of their opponents in the country and made very little headway. The Yorkist lords also attempted a similar ploy for regaining Lancastrian occupied castles in the north of England. On 24 August, the earl of Northumberland was ordered to surrender the castles of Pontefract and Wressle in Yorkshire to Salisbury.[35]

Salisbury was eager to gain control of these particular castles as he had a vested interest in both of them. Pontefract was one of the finest castles in the north of England and an important centre for local administration in the West Riding of Yorkshire. In the eleventh century it had the form of a motte and bailey castle, which was later rebuilt into an impressive masonry enclosure castle. Its main defining feature was its fine keep, with extensive works carried out by John of Gaunt, duke of Lancaster, in the late fourteenth century, and during the reigns of the Lancastrian monarchs from Henry IV to Henry VI. Despite being a royal castle, Salisbury had nevertheless held the stewardship of the lordship since 1425. By contrast, Wressle was a much newer castle. It had been founded by Sir Thomas Percy, a younger brother of Henry, first earl of Northumberland, in the late fourteenth century. Wressle had a quadrangular form, with four ranges flanked by corner towers. The entrance was via a gate tower in the middle of the east range, and the whole structure was surrounded by a moat. Wressle had previously belonged to Ralph, Lord Cromwell, whose niece, Maud Stanhope, had married Sir Thomas Neville, Salisbury's second son. The latter had thereby acquired an interest in the castle. However, following Cromwell's death in 1456, Wressle was granted for life to Egremont, who was himself later killed at Northampton. The castle should have thereafter reverted to royal ownership, but the chaos caused by the civil war gave Northumberland an opportunity to seize it for himself. The latter's dominant position in Yorkshire, meant that he could not be easily dislodged from either castle, without the use of significant military force. Northumberland therefore simply ignored any commands issued by the Yorkist-controlled government.[36]

This cold war between the two sides eventually came to an end following the belated return of the duke of York to the realm. He made landfall in Chester, where he appointed Robert Bold as constable of Denbigh Castle on 13 September (although it was still held by his enemies). Afterwards he gradually made his way eastwards through the Welsh Marches and the Midlands visiting Shrewsbury, Ludlow, Hereford, Coventry and Leicester. This was said to be on account of 'strange commissions' issued to him in the name of the king to 'punish them by the faults to the king's laws'. York subsequently proceeded to the capital to attend Parliament accompanied by a large entourage. He arrived there on 10 October and boldly asserted his claim to the throne, but met with opposition from the Lords who were hesitant to depose the king. Eventually a settlement was reached with Henry retaining his crown for his lifetime, but with York recognised as his heir, which was passed by Parliament as the Act of Accord. The latter was therefore recognised as Prince of Wales by Act of Parliament, which included the bestowing of extensive lands and castles in the principality of Wales and elsewhere. Prince Edward was the chief loser from this agreement, as he was thereby disinherited by his own father. This was unacceptable to Queen Margaret or other supporters of the Lancastrian dynasty and so made renewed conflict inevitable.[37]

These developments coincided with fresh efforts to increase the pressure against the Lancastrians in the north of England. On 8 October further orders were issued by the Chancery in the name of the king. John, Lord Clifford, was told to surrender the custody of Penrith Castle in Cumberland to Salisbury. The same command was also sent to the earl of Northumberland in respect of the castles of Wressle and Pontefract. Both Clifford and Northumberland were ordered to remove all evildoers from these castles, who were allegedly responsible for various crimes including murder, and to permit no armed gatherings except against the Scots. On the same day, commissions were issued to the civic authorities of York and Newcastle upon Tyne to demand their obedience against disturbers of the peace. Later, on 14 October, notable men from the northern counties of England, who included Ralph, Lord Greystoke, Henry, Lord FitzHugh and Sir Thomas Lumley, were charged with the task of gaining control of Wressle, Pontefract and Penrith. They were authorised to issue proclamations against the occupiers of these strongholds, threatening the forfeiture of their lands should they fail to comply. Furthermore, they were empowered to use force against them and to assemble men from Yorkshire and the adjacent counties to lay siege to the castles if necessary.[38] Nevertheless, the Lancastrians remained defiant. The sheriffs of London were therefore ordered to issue a proclamation regarding the conduct of the earl of Northumberland by the authority of the lords and bishops assembled at Parliament. It was explained that Northumberland had occupied Pontefract and Wressle with 'great strength and might' and had refused to obey royal commands to surrender them to Salisbury. Not only had the earl refused to comply with the most recent instruction sent to him, but his servants had murdered the king's messenger, John Drayton, after he had delivered his writ. The sheriffs were to announce that unless the castles were surrendered within twenty days, Northumberland would suffer the forfeiture of his lands.[39]

Queen Margaret's Revenge

In the meanwhile, their opponents had been busy gathering together an army to avenge the defeat at Northampton. According to the author of the *Annales*, the earl of Northumberland, Clifford, Randolph, Lord Dacre, and John, Lord Neville held a council in York in November.[40] The details of this meeting are not recorded but their subsequent actions suggest that they intended to seek revenge against the Yorkist lords. Commissions were issued throughout the region in the name of Northumberland and Neville for all men between the ages of 16 and 60 to turn out in their most defensible array. They were to await upon the said lords for the purpose of bringing the king 'out of prison and out of his enemies' hands upon pain of forfeiture of life and limb'.[41] Northumberland appears to have used York as his base of operations, whereas Neville spent much of his time at his family's castle of Raby. These men between them could draw upon the allegiance of many men from the northern counties of England. This can be seen from the accounts of Henry Preston, the chancellor and receiver-general of the bishop of Durham and constable of the castle. His accounts record that an armed watch was kept at the north gate of the city from 14–16 November. This was due to the passing by of 'diverse persons from the counties of Northumberland and Westmorland in a warlike array' who were travelling towards Pontefract and other places in Yorkshire. By December, the Lancastrian lords had succeeded in assembling a sizeable force. Yet, with the memory of Northampton still fresh in their minds, they decided to await reinforcements from elsewhere before moving against the Yorkists. They instead occupied themselves with devastating the northern estates of York and Salisbury.[42]

According to *Gregory's Chronicle*, Queen Margaret was also said to have been active in sending messages to supporters throughout the kingdom to join the rapidly growing Lancastrian army. Her chief officers were enjoined to warn all those servants that loved her and were loyal to join the muster at Hull at the appointed time. This included men from the south-west of England, such as Courtenay and Somerset. The latter had been engaged in combatting the Yorkists in the Pale of Calais, but military defeats and dwindling funds forced him to come to terms with his opponents in July, which necessitated the surrender of Guînes Castle. In October, Somerset returned to England and went to his castle at Corfe. Upon receiving his instructions from Margaret, he began to recruit men from the region for the Lancastrian cause. Somerset was recorded as being present at Exeter on 10 November, and afterwards was at Bridgwater in

Somerset gathering further supporters. These contingents from the south-west subsequently travelled northwards via Bath, Cirencester, Evesham and Coventry, before reaching York. This considerable gathering of Lancastrian forces in Yorkshire took place with such speed and secrecy that their enemies were said to have been caught unawares.[43]

The Yorkist-dominated Parliament did pass a bill ordering the sheriffs and other royal officials in the counties to obey the instructions of York by late November. This was as the duke had been given the 'charge and task of riding into the regions of the said realm of England and Wales ... to repress, subdue and pacify them'. To confront the Lancastrians in the north, he quickly raised a small army of men who predominately came from the south-east of England, with the intention of recruiting further men en route through the use of commissions of array.[44] York had also received reports of the activities of Somerset and other Lancastrians in the south-west. This prompted him to send two commissions to the civic authorities of Bristol on account of the 'malice' of Somerset. York's eldest son, the earl of March, had only recently been appointed as constable of Bristol Castle on 14 November. Nonetheless, the mayor and common council were instructed to 'take upon them the rule governance and defence of the king's castle', as Somerset intended to 'have entry and rule of the said castle'. This uncertainty about the intentions of his opponents prompted York to send March to the Welsh Marches, whilst he himself focused on the situation in the north of England.[45]

In early December, York left the capital with his army accompanied by Salisbury and his son the earl of Rutland, together with a field train of artillery, with Warwick left behind to guard the capital. He proceeded northwards via Nottingham towards Sandal Castle in Yorkshire, which he reached on 21 December. This was York's principal castle in the region and could serve as a secure base for operations against the Lancastrians. Furthermore, Sandal's location on a prominent sandstone ridge meant that his watchmen could obtain good views of the surrounding area. This was particularly true of the motte of the castle, which rises some 15m high, and was topped by a shell keep enclosed by four towers. The keep itself could only be accessed from the bailey via an elaborate entrance system. This involved crossing a bridge over the inner ditch to a barbican encircled by a wall and then making a 90-degree turn to cross another bridge, to reach a twin-towered gatehouse at the bottom of the motte. Finally, a visitor would need to walk up a ramp to reach the twin-towered inner gate at the top. The duke most probably stayed in his comfortable residential chambers in the shell keep, as did Salisbury and Rutland. Most of their servants and other members of their households perhaps took up residence in the buildings in the bailey, but the constricted size of the castle meant most of his army would have taken up lodgings nearby in the town of Wakefield.[46]

In December 1460, the castle was held by York's constable, Edmund Fitzwilliam. Fitzwilliam had garrisoned Sandal at his lord's command and had carried out minor repairs. Nevertheless, the financial accounts of the lordship of Wakefield reveal that the area had been plundered by the Lancastrians, and therefore he had few provisions with which to supply the newly arrived army. The author of the *Annales* implies that the Yorkists were forced to resort to foraging from the surrounding area; if so, it was to prove a costly mistake. York appears to have been badly informed about his enemies' movements and unaware of their numerical superiority. This may have been because some of his scouts were ambushed and killed by Somerset's men at Worksop in Nottinghamshire during the march northwards. The Lancastrians had meanwhile gathered at nearby Pontefract Castle only 10 miles away and waited for an opportunity to strike. This came on 30 December, when the Yorkists left Sandal, apparently in search of provisions. They were then attacked by a larger Lancastrian army led by Northumberland, Somerset, Courtenay, Clifford and other lords. Taken by surprise by their more numerous opponents they were defeated, with York and Rutland killed during the fighting. Prisoners, including Salisbury and the London captain John Harow, were taken to Pontefract Castle and beheaded. According to the account of *An English Chronicle*, Salisbury's life was to be spared upon the payment of a large ransom. However, the common people of the area hated him so they dragged him out of the castle and decapitated him. Afterwards the corpses of the slain lords were cut up and taken to the city of York, where they were displayed in various locations, with a paper crown mockingly placed upon the duke's head.[47]

The Triumph of Edward

Margaret was still in Scotland when she received news of the Battle of Wakefield. She was undoubtedly elated by the victory achieved and eager to exploit the disarray of her enemies. An agreement was quickly made with Mary of Gueldres, regent for her young son James III, at Lincluden College near Dumfries in Galloway on 5 January, with the Scots apparently offering some form of military assistance. Margaret afterwards returned to England by ship, most probably landing at Hull. She subsequently took charge of the Lancastrian war effort and began planning for an invasion of the south. At a council meeting held at York on 20 January, attended by ten peers and two bishops, it was agreed that they would march on London to rescue the king from his enemies. A short time later, the Lancastrian army moved southwards via the East Midlands towards the capital. The northern soldiers appear to have been particularly ill-disciplined, as they plundered the towns in their path, including Gran-tham and Peterborough. Rumours of these outrages caused considerable alarm in the more southerly regions of the kingdom. One contemporary writer asserted that the 'people in the north rob and steal, and been appointed to pillage all this country, and gift away men's goods and liveli-hoods in the south country'.[48]

Warwick had meanwhile been raising an army with which to counter the Lancastrians. Urgent instructions were despatched for men to assemble on account of the 'misruled and outrageous people in the north parts ... intending as well the destruction of ... our true subjects'. Assistance was provided by the Londoners, who contributed a loan of 2,000 marks (£1,333 6s. 8d.) and a consignment of bows, bowstrings and other supplies. Measures were taken to dissuade men from joining their enemies, with a proclamation issued in Middlesex and Hertfordshire, forbidding men from wearing any badges or liveries of any lords, except those who intended to serve in the Yorkist army. Attempts were also made to hinder the southward advance of the Lancastrian army. The burgesses of Stam-ford were ordered to prepare the defences of the town on 17 January, by maintaining a continual watch and to muster the inhabitants in arms. On 3 February, with the Lancastrians drawing ever closer to the capital, instructions were sent to two esquires, Nicholas Morley and John Bensted, to array the men of Hertfordshire, Cambridgeshire and Hunt-ingdon and to garrison them in castles and other fortifications. Another area of concern was East Anglia where Lancastrian supporters were said to be assembling in large numbers. It was reported that there was a great gathering of hostile armed people at Castle Rising in Norfolk, who were intent on robbery. Therefore, a commission was given to notable men of the county on 26 January to assemble a force to suppress 'evildoers' who had garrisoned and provisioned castles. They were also ordered to carry out searches to ensure that no arms or other goods could be supplied to the men holding the castles, and to arrest anybody caught doing so. Yet, the situation remained volatile as less than two weeks later, Richard Cropwell, the escheator of Norfolk, was ordered to seize Castle Rising and to install a garrison in it. William Ely, bishop of Ely, was also said to have installed a garrison in his castle of Wisbech on the Isle of Ely.[49]

In mid-February, the Yorkist army moved northwards to St Albans to block the Lancastrian advance on London. Warwick was accompanied by John Mowbray, duke of Norfolk, William Neville, Lord Fauconberg, and the king, with his forces comprising men raised from southern England, together with an artillery train. Initially they constructed a fortified camp near to the city, but subsequently decided to move to a new site close by, apparently unaware of the proximity of the Lancastrian army. This proved to be a costly mistake. They were caught off-guard by their enemies, who attacked them on 17 February and were soon routed. Warwick and Norfolk escaped, but other prominent Yorkists, including Bonville and Kyriell, were captured and executed. The Lancastrians also succeeded in rescuing the king, who thereby went over to their side. Henry's so-called defection was characterised as an act of betrayal by the Yorkists, with the author of *A Short English Chronicle* stating that he 'wickedly ... went to the contrary party of the north' and so forsook his 'true lords'. The way to London was now open, yet the Lancastrians did not immediately advance on the capital. Instead, Margaret sent envoys to treat with the civic authorities. She intended to gain admittance to the city without bloodshed, particularly as the Lancastrians were experiencing difficulties in keeping their army together. What was more, the expectation must have been that the inhabitants would have no choice but to submit, given the Yorkist defeats at Wakefield and St Albans. Instead, the Londoners played for time. They agreed to send carts of goods to provision the Lancastrian army, but they also prepared the defences of the city, with the citizens mustered in arms and a garrison placed in the Tower. This was because they had received news that the earl of March was rapidly marching to their rescue at the head of another Yorkist army.[50]

March was at Shrewsbury when he learnt of the Yorkist defeat and his father's death at Wakefield. He at once began to raise an army from the counties of western England and the Welsh Marches. Yet, before he could move eastwards to join forces with Warwick, he received tidings of the approach of a Lancastrian army from the west led by Jasper Tudor and the earl of Wiltshire, which primarily comprised men from south Wales. The two armies encountered each other at Mortimer's Cross, near to March's castle at Wigmore. Prior to the battle, three suns were seen in the sky, which was said to have been taken as a good sign by the Yorkists, with the Lancastrians subsequently defeated. Prominent prisoners, including Owen Tudor, Jasper's father, were taken to Hereford by the Yorkists where they were beheaded. March then headed for London with his army, where he was met en route by Warwick with reinforcements. News of his imminent arrival prompted Margaret to retreat northwards with her army. March entered the capital on 4 March where he was acclaimed as King Edward IV by the inhabitants. King Henry having been deemed to have forfeited his crown due to his actions following the Second Battle of St Albans. Edward then gathered his forces to pursue the Lancastrians, who had meanwhile regrouped in Yorkshire.[51]

The two sides now sought to bolster their respective forces for the decisive clash of arms. *Gregory's Chronicle* states that messengers were sent from region to region and 'both the new king and the old were full beside to make their party strong'. On 6 March, a proclamation was issued in the name of King Edward commanding all men between the ages of 16 and 60 to join his army in their most defensible array. This was on account of the numerous crimes said to have been committed by the Lancastrian lords, to whom no assistance should be provided. Orders were also issued for a fleet to be sent to the northern part of the realm. Having refreshed his army, Edward left the capital on 13 March and advanced towards York, with Warwick sent to raise additional forces in the west of the country. The army was said to have been divided into three contingents led by Edward, Norfolk and Fauconberg, which used different roads, before re-uniting in Yorkshire. Their opponents attempted to block their crossing of the River Aire at Ferrybridge on 28 March, but they were defeated. On the following day the two sides met in battle near to the village of Towton, some 12 miles to the south-west of York. This was most probably the biggest engagement of the Wars of the Roses, with large numbers of soldiers present on both sides. The fighting was said to have taken place in poor weather conditions during heavy snowfall. Eventually the Yorkists gained the upper hand and routed their opponents. The Lancastrians suffered heavy losses, with Northumberland, Clifford and Lord Neville killed at the battle. Henry, Margaret, Prince Edward, Somerset and some others managed to make their escape to Scotland, but their army had ceased to exist. Edward had therefore won a decisive victory against his enemies.[52]

Chapter Four

Securing the Realm

Following his victory, Edward proceeded to York where he received a grand reception from the inhabitants, who were eager to make amends for their adherence to the Lancastrian cause. Prominent prisoners captured at the battle were taken to the castle, where some, including Courtenay, were beheaded. Edward subsequently stayed in the city for three weeks to celebrate Easter. Meanwhile, the task of securing the realm was already being carried out by his supporters. Prior to the Battle of Towton, Sir John Wenlock had been entrusted with capturing Thorpe Waterville Castle in Northamptonshire. This was little more than a fortified manor house, which belonged to the Lancastrian magnate Henry Holland, duke of Exeter. Wenlock appears to have begun the siege in mid-March, perhaps having been detached with his forces from the main army during Edward's march northwards. The castle was said to have been held by 'diverse ... great rebels', but Wenlock still had sufficient manpower to send men to search for fugitive Lancastrians, such as William, Lord Beaumont, and Sir William Tailboys, then 'said to be in secret places' in the county of Lincoln. On 31 March, instructions were issued for carters, horses and oxen to be procured for the transportation of three bombards for the siege, with a commission granted to Wenlock on the following day for him to summon the gentry of East Midlands to assist him. Nevertheless, these measures appear to have been unnecessary, as the defenders of Thorpe Waterville had surrendered by 4 April. Following its capture, Wenlock installed a small garrison of thirteen men to hold the castle.[1]

Over the next few months, the king issued instructions for other castles that had been held by the Lancastrians to be seized by trusted supporters. On 12 May, John, Lord Bourchier, Sir Robert Harecourt, Walter Blount and others were ordered to take control of the castles of Eccleshall and Stafford, with authority to arrest anybody who offered resistance. In most places this task appears to have been achieved without bloodshed, as there is little evidence of the king's men encountering opposition. A rare exception was at Buckenham Castle in Norfolk. Edward's representatives found their entry barred by the occupant, Alice Knyvet, who held it with a garrison of fifty men in the name of her husband John. From a tower over-looking the raised drawbridge, she was said to have threatened bloodshed if they attempted to seize it. This show of force prompted the Yorkists to withdraw empty-handed. Elsewhere, uncertainly about the security of the new regime and the prospect of a Lancastrian counterattack prompted the placing of garrisons in castles throughout England. Sir Robert Harecourt took charge at Wallingford, later receiving £100 for the wages of soldiers that served there and for repairs to the fortifications. Similar expenses were incurred by Thomas Higford and William Sade at Kenilworth, with William Rastryk subsequently paid for having kept Corfe with a garrison of thirty men for some five months. Lancastrian resistance in the Pale of Calais was also subdued, with the defenders of Hammes Castle surrendering to a Yorkist force in October.[2]

One place of special interest was the Isle of Wight and its principal fortress, Carisbrooke Castle. This was a strategic island due to its location off the south coast, which meant that it could potentially be used as an entry point for a foreign army. Therefore, gaining control of it was an important objective. This mission had been entrusted to Geoffrey Gate, a member of the gentry in Kent, who had taken part in the siege of the Tower of London. On 16 December 1460, he was appointed as lieutenant and keeper of Carisbrooke Castle and the lordship of the Isle of Wight. Gate was instructed to assemble men from the island and the adjoining counties of Hampshire, Surrey and Sussex for its defence, with the assistance of the abbot of the nearby Quarr Abbey, John Cheselburgh, and other local notable men. He was also ordered to expel the current occupants of the castle and if they used force to resist him, was authorised to arrest and imprison them. These commissions were ostensibly to protect the island from the threat posed to it by French invaders. In fact, it was to wrest control of it from the Lancastrians. Since October 1457, Henry Beaufort, duke of Somerset, had held the keepership of the castle and lordship, as part of a move by the government of Henry VI to reinforce royal influence in the region. At some point in 1460, the duke despatched his younger brother, Edmund, to reinforce the defenders of the castle.[3]

The regular garrison consisted of a force of ten men-at-arms and thirty archers, whose wages were financed by the Exchequer. Edmund appears to have had approximately twenty men in in his own retinue, therefore his arrival significantly increased the number of defenders, who were well equipped with guns and other weaponry. Carisbrooke was an impressive castle with strong defences. It is situated in the centre of the island on an area of high ground that still dominates the surrounding area. The highest part of the castle is the shell keep, built on the site of the motte of the Norman fortress, surrounded by a large walled enclosure. Gate eventually assembled a force of 5 men-at-arms and 120 archers with which he besieged the castle. Despite being cut off from outside assistance, the siege continued throughout the first half of 1461. News that a French fleet had captured Jersey in the Channel Islands prompted the besiegers to redouble their efforts. On 28 May, Gate and other prominent local men were empowered to array the inhabitants of the island for its defence. Two days later, further instructions were issued with the sheriffs of Hampshire, Sussex and Surrey ordered to render assistance to Gate. Eventually the defenders were forced to surrender, most probably due to a shortage of supplies. The attackers may have used artillery during the siege, however, as Gate was later reimbursed for spending £23 10s. on rebuilding a wall that had collapsed in the castle. Edmund and the sixty-one other members of the garrison were then imprisoned in Carisbrooke for thirty-one days. Afterwards they were sent by ship to Calais for safekeeping, with a carvel and barge used to transport them.[4]

In the meantime, Edward had travelled northwards to Durham by 22 April. Whilst there he received news that James Butler, earl of Wiltshire, had been captured at Cockermouth. He then went to Newcastle upon Tyne, where the earl had been sent, to oversee his execution on 1 May. Edward then slowly returned to the south-east, first making a detour to Lancashire, before proceeding towards London. He eventually entered the capital on 26 June for his coronation. Edward was greeted by the mayor, aldermen and 400 citizens who escorted him from Lambeth Palace to the Tower. There he dubbed twenty-eight knights that evening and four more the following day. Amongst the recipients were his brothers, George and Richard. The coronation took place on 28 June in Westminster Abbey with great pomp and ceremony, after which the king ennobled some of his prominent supporters. These new peers included John, Lord Wenlock, William, Lord Hastings, Robert, Lord Ogle, Thomas, Lord Lumley, and Walter Devereux, Lord Ferrers.[5]

The Conquest of Wales

Large areas of the kingdom remained under the control of supporters of Henry VI. Despite the crushing Lancastrian defeat at Towton, there were still many who were determined to resist the new regime. They sought to reverse the Yorkist takeover of power and to restore Henry VI to the throne using military force. This was especially the case in Wales, where support for the old king remained strong. The principal Lancastrian commander in the country was Jasper Tudor who had retreated to Tenby in Pembrokeshire after his defeat at the Battle of Mortimer's Cross. From there he wrote to his deputy at Denbigh Castle, Roger Puleston, to encourage him to remain resolute. In his letter dated 25 February, Jasper wrote of the 'great dishonour and rebuke' he had experienced in battle, which he intended with the assistance of God and 'other our kinsmen and friends, within short time to avenge'. He expressed the hope that Roger would be 'well-willed' as 'our especial trust is in you'. Five months later, Jasper sent another message to Puleston concerning Denbigh. The latter was to perform his 'faithful diligence for the safeguard of it', with money to be provided by the receiver of the lordship, Griffith Vychan, for the provisioning of the castle. Jasper undoubtedly sent similar letters of encouragement to other Lancastrian castellans, such as those holding Carreg Cennen and Kidwelly in the south, and Conwy in the north.[6]

The losses suffered at Mortimer's Cross seemingly prevented or discouraged Jasper from raising an army for offensive operations, and instead he oversaw the defence of Pembrokeshire, particularly his castles of Tenby and Pembroke. These were both formidable fortresses, which if sufficiently manned and supplied could withstand lengthy sieges. Tenby is situated on a wide promontory that juts into the sea, which overlooks the harbour of the settlement. Its masonry fortifications date from the thirteenth century and it is connected to the adjoining walled town by a thin stretch of land. Pembroke had even more formidable defences, situated on a high ridge encircled by water defences and overlooking the adjacent borough. It has an outer and inner ward, with a four-storey round keep located in the latter. These castles had the advantage of being situated in the far south-west corner of Wales, which meant that they could be reached by ships going to or from Ireland, France or Scotland. This was significant as, by the summer of 1461, the Lancastrians were eager for outside military assistance to swing the balance of power against their opponents who were now in the ascendant. This appeared to be a realistic possibility, with Charles VII of France seemingly willing to provide military support to his relative, Queen Margaret. On 2 June, the Milanese ambassador to the French court, Prospero di Camalio, claimed that an army of 20,000 soldiers had set sail from Normandy and intended to land in Wales, where they hoped for assistance from the inhabitants. This invasion failed to materialise due to the unexpected death of the French king but, nevertheless, the danger of outside intervention remained.[7]

It was essential for Edward IV to neutralise this threat by gaining control of Wales. Rather than dealing with this matter in person, he instead delegated it to trusted lieutenants. For the important task of subduing south Wales, he chose Sir William Herbert to lead the campaign, who on 13 May was given full authority to pardon rebels in that country. Two months later, he was raised to the baronage by the king who issued him with a personal summons to Parliament. Herbert had been a long-time supporter of the Yorkist cause and had a proven track record of military success. He was to work in conjunction with William Stanley, who took charge of operations in north Wales, where many castles were held by pro-Lancastrian constables. William came from an important family that held many estates in north-west England, in Lancashire and Cheshire, and the Isle of Man. On 1 May, he was appointed as chamberlain of Chester, sheriff of Flintshire and as constable of Flint Castle, later receiving a knighthood in July. These appointments provided him with significant military resources, which he soon employed against the Lancastrians. It was to be two-pronged offensive into Wales, with Stanley operating from Chester and Herbert from Hereford.[8]

Preparations for the expedition to the south began in the summer. On 8 July, Herbert, Devereux and James Baskerville were sent instructions to array the men of the border counties of Herefordshire, Gloucestershire and Shropshire for its defence. These preparations intensified in the following month. On 10 August, Herbert and others were ordered to take control of the earldom of Pembroke and all other castles and lands belonging to Jasper Tudor. They were also instructed to seize control of the castles of Dunster in Somerset and Goodrich in Herefordshire, which had been forfeited by their owners for their adherence to the Lancastrian cause. Two days later, further commissions were issued by the king to notable landowners in the Welsh Marches and the west of England. They were to exhort the men of these regions to array a force at their own expense that would muster at Hereford on 8 September. On the same day, Herbert was also appointed as steward of the castles of Monmouth, White Castle, Skenfrith and Grosmont in Monmouthshire, which he was commanded to seize in the name of the king. The army was to be supported by a fleet of ships assembled from south-west England, which included many vessels from Bristol. By 30 August, it was reported that the campaign was underway, with the original date of 8 September having apparently been abandoned, as the army had already advanced into Wales and the fleet had set sail. Meanwhile, Stanley had begun his offensive by attacking Chirk Castle, some 20 miles to the south-west of Chester. Chirk had been constructed in the late thirteenth century, as a courtyard castle with four round towers at each corner, which served as the seat of the Marcher lordship of

Chirkland. Stanley evidently faced resistance, as he was required to send for guns from Chester to assist with the siege. It is unrecorded whether they were used or not, but the castle appears to have been captured by the end of the month.[9]

Herbert's army marched steadily from east Wales towards the south-west throughout September. Efforts continued to be made to augment the fleet, with royal commands issued for commissioners to recruit sailors for ships from Minehead, Bridgwater and Bristol. On 7 September, Herbert was sent instructions to seize control of Brecon Castle and other estates that had belonged to Humphrey, late duke of Buckingham. Furthermore, he was appointed as steward of these lands during the minority of Henry, son and heir of the deceased duke, and to the same office for the castle of Clifford in Herefordshire.[10] By 9 September, it was reported that Herbert and Devereux with 'diverse many other gentlemen' had been sent to 'cleanse the country afore us'. The king having decided to travel from Hereford, where he had been staying, to Ludlow rather than participate in the campaign.[11]

By the end of September, the Yorkist army had arrived at Pembroke. Jasper had entrusted the safeguard of the castle there to Sir John Skydmore, a hitherto loyal member of the Herefordshire gentry, who had served with him at the Battle of Mortimer's Cross. The strong defences of Pembroke meant that it should have been able to resist a lengthy siege. This was especially the case as the castle was said to have been 'victualled, manned and apparelled for long time after'. Nevertheless, the garrison capitulated without offering any resistance. Skydmore surrendered the castle under terms and agreed to become Edward's liegeman, in return for his life, goods and lands, as well as the promise, allegedly, that he would benefit from the new king's largesse. This agreement was set out in a letter of pardon given to him, which was authenticated by Herbert's seal on 30 September. Yet, Skydmore was apparently unaware that he had been specifically excluded by royal command from any pardons that the Yorkist commanders in Wales could offer him, for having fought at the Battle of Mortimer's Cross. Herbert and Devereux were therefore ignorant, or more probably disingenuous, in accepting the terms of his surrender. This meant that Skydmore, as he was to bitterly complain to the king some years later, subsequently suffered from the confiscation of his lands.[12]

Meanwhile, Jasper retreated northwards to Harlech, thereby abandoning the defence of Tenby. His flight was perhaps precipitated by the rapid surrender of Pembroke and the size of Herbert's army. On 4 October, it was reported that Jasper and the duke of Exeter had fled to the mountains of Snowdonia, with the Yorkist lords in hot pursuit. Furthermore, it was stated that the 'most part of gentlemen and men of worship are coming in to the king' to make their submission.[13] Despite this setback, it seems that Jasper and Exeter made a counterattack against another Yorkist force, which had advanced across north Wales as far west as Caernarfonshire. In the parliament that was held later that year, it was stated that on 16 October, at a place called Twt Hill next to the town of Caernarfon, they had 'raised war against our same sovereign lord, intending then and there to proceed to his destruction by treacherous and cruel violence, against their faith and allegiance'. It is unclear exactly what transpired outside Caernarfon, whether this was pitched battle that took place between the two sides, or simply an armed demonstration. Yet, the outcome was clearly a defeat for Jasper and Exeter as they afterwards fled to Scotland. Furthermore, it is unclear whether Caernarfon was still being held by the Lancastrians or had already fallen to the Yorkists.[14]

Whilst these events had been taking place, Stanley was busy mopping up resistance in the north-east of Wales. By November the last remaining Lancastrian-held castle appears to have been Rhuddlan in Flintshire. This was a royal castle that had been built by order of Edward I in the late thirteenth century. It takes the form of a courtyard castle, with a quadrilateral-shaped outer ward and diamond-shaped inner ward, with twin-towered gatehouses. During its construction, the adjacent River Clwyd was dredged and straightened to make it navigable for shipping, with the dock fortified. Since 1439 the constableship had been held by John, Lord Beauchamp, with the castle defended by a permanent garrison of six soldiers. The strong defences of Rhuddlan meant that Stanley took pains to ensure that the siege was carefully planned and carried out in accordance with royal instructions. Therefore, he sent two men, Thomas Kendale and Christopher Holauste, from Chester to Warwickshire to seek the advice of the king and council for the forthcoming operation. Stanley eventually employed a sizeable force of 464 soldiers accompanied by artillery for the siege. The siege lasted for thirteen days after which the defenders of Rhuddlan, who were isolated and cut off from assistance, seem to have surrendered. Their commander, Nicholas Wyrall, and the other members of the garrison were then escorted to Chester, before being sent to London with Stanley. The fall of Rhuddlan was soon followed by the capture of the castles of north-west Wales, with the exception of Harlech. This appears to have happened in December as Yorkist garrisons are recorded as having received wages at this time.[15]

Despite these successes, fears of a Lancastrian resurgence with French assistance prompted the Yorkists to undertake defensive measures. Herbert had remained at Pembroke until at least mid-October, where he received oaths of allegiance on behalf of Edward IV from the members of the former garrison. He appointed his half-brother, also called William, to oversee the area as treasurer of the county of Pembroke, who on top of his salary of £20 received an annual bonus of £20 as his reward for residing in the castle. John ap Howell ap Jankyn served as his constable for Pembroke Castle with a garrison of forty-seven men including two gunners. Over £35 was spent on making the fortress habitable for the soldiers, with carpenters, masons and others paid to repair the houses and other buildings, with 1,000 quarrel heads purchased for crossbow bolts. Tenby Castle was entrusted to John ap Glo Thomas, who served as constable with a force of twenty men. These precautions were necessary as the region was still threatened with attack. At least four men were taken prisoner at sea by Genoese and Breton sailors with efforts made to pay their ransoms. Fears of an imminent attack on Tenby by a Breton fleet even prompted John ap Howell to temporarily reinforce the castle with a force of thirty-six soldiers drawn from the garrison of Pembroke, with the men of the region arrayed for the defence of the country.[16]

Yet pockets of Lancastrian resistance remained further to the east. It was for this reason that a garrison was installed in Carmarthen Castle on 14 October. This initially consisted of a force of eighty-four men which was gradually reduced to thirty-four men by the following January, after which they were dismissed, presumably as the situation had improved. By the spring of 1462, the last remaining castle held for the Lancastrians in south Wales was Carreg Cennen. Carreg Cennen was formidable due to its dramatic location and the strength of its fortifications. It is situated on an area of high ground that overlooks the surrounding area and is flanked on one side by a steep cliff making it difficult to approach or besiege. Originally Carreg Cennen had belonged to the Welsh princes of Deheubarth but was extensively rebuilt following the conquest of Wales in the late thirteenth century. Eventually it passed into royal hands as part of the lordship of Kidwelly, which was part of the duchy of Lancaster. Following the Lancastrian defeat at Mortimer's Cross, it was entrusted to, or was possibly seized by, Thomas and Owen ap Gruffydd. These men were the sons of Gruffydd ap Nicholas, who had died at some point in 1460. They appear to have had less influence in the region than their father had managed to achieve, but nevertheless were said to have had a 'great

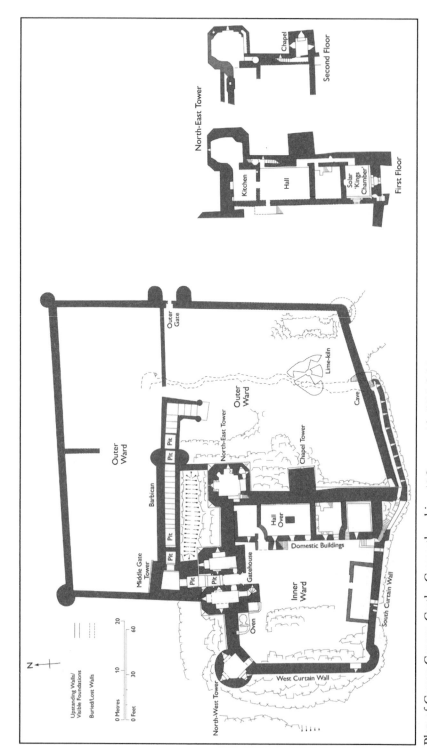

Plan of Carreg Cennen Castle, Carmarthenshire. (©*Crown copyright (2019) Cadw*)

number' of men under their command. The brothers could therefore have put up a lengthy resistance.[17]

Yet, the hopelessness of the Lancastrian cause prompted them to come to an accommodation with the Yorkists. This led to Herbert sending a force of 200 gentlemen and yeomen led by his half-brother, Sir Richard Herbert, and Sir Roger Vaughan to Carreg Cennen from his castle of Raglan in April. There they met with Thomas and Owen ap Gruffydd who, along with their men, agreed to swear allegiance to Edward and to deliver up the castle. After they had departed, Lord Herbert placed a small contingent of nine soldiers there, who were supplied with provisions. This was because it was 'of such strength that all the misgoverned men of that country there intended to have inhabited the same castle and to have lived by robbery and spoiling our people'. This garrison remained in place from 1 May until 8 August. However, it was subsequently decided that it would be more convenient, and doubtlessly cheaper, for the fortress to be demolished. A labour force of over 500 men was recruited for this task, who used pickaxes and other tools to knock down the walls thereby rendering it uninhabitable. This decision testifies to the strength of the fortress and Lancastrian sentiment in the region, as it was the only castle to be slighted in the Wars of the Roses. Nevertheless, the situation in Carmarthenshire remained tense. It was stated that at the Justiciar's Session held at Carmarthen Castle, all the gentlemen 'stood divided in two parties like to have grown to great mischief and manslaughter'. Lord Herbert attended in person with 'great power and multitude of people', where he tarried for four days at the request of the gentry and common people 'to set rest and peace amongst them'. This show of force appears to have had the desired response in quelling the unrest. Therefore, by the summer of 1462, almost all of Wales was in the hands of the Yorkists.[18]

War in the North

Another region where the Yorkists were forced to contend with continued resistance from the Lancastrians was in the far north of England, particularly in Northumberland. The latter was a particularly militarised county, with many castles kept in a defensible condition, and where the pro-Lancastrian Percy family had great influence. This meant that many of the inhabitants remained loyal to the cause of Henry VI. As we have already seen, Edward refrained from going any further north than Durham, choosing instead to leave the task of subduing the region to his Neville relatives. This was because he was keen to secure his position in the heartlands of the realm rather than becoming embroiled in protracted campaigning in the fringes of the kingdom. Furthermore, in the aftermath of the Battle of Towton, the Lancastrian cause appeared to be all but spent. Henry VI, Queen Margaret, Prince Edward and some of their closest followers had fled across the border to Scotland. Yet, the lords and knights with them, principally the dukes of Somerset and Exeter, Jasper Tudor, and Thomas, Lord Roos, were only accompanied by a small number of men. They no longer had an army with which to challenge the Yorkists themselves. Instead, they turned to the Scots for military assistance, with a treaty soon agreed. However, the price of their support was the surrender of Berwick-upon-Tweed, which occurred on 25 April. This was an unpopular concession that damaged the prestige of the Lancastrian cause, but given their desperate circumstances was a necessary evil.[19]

Their opponents wasted no time in capitalising on the situation in their propaganda. In a letter written to the corporation of the city of London, Edward outlined the supposed misdeeds of Queen Margaret in making such an alliance. She was stated to have agreed to hand over seven sherifwicks (counties) to Scotland, to marry her son, Prince Edward, to a sister of James III and to hand over the livelihoods of the English nobility and gentry to the Scots and French. As a consequence of this, the realm was to be placed under the domination of the latter, who 'she hath excited and provoked to show them of the greatest and largest cruelty and tyranny against our said subjects that they can, unto the execution of the end of her insatiable malice toward them'. In addition, the Scots were said to be planning to invade the realm to besiege Norham Castle with a large artillery train. Edward therefore requested the assistance of the Londoners in resisting this invasion, although in the event the attack on Norham failed to materialise. Similarly, at the parliament held later that year, the Lancastrians were characterised as traitors who had invited outsiders to invade the kingdom. They were said to have 'urged, importuned and provoked the foreign enemies of our said sovereign lord King Edward IV to enter into his said realm with great armies'.[20]

The threat from the Scottish allies of the Lancastrians prompted the Yorkists to carry out defensive measures to defend the far north of England. A garrison was installed in Newcastle in late April or early May, which included a contingent of twenty-four soldiers sent from Beverley. Following the surrender of Berwick, Newcastle was the most northerly settlement held by the Yorkists in the north-east of England. It was therefore of strategic importance, due to its port facilities, which meant that soldiers and supplies could be transported by sea to Northumberland with relative ease, as well as it being a centre for the export of coal. Newcastle's name derived from its castle, whose principal feature was its imposing twelfth-century keep, where these soldiers were most probably stationed. The castle of Tynemouth, at the mouth of the River Tyne, was also garrisoned with a force of forty men on 2 May. They were placed under the command of Sir George Lumley, the son and heir of Thomas, Lord Lumley, who owned the castle of the same name in the County Palatinate of Durham. Tynemouth Castle has strong natural defences due to its location on a headland that juts out into the sea. The defensive potential of the site is the reason why it was fortified, despite the presence of a priory in the same place. Lumley oversaw a programme of works to refurbish the fortifications, which included the scouring and cleansing of the ditches, the repair of the walls and the making of large wooden shields called pavises for the soldiers.[21]

Attempts were also made to make inroads into Northumberland. Despite the strong Lancastrian sympathies of many in the county, some important members of the local gentry such as Robert, Lord Ogle, adhered to the cause of Edward IV. Ogle came from a prominent Marcher family that had long been involved in the defence of the region against the Scots. He owned the castles of Ogle and Bothal in his own right and held the constableship of Norham Castle, which belonged to the bishop of Durham. Ogle soon received instructions from the king to go onto the offensive against the Lancastrians. On 2 May, he was ordered to seize control of the castle of Harbottle and lordship of Redesdale, which belonged to Sir William Tailboys, as well as Ford Castle, that had previously been held by Sir John Heron of Ford, who had been killed at Towton. Ogle was authorised to crush any resistance he encountered. Whether he faced any opposition or not is not recorded, but his efforts were nevertheless rewarded, as he was later raised to the baronage by the king.[22]

The Yorkists were also busy subduing Lancastrian resistance further south in Yorkshire. On 10 May, commissions of array were issued to the earl of Warwick, his brother, John, Lord Montagu, and their uncle, William Neville, Lord Fauconberg, as well as to other notable figures, such as Thomas, Lord Lumley, Ralph, Lord Greystoke, and Sir James Strangeways in all three ridings in Yorkshire. Three days later, they were given powers to arrest and imprison rebels. Further commissions for arraying men were issued at the end of the month across the county. They faced at least some opposition, including armed resistance at Skipton Castle in the West Riding of Yorkshire. Skipton was of strategic importance due to its location in the Aire Gap, a pass through the Pennines, which allowed access between the Vale of York to the east and Lancashire to the west.

The castle has an inner and outer ward, with the latter entered via a striking gatehouse flanked by two large drum towers. Skipton belonged to John, Lord Clifford, who was killed fighting on the Lancastrian side at the Battle of Ferrybridge, but the castle appears to have been held by his partisans following the battle. In May, Warwick sent a contingent of soldiers to seize control of the place, but the garrison refused to admit them. Unfortunately, next to no information is known about what took place. The sole reference is provided from the accounts of the lordship of Knaresborough, which records the expenditure of £2 6s. 7d. on the provisions and expenses of soldiers serving at the siege in May. By the end of July, it was reported by an Italian observer, Giovanni Pietro Casnolla, that Yorkshire had been pacified despite the pro-Lancastrian sympathies of the inhabitants.[23]

Meanwhile, the Lancastrian leadership, who now had Scottish military assistance, had launched a counteroffensive across the border into Cumberland in June. It was claimed that Queen Margaret, Prince Edward, the duke of Exeter, Sir Humphrey Dacre, Sir Edmund Hampden, Sir Richard Tunstall and others had incited the Scots to invade England and had brought them to the city of Carlisle. This was described as the 'key to the west marches of England', which they allegedly promised to hand over to them once it was captured. The defence of Carlisle was led by Richard Salkeld, esquire, who had recently seized the settlement for the Yorkists. Fortunately for the defenders it had strong fortifications, which had been kept in a good state of repair due to its proximity to the Scottish border, with the walled settlement adjoined on its north side by a formidable castle. This fortress is situated on high ground overlooking the city, and has a large outer ward and smaller inner ward, with the latter including an imposing twelfth-century keep. The Scots were said to have caused considerable damage to the suburbs of Carlisle and its surrounding area during their siege. They may have employed artillery as damage was later recorded as being inflicted on the fortifications at this time. Yet, relief was soon at hand for the hard-pressed garrison. The siege was broken by an army led by Montagu, with the Scots routed and supposedly 6,000 of them slain. By 24 June, Warwick had reached the city to oversee its defence, where he retained a gunner, John Faucon, in his service.[24]

Yet, undaunted by this setback, the Lancastrians also launched an attack into north-east England. This appears to have taken the form of a mounted raid deep into Yorkist-held territory. At the parliament held later that year, it was stated that Henry, late king of England, Lord Roos, Tailboys, Sir Humphrey Neville and others 'with standards and banners displayed, raised war against our said lord King Edward' at Ryton and Brancepeth in the Palatinate of Durham on 26 June.[25] Their motivation in carrying out this daring enterprise is not clear. It could have been an attempt to spark a rebellion in the area or to capture the city of Durham itself. Brancepeth may have been chosen as the castle there belonged to the senior pro-Lancastrian branch of the Neville family. Humphrey Neville, who was the nephew of the earl of Westmorland, may therefore have sought to exploit his family's connections in the region. They also appear to have used compulsion to force men to join their ranks, as is suggested by a letter sent by the prior of Durham to Warwick. The prior explained that his kinsman, Richard Billingham, had joined with Humphrey Neville. Yet, as he claimed, this was either because Richard believed that Humphrey was loyal to Edward IV, or otherwise had only accompanied him due to fear for his life if he refused to do so. Whatever their motives, the Lancastrians were soon forced to beat a hasty retreat. This was due to the actions of Lawrence Booth, the bishop of Durham, who led the defence of the region. In recognition of this, he was later compensated by the king for the expenses he had borne in resisting the 'late king Henry and his adherents'. Humphrey, who appears to have been captured by the Yorkists during the raid, was sent to the south and imprisoned in the Tower.[26]

Having repulsed these Lancastrian attacks, the Neville brothers then advanced northwards to the Scottish border. Their forces having been augmented by reinforcements from the south, which included a contingent of forty men sent by the city of Coventry. On 31 July, Warwick, who already held the wardenship of the west march, was also appointed as warden of the east march. Eight days later, Lord Ogle was granted the offices of steward and constable for the Percy castles of Alnwick, Warkworth and Prudhoe in Northumberland. By the end of the year the Yorkists had succeeded in capturing the Lancastrian-held castles of the far north of England. Sir William Bowes had taken control of Alnwick Castle by 13 September, which he held with a garrison of 100 men, whereas Cockermouth Castle in Westmorland had been occupied by Sir John Hudleston with a force of 80 men by December. The existing garrisons further to the south were also kept in existence. Thomas, Lord Lumley, was in command at Newcastle with a force of 120 soldiers, with provisions sent by sea from Norfolk and £300 lent by a wealthy merchant of the town, Alan Birde, for the purchase of ordnance. The garrison at Tynemouth Castle, which was led by Sir George Lumley, was also maintained, although it was reduced from forty to twenty-four soldiers after

13 September. At the end of the year, commissions of array were issued for the defence of the border counties against the Scots and their English allies.[27]

Over the winter of 1461–2, the Lancastrians succeeded in regaining control of some of the border castles, including Alnwick in Northumberland and Naworth in Cumberland. The latter was another castle that belonged to the Dacre family, which explains why Sir Humphrey Dacre apparently oversaw its capture and subsequent defence. Naworth was a quadrilateral fortress, which had strong natural defences, due to its location on a spur between two streams, thereby rendering it difficult to approach except on one side. It is unclear how the Lancastrians took these places but given the military superiority of the Yorkists it is unlikely that the castles were captured after formal sieges, particularly as they had impressive fortifications. Instead, it seems more probable that they were taken by subterfuge or by treachery. In July, the Yorkists counterattacked by laying siege to both castles. The *Annales* relates that Naworth was surrendered by appointment, in other words under terms, by Dacre to Montagu. Similarly, the same account states that a Yorkist force led by William, Lord Hastings, Sir Ralph Grey and many others laid siege to Alnwick Castle, where Tailboys was the captain. Alnwick was the main seat of the Percy family who had lavished large sums of money on its buildings and defences. It was a sizeable site incorporating some 7 acres that had an inner and outer bailey with the gatehouse of the latter being defended by a barbican. The castle's most prominent feature was a twelfth-century shell keep. It should have been capable of withstanding a lengthy siege. Nevertheless, Tailboys was said to have capitulated in return for the sparing of the lives, limbs, horses and weaponry of the members of the garrison. A more prominent role in the taking of Alnwick is ascribed to Hastings by the author of the *Great Chronicle of London*. According to this account, the king gave him the 'rule of his soldiers' on account of his manliness, and under his able leadership the troops launched furious assaults against the rebels, which forced them to surrender the castle by the beginning of August.[28]

Margaret's Invasion

Despite these successes in the north, the continued prospect of a French invasion and of conspiracies by supporters of the deposed king, meant that the realm remained troubled. Arrests were periodically made of Lancastrian agitators and commissions of oyer and terminer were established to investigate treacherous activities. In February 1462, a conspiracy led by

John de Vere, earl of Oxford, was supposedly uncovered. The earl was alleged to have plotted against the king, with the author of the *Annales* claiming that he intended to kill him whilst they were campaigning in the north of England. Oxford, together with his eldest son, Aubrey, and others, including Sir Thomas Tuddenham, were therefore arrested by royal command and sent to the Tower. After being put on trial before John Tiptoft, earl of Worcester, the newly appointed constable of England, they were condemned to death and executed at Tower Hill. Measures were taken to protect coastal regions, with commissions of array issued, watches kept at vulnerable landing sites, and ships sent to patrol the coastline. In Hastings in East Sussex there was even the belief that foreign spies were operating in the town and gathering information and spreading rumours. A commission was therefore issued to three men to arrest all people suspected of these crimes in the settlement and to interrogate them.[29]

The feared French invasion eventually materialised in the autumn of 1462. An earlier scheme to support the Lancastrians had been frustrated by the unexpected demise of Charles VII in the previous year. The new king, Louis XI, was hesitant to intervene in English affairs and initially had imprisoned Henry's envoys, Robert, Lord Hungerford, and Robert Whittingham, at Dieppe. This situation was only transformed due to the actions of Queen Margaret. In the spring of 1462, she left Scotland with her son and sailed to France, having received a commission from her husband to act as his envoy. This was a risky venture, as the sea lanes were controlled by the Yorkists, but was borne out of desperation, as the Scots had proved to be ineffectual allies. Nevertheless, it paid off as she concluded an agreement with Louis XI on 23 June at Chinon, whereby he lent her a large sum of money, with Calais offered as security for its repayment, should the Lancastrians recover it. This was used to recruit an army and fleet from Normandy led by the experienced French captain Pierre de Brézé, who had sacked Sandwich five years earlier. However, this was a far smaller force than had originally been envisaged. Instead of a great army capable of regaining her kingdom, it appears to have numbered in the hundreds rather than thousands of men.[30]

In anticipation of her arrival, efforts had been made by Lancastrian sympathisers in northern England to prepare for a rising. Earlier in the year, people were said to have uttered seditious speeches and incited rebellion in the counties of Cumberland, Westmorland and Northumberland. The civic authorities of York played an active part in attempting to thwart Lancastrian conspiracies. In the summer, they had sent a messenger to Warwick, whilst he was at his castle of Middleham, to inform him that they had arrested a man from the north, who was found with incriminating letters. Subsequently, the mayor exchanged further correspondence with the earl, during his stay at Knaresborough Castle, where he was constable. The French fleet, which according to *Gregory's Chronicle* numbered fifty-two ships, eventually set sail from Normandy in October making its way northwards along the eastern coastline of England. This was a voyage potentially fraught with peril due to adverse weather conditions and Yorkist naval patrols. Nevertheless, they successfully evaded these threats and made landfall off the coast of Northumberland near to Bamburgh on 25 October. This led to the outbreak of a rebellion, with the Lancastrians soon able to assume control of much of the county. This appears to have taken place with relative ease, although the author of the *Annales* relates that Alnwick Castle was captured after a siege, with the Yorkist garrison surrendering due to a lack of provisions. They also managed to take other nearby fortresses including Bamburgh, Warkworth and Dunstanburgh. Possession of these castles, as explained by the Warkworth chronicler, thereby gave them 'the most part of all Northumberland'. Concerns that the rebellion could spread further afield even prompted Montagu to temporarily install a garrison at Knaresborough Castle.[31]

Edward responded by issuing orders for an army to be assembled to recover the castles. A large loan was offered by the citizens of London to finance the expedition, bows and arrows supplied by bowyers and fletchers, guns procured for the royal artillery train and ships obtained to support the land forces. The king also sent a commission to Warwick to act as his lieutenant in the north, with instructions to raise his standard against the rebels and their foreign allies. Edward eventually raised a substantial army, which was said to have included the retinues of two dukes, seven earls, thirty-one barons and fifty-nine knights. News of the imminent arrival of this huge force seems to have unnerved Margaret, who decided to flee to Scotland. Leaving behind some of her French soldiers to garrison the castles, she embarked with the rest. Yet, her small fleet soon encountered a tempest. Margaret was forced to abandon her ship, with the loss of her possessions, and to carry on the voyage to Berwick in a boat. Three other large vessels were said to have sunk, with the survivors taking refuge on Holy Island. This tidal island can be seen from Bamburgh Castle on the mainland, but the Lancastrian garrison of the latter were powerless to aid their comrades. The stranded French soldiers were soon attacked by a Yorkist force led by the Bastard of Ogle and John Manners who forced them to surrender.[32]

The king only managed to travel as far north as Durham, where he fell ill, possibly from contracting measles. Warwick therefore took charge of the army and led it into Northumberland. The first target appears to have been Warkworth, which had belonged to the Percy family since the fourteenth century. Warkworth has an outer and inner ward, with an unusual and striking cross-shaped keep situated in the latter. Despite its strong fortifications, it was quickly occupied by the Yorkists, who then moved on to besiege the other Lancastrian-held castles. A detailed insight into how these sieges were conducted, can be seen from a surviving letter written by one of the Yorkist soldiers on 11 December. Warwick was said to have used Warkworth Castle as his headquarters for the campaign. From there he rode every day to each of the besieged castles to supervise the activities of his lieutenants. The earl of Worcester and Sir Ralph Grey were in command of the besiegers at Dunstanburgh Castle, Montague and Lord Ogle at Bamburgh Castle, and William Neville (who had now been raised to the rank of earl of Kent) and Anthony Woodville, Lord Scales, at Alnwick Castle. Strict discipline was said to have been maintained, with leave denied for soldiers in the army and those caught trying to desert being sternly punished. Ships were used to freight provisions and armaments by sea to Newcastle. From there they were carted by land to Warkworth whilst escorted by soldiers. The duke of Norfolk was allocated the task of supervising at least one of these deliveries, and sent men, including John, Lord Howard, Sir William Peche and others, to transport these supplies to Warwick. Amongst the military equipment conveyed from Newcastle were guns intended for both use in the sieges and on the battlefield, the latter in case the Scots intervened, as was expected. Other supplies were obtained or seized from the local area. For instance, the abbot and convent of Alnwick Abbey later received compensation of £100 for goods taken from them during the siege of the nearby castle.[33]

The Lancastrian defenders were heavily outnumbered by their opponents. Large numbers of men from different parts of England were present in the Yorkist army. This included 400 archers serving under Sir William Stanley at the siege of Alnwick, together with contingents ranging from places such as Stoke, Boxford and Felixstow in Suffolk, and Ainsty in Yorkshire. According to one account, the Yorkist army consisted of 30,000 soldiers in total, with 10,000 allocated for each siege. By contrast, the Lancastrian defenders were said to have been far fewer in number. Bamburgh Castle was garrisoned by 300 men, commanded by the duke of Somerset, Jasper Tudor, Lord Roos and Sir Ralph Percy. Dunstanburgh by 120 men led by Sir Richard Tunstall and Thomas, Lord

Fyndern, and Alnwick by 300 men, whose commanders were unknown to the chronicler. The Yorkists also had a strong artillery train, including one bombard from Warkworth, which was accompanied by a team of gunners. Yet, they made little attempt to storm or bombard the castles, instead choosing to starve their garrisons into surrender. This was to ensure that they could be captured intact without their fortifications being damaged or the lives of the soldiers in the Yorkist army being unnecessarily risked. The latter was an important consideration as they had strong defences. This can be seen with Dunstanburgh, situated on the Northumberland coastline some 10 miles to the south-east of Bamburgh. The castle is located on a headland flanked by cliffs, with its most striking feature being an impressive twin-towered gatehouse whose towers were five storeys high. It was also surrounded by extensive water features, which made it difficult to approach.[34]

The blockade soon began to take effect, as the garrisons, despairing of outside assistance and with food supplies running low, entered into negotiations to surrender. Despite their desperate circumstances, being cut off and surrounded, they were able to achieve generous terms. The defenders were offered pardons in return for accepting Edward's allegiance, which was taken up by notable figures, such as the duke of Somerset and Sir Ralph Percy. Alternatively, those who found these terms unacceptable, such as Jasper Tudor and Lord Roos, were escorted to the border with Scotland. These negotiations led to the surrender of Bamburgh Castle on 26 December and Dunstanburgh Castle on the following day. Yet, the defenders of Alnwick were evidently more determined to resist than their comrades, as they refused to capitulate. This decision may have been motivated by the news that the eagerly awaited Scottish army was marching to their rescue. It was led by George Douglas, earl of Angus, who had assembled what was said to be a large force and was accompanied by Pierre de Brézé. News of their approach soon reached the Yorkists. From his sickbed in Durham, Edward wrote a letter on 28 December to his chancellor, George Neville, bishop of Exeter, to advise him that the Scots would soon invade to rescue the French soldiers at Alnwick castle. Three days later, he sent him another message with an order to assemble the clergy of his province in arms to meet them in battle.[35]

On 5 January, the Scottish army arrived in the vicinity of Alnwick. Despite having been forewarned, their approach appears to have thrown the besiegers into disarray. Rather than moving to confront the Scots, the Yorkists instead abandoned their camp and withdrew a short distance away. According to the author of the *Annales*, they moved to a location near to the coast so as to offer battle to the Scots, presumably where the ground was more favourable to them. This withdrawal allowed some of the defenders of Alnwick, including Lord Hungerford, Sir Richard Tunstall and Sir Robert Whittingham, to flee the castle and join the Scottish army. Yet, the Scots chose not to engage with the Yorkists and retreated back to Scotland. Some of the London chroniclers attributed this to their fear of meeting the English in battle, who outmatched them. By contrast, the Warkworth chronicler emphasised that the Scots had missed a great opportunity to inflict a decisive blow against their opponents. If they had 'come on boldly, they might have taken and distressed all the lords and commoners'. This was because the Yorkists soldiers 'had lain so long in the field, and were grieved with cold and rain, that they had no courage to fight'. Following the departure of the Scottish army, the remaining defenders of Alnwick surrendered under terms a short time later. This meant that all of the castles of Northumberland had been recovered by the Yorkists.[36]

The Struggle Resumed

This situation was not to last long. Edward, as we have already observed, had pardoned and accepted into his service men from the garrisons of the Lancastrian-held castles. For Dunstanburgh Castle this included Thomas Carre who had served as the captain and Thomas Clenell as the constable. The king even went so far as to allow Sir Ralph Percy to remain in command of Bamburgh and also, according to *Gregory's Chronicle*, to take charge of Dunstanburgh. In addition to this, he was given the authority to receive the submission of rebels on the king's behalf. This decision was perhaps borne as much out of pragmatism as generosity. Medieval rulers were dependent upon the cooperation of local elites to exercise effective governance. Edward could already rely upon the support of some of the Northumbrians, such as Ogle, but he was keen to persuade adherents of Henry VI to defect to him. Not only did this strengthen his grip on power, but it thereby reduced yet further still the dwindling band of Lancastrian exiles. However, it proved to be a mistaken one, as the loyalty of some men to the cause of Henry VI proved to be remarkably tenacious. In March 1463, the garrisons of the castles of Bamburgh and Dunstanburgh defected to the Lancastrians. Their former commanders had been left in charge of these fortresses, so this was easy enough for them to accomplish, with any internal opposition amongst the soldiers quickly quelled.[37]

By comparison, the captaincy of Alnwick had been entrusted to Sir John Astley. The latter had won great renown some years earlier, in 1442, when he had defeated a knight from Catalonia in a duel at Smithfield. Astley was also an adherent to the Yorkist cause and had received rewards from the king, including an annuity of £40. His appointment as captain was said to have infuriated Sir Ralph Grey, according to the author of the *Annales*, as the latter wished to have the office for himself, although he was given the constableship. Grey had hitherto been a Yorkist who had served with Hastings at the siege of Naworth, but now he plotted against his erstwhile comrades. This was unknown to Astley, who on 17 March was authorised to procure goods and to arrange for their transportation to ensure that Alnwick was supplied with provisions, a defensive measure almost certainly taken in response to the loss of the castles of Dunstanburgh and Bamburgh. Yet, his attempts to prepare the defences of Alnwick were undone by the treachery of Grey. *Gregory's Chronicle* states that the latter used deception to gain control of the castle and imprisoned Astley in May. His unfortunate prisoner was afterwards sent to France where he languished in prison for some time before being ransomed. At around the same time, according to a French report, Henry and Queen Margaret travelled southwards from Scotland with a force of 2,000 men to Bamburgh. They then advanced southwards to Newcastle but after being defeated in a skirmish returned to Lancastrian-held territory. Attempts were also made to send supplies to Bamburgh from France by sea. Yet, these efforts were unsuccessful, with four large French vessels captured by English ships from Newcastle.[38]

The rapid loss of such strategically important castles, which had only a few short months earlier been won at such a great financial expense, was undoubtedly a setback. This was compounded by the actions of the Scots, who decided to launch another invasion. Their objective this time was Norham Castle, situated some 7 miles west of Berwick. This was a strategic border fortress located on the south bank of the River Tweed, the significance of which had been further enhanced following the loss of Berwick and the destruction of Roxburgh in recent years. Norham dated from the twelfth century, with its principal feature being a large five-storey keep located in the inner ward. Access to the latter was via a drawbridge across a moat from the outer ward of the castle, which in turn had its own curtain wall. Lord Ogle, as constable of Norham, was responsible for its defence, with additional funding for its garrison provided from royal revenues. Yet, the castle was vulnerable to attack as an isolated outpost, the defenders of which were some distance from other friendly forces, despite its strong defences. Nevertheless, its location meant that the garrison posed a threat to the line of communication between the Lancastrian-held

castles further south and Scottish-occupied Berwick. Norham was therefore an important target for the Scots and their Lancastrian allies, as its
capture would allow them to operate with greater ease in Northumberland. In July, a large Scottish army accompanied by Henry VI, Queen
Margaret and Brézé crossed the border and advanced to Norham.[39]

News of their incursion soon reached the Yorkists. From his castle at
Middleham, Warwick wrote to the bishop of York to request military
assistance on 11 July. This was because the Scots 'with his traitors and
rebels have entered this land with great power intending to do ... all the
hurt and damage they can imagine'. He therefore ordered him, as the
king's lieutenant, to assemble the clergy of his province in their most
defensible array to meet with him at Durham four days later. Edward also
issued instructions for a fleet to be assembled and began to gather an army
for an expedition to the north. Yet, it would take time for forces from the
south to mobilise. Fortunately for the hard-pressed garrison, relief was
soon at hand. After a siege that supposedly lasted eighteen days, they were
rescued by the forces of Warwick and Montagu who routed the Scots.
This was described in a letter written by Lord Hastings to the Seigneur
de Lannoy on 7 August. Hastings boasted that the Scots had besieged the
castle with the full power of their kingdom, but were put to flight by
Warwick, who was only accompanied by the men of the border region.
Margaret and Brézé with their companions were forced to abandon their
horses and armour, so hotly were they pursued, before sailing overseas to
Sluis in Flanders. The victorious Yorkists then pursued their enemies
across the border into Scotland, where they were said to have caused great
destruction, before withdrawing southwards.[40]

Edward meanwhile continued preparations for an expedition to punish
the Scots. On 15 August he wrote to the civic authorities in Salisbury
from Fotheringhay Castle in Northamptonshire. The king ordered them
to send a company of soldiers from the city to arrive at Newcastle by
13 September for 'our voyage against our enemies of Scotland to proceed
against their accustomed pride'. In response, the citizens agreed to provide a contingent of twenty-three men led by a captain with wages for two
months.[41] Funds were also allocated for the purchase of provisions to be
transported by sea so that the army would be suitably supplied in Scotland. Yet, the planned expedition never took place. As bitterly noted by
the author of *Gregory's Chronicle*, despite the king having 'ordained a great
navy and a great army ... all was lost and in vain, and came to no purpose'.
The reason for its abandonment was because a truce was negotiated with
the Scottish government in December. This meant the Lancastrians were

now diplomatically isolated, with Louis XI having entered into a similar arrangement two months earlier. However, they remained determined to carry on the struggle. Furthermore, some of their supporters who had entered the service of the Yorkist king returned to their previous allegiance. Most prominent amongst them was the duke of Somerset.[42]

Edward IV had made great efforts to win the loyalty of the duke. According to the author of *Gregory's Chronicle*, he hunted and shared a bed with him, arranged a tournament in his honour and even formed a 'king's guard' from his entourage. Later, after Somerset was almost lynched by the inhabitants of Northampton, who were angry at the affection shown to him, the king sent him to a castle in north Wales for his own safety. Nevertheless, around Christmas time, the 'false duke' left Wales and secretly travelled northwards with a group of followers. His plan being to seize control of Newcastle with the assistance of some of his men who were serving in the garrison in the town. Yet, he was detected whilst passing through Durham and was forced to flee from his bed wearing only a shirt and barefoot, leaving behind his armour and other possessions. When his followers in Newcastle learnt of the failure of this plot, they took flight, but some of them were apprehended and executed by the Yorkists. Subsequently, Edward sent a force of sixty-two men from his household, under the command of John, Lord Scrope, to secure the settlement, who 'kept it surely all that winter'.[43]

The Siege of Bamburgh Castle

Despite the failure of this plot, the Lancastrians succeeded in strengthening their position in Northumberland. This can be seen from a letter of protection granted by Henry at Bamburgh Castle on 8 December 1463. It was given to William Burgh, his sons, William and Christopher, and six other persons with them, which was to last until the feast of St John the Baptist (24 June). This was remarkable as William Burgh, senior, had held the office of constable of Yorkist-held Prudhoe Castle since February 1462. Prudhoe had been forfeited by the Percy family, with its ownership afterwards transferred by Edward IV to his brother, George, duke of Clarence. An indenture dating from 26 March 1463 between Burgh and Clarence specified that the former would hold the castle 'at his proper charges and costs at his own peril to the use of the said duke unless that such casualty fall by misfortune of war that it shall pass his might and power so to do'. In which case Clarence would take on financial responsibility. Burgh's agreement with Henry was unlikely to have been authorised by Edward and was potentially treasonous. His decision to take such a risk indicates that he had been placed under military pressure by his opponents. A resurgence in Lancastrian power also appears to have prompted some notable men from the region who had previously accepted pardons from Edward IV to defect back to Henry's allegiance. These individuals included Sir Humphrey Neville, who had previously escaped from the Tower, as well as members of the Northumberland gentry, such as William Lermouth and Thomas Elwick, both from Bamburgh, Gawen Lampleugh of Warkworth, together with Archibald Ridley and Gilbert Ridley from Langley.[44]

In the winter of 1463–4 the Lancastrians went onto the offensive, despite having been deserted by their French and Scottish allies. They succeeded in capturing the Tower of Hexham and the castles of Langley and Bywell in Northumberland, thereby threatening communications between Carlisle and Newcastle, as well as taking Norham Castle. The Lancastrians also carried out raids into Cumberland, which meant that the Yorkist sheriff, Sir John Hudleston, constable of Cockermouth Castle, was unable to render his accounts for the county. This was because he was said to have borne 'great charges and costs ... in resisting and subduing of our traitors enemies and rebels'.[45] A contemporary survey of the estates of Naworth Castle also reveals that the land had been laid waste by the Scots and rebels. The Lancastrians even managed to penetrate as far as the West Riding of Yorkshire, where they seized Skipton Castle. These advances prompted the Yorkists to undertake measures to defend fortifications in the region. This included the placing of a force of twenty men in Ponte-fract Castle to ensure its safely, 'at such time as the castle of Skipton in Craven was taken by our traitors', for sixteen weeks, as well the installation of a garrison in Durham.[46]

Negotiations between the English and Scottish governments had been ongoing throughout the spring to extend the truce or even to negotiate a peace treaty. It was decided that the Scots would send ambassadors to Newcastle, later changed to York, to agree a settlement. Yet, the decision to send these men overland, rather than by sea, posed a problem as much of Northumberland was controlled by the Lancastrians. Therefore, Montagu was sent northwards with a force to meet the commissioners at the border and to escort them southwards. Understandably, the Lancastrians were keen to disrupt these negotiations and attempted to intercept the Yorkists. On 15 April, a force led by Somerset, Hungerford and Roos engaged the Yorkists at the Battle of Hedgeley Moor but were routed, with Sir Ralph Percy slain. Following this victory, Montagu escorted the ambassadors to York, where talks led to an extension of the Anglo-Scottish truce. Despite this setback, the Lancastrians decided to go onto the offensive once again. Advancing southwards, they met with Montagu's forces at the Battle of Hexham on 15 May. This time they suffered an even greater defeat, with many of their men said to have been killed and their army effectively destroyed. One of the few prominent Lancastrians to escape from this debacle was Henry, who had been staying in nearby Bywell Castle. Even so, he was forced to flee in such a hurry that he abandoned his helmet, crown and sword, as well as a hat called a bycocket encrusted with jewels. His supporters were less fortunate. Unlike on previous occasions, their commanders were shown no mercy. Somerset was taken to Hexham where he was beheaded, with the same fate befalling Hungerford and Roos at Newcastle, with other men executed at Middleham and York. The latter included Tailboys, who was said to have been captured in a coal pit with £2,000 worth of money. These executions decimated the leadership of the northern Lancastrians and showed that Edward's earlier policy of clemency had been abandoned.[47]

Whilst these events were taking place the king was preparing an expedition to the north. On the same day as the Battle of Hedgeley Moor, he wrote a letter to the city of Salisbury, where he announced his intention to 'bring in to our obedience our castles kept by our traitors and rebels'. Edward therefore requested that a contingent of soldiers be sent to meet with him at Leicester on 10 May. He eventually made his way to Pontefract on 22 May, where he was presented with Henry's bycocket by Montagu. The latter was duly rewarded for his achievements in defeating the Lancastrians, with the king granting him the earldom of Northumberland. Meanwhile, Thomas, Lord Stanley, and his brother Sir William, had been busy subduing Lancastrian resistance in Yorkshire. This culminated in the siege of Skipton Castle, which they captured after bombarding the defenders.[48]

Despite the heavy losses that they had suffered in battle, the Lancastrians still held three major castles in Northumberland. In the immediate aftermath of the Battle of Hexham, Bywell, Langley and the Tower of Hexham had been surrendered, but they still retained Alnwick, Dunstanburgh and Bamburgh. The task of regaining these fortresses was left to Warwick and Montagu who on 11 June were given the authority to pardon rebels, except for Sir Ralph Grey and Sir Humphrey Neville who were expressively excluded. Later in the month, the Yorkists advanced on Alnwick and Dunstanburgh, which were both surrendered under terms. This left Bamburgh as the remaining Lancastrian-held stronghold in the north, where fugitives from the rout at Hexham, including Sir Ralph

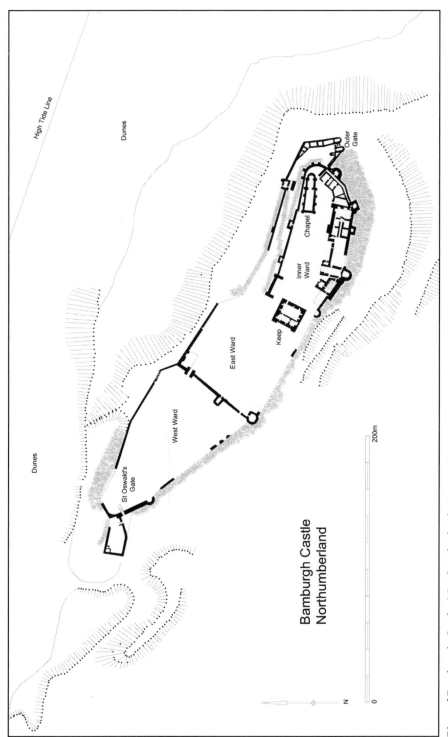

Plan of Bamburgh Castle, Northumberland. (*Drawn by James Wright*, © *Dan Spencer*)

Grey, had congregated. Despite the hopelessness of their situation, they were resolved to put up a determined resistance. Bamburgh was a formidable fortress due to its location on a volcanic outcrop, which made it difficult to assault. Furthermore, it had extensive masonry defences, which occupied a large site, with three wards and a twelfth-century keep.[49]

A detailed account of the siege is preserved in a manuscript kept at the College of Arms. According to the unnamed author, proceedings began with Chester and Warwick heralds sent to deliver an ultimatum to the defenders on 25 June. If the castle was delivered immediately then a pardon would be offered to all members of the garrison except for Sir Ralph Grey and Sir Humphrey Neville. Grey was said to have replied that he would live or die within the castle. In response, the heralds stated that he would be responsible for any offence committed against God or the shedding of blood, with Warwick and Montagu having pledged to sustain a siege for seven years. They went on to say that 'if you deliver not this jewel, the which the king our most dread sovereign lord ... especially desires to have it whole unbroken with ordnance. If you suffer any great gun laid unto the wall and be shot and prejudice the wall, it shall cost you the chieftain's head and so proceeding for every gunshot to the least head of any person within the said place'. Warwick then ordered that the artillery, which included three bombards called *Newcastle*, *London* and *Dysyon*, should be fired at once at the defenders. This bombardment caused such destruction that stones from the castle were knocked into the sea and gunstones repeatedly smashed through Grey's chamber. Eventually the gunfire from the Yorkist guns so overwhelmed the defenders, that the men-at-arms and archers in the besieging army succeeded in storming the fortress. Grey was taken prisoner and brought before the king at Doncaster where he was put on trial and after being found guilty was executed. The fall of Bamburgh led to the end of Lancastrian resistance in Northumberland.[50]

Henry had meanwhile fled north of the border following the Battle of Hexham, where he was sheltered by the Scots, notwithstanding the truce between England and Scotland. Yet, his safety was precarious due to the improved state of Anglo-Scottish relations. This prompted him in the following year to make the ill-advised decision to secretly return to England. He was sheltered for some time by his supporters in Lancashire before he made his way to Waddington Hall in the far west of the West Riding of Yorkshire. There he was betrayed to the Yorkists and was captured by Sir James Harrington, along with two companions. Henry was said to have been taken by horseback to London, with his legs bound to his stirrups. Warwick met him at Islington just outside the city, after which he escorted him through Newgate and Cheapside before reaching the Tower on 24 July. The Warkworth chronicler records that he was thereafter guarded there by two squires and two yeomen of the Crown with their men, with visitors only allowed to speak to him with their permission.[51]

The Defiance of Harlech

As explained by the Warkworth chronicler, the capture of Bamburgh meant that all of England (and Wales) recognised the authority of King Edward. Except, as he went on to add, for a castle in north Wales called Harlech. This was now the only part of the realm that remained under the control of the supporters of Henry VI. Safe in their remote fortress in the wilds of Snowdonia they remained defiant, even after the rest of Wales had long since submitted to the Yorkists. Harlech's remote location and strong defences meant that it could only be captured by a sustained and concerted effort. Yet, neither the king, nor his chief lieutenant in Wales, Lord Herbert, initially showed much interest in reducing Harlech to his obedience. Their priorities lay elsewhere. The former allocated the bulk of royal resources to the prosecution of the war in the north, whereas the latter focused his efforts on asserting his authority in Wales where he was now the dominant magnate. However, the failure to neutralise this outpost of Lancastrian resistance did have consequences. It was responsible for continued unrest and instability in Wales, parts of which remained in a state of warfare. Furthermore, the defiance of the garrison provided a focal point for Lancastrian dissenters throughout the kingdom.[52]

The effects were most keenly felt in the north of the country, particularly in the county of Merioneth. In the parliament of 1461, a petition from the inhabitants of the region was presented to the king by the House of Commons. They claimed that every day they had suffered from the activities of the Lancastrians in the area. Their crimes included imprisoning and ransoming people, 'as if it were a land at war', as well as acts of robbery, in defiance of the law. These outrages were carried out by Dafydd ab Ieuan ab Einion, various members of his family, including his brothers, Gruffydd, John, Thomas and Grommys, as well as other individuals. Dafydd claimed to be acting as constable of Harlech in the name of Henry VI. By both word of mouth and through his writings, he asserted that the keeping of the castle had been entrusted to him by Queen Margaret and her son Prince Edward. This presumably took place during their stay at Harlech in 1460. Dafydd had sworn to guard the castle and would only transfer custody of it at their command. His men were also said to have seized oxen, sheep, wheat and other goods from the local population for provisioning the castle. Dafydd and his principal supporters were issued with an ultimatum to deliver the castle to the king's representatives, and to travel in a peaceful manner to the town of Caernarfon where they would present themselves to the chamberlain of north Wales. If this did not take place by 2 February 1462, they were to be considered as traitors, which would be proclaimed throughout the counties of Merioneth and Caernarfon, and would suffer the forfeiture of their lands. Yet, without employing force against them this was an empty threat.[53]

Instead the main measure taken by the Yorkists was to reinforce the garrisons of the principal royal castles in north Wales. William, Lord Hastings was given the task of safeguarding Beaumaris Castle on the island of Anglesey with a force of forty-eight soldiers to defend both the castle and town. The same number was also allocated for the defence of the castle and town of Conwy under the command of Sir Henry Bold. Sir Thomas Montgomery, the constable of Caernarfon, had a smaller force, with twenty-four men to guard the castle and twelve men for the town. In addition, two watchmen were employed to keep a careful watch for rebels in case they attempted to attack the settlement. By contrast, the force at Aberystwyth in West Wales remained at the long-established number of one mounted man-at-arms and twelve archers, serving under Devereux. Nevertheless, the deputy chamberlain of south Wales, John Hunteley, travelled there from Carmarthen with an escort of horsemen twice a year to muster the soldiers and supervise repairs. These garrisons ensured that the castles remained under Yorkist control, but did little to counter the depredations of the Lancastrians operating from Harlech.[54]

The supporters of Henry VI continued to plot and to plan rebellions elsewhere in Wales. In the winter of 1463–4, Lancastrian conspirators attempted to launch uprisings throughout the country, at the instigation of the duke of Somerset. As we have already seen, he secretly left north Wales before Christmas in 1463 in an unsuccessful attempt to seize Newcastle. Somerset was said to have the support of many gentlemen in the region, who had assisted him in his flight to northern England. The leaders of the northern rebels included John Hamner, a gentleman who had previously been recorded as serving with the Lancastrian garrison at Harlech, and Roger Puleston, who had served as Jasper's constable at Denbigh. John Mowbray, duke of Norfolk, was assigned the task of subduing unrest in the region with the power to execute or pardon rebels. His kinsman, John, Lord Howard, who appears to have acted as his deputy, went on ahead into Wales in late October, with the duke following later.

The campaign was directed from Mowbray's castle of Holt where Howard served as his constable, with forays made into the surrounding area. A major attempt to capture Hamner took place at the beginning of 1464. Howard's household accounts record that he left the castle with a force of 1,200 men at midnight on 5 January. This expedition was unsuccessful as Hamner was still at large two months later. Nevertheless, the region appears to have been pacified by the summer.[55]

Lancastrian sympathisers also sought to raise a rebellion in south Wales. In a session of Parliament it was later stated that these individuals included two members of the gentry from Gower, Philip Mauncell and Hopkin ap Rhys, as well as a monk called Lewis ap Rhydderch ap Rhys. At Dyffryn in Carmarthenshire, they were said to have 'incited, encouraged and prompted' Queen Margaret and other Lancastrians to invade the realm to depose King Edward. However, this uprising proved to be abortive, with the principal participants suffering the forfeiture of their lands. There were also renewed attempts to persuade the defenders of Harlech to surrender. The garrison led by Dafydd was said to have 'caused commotions and uprisings' in the region and to be harbouring two attainted fugitives, Thomas Danyell and John Dowbegyng. Proclamations were ordered to be made upon three consecutive days in Chester calling upon them to yield the castle, upon pain of forfeiture of their lands. Herbert and Devereux were also authorised to grant pardons and to receive the members of the garrison into the king's allegiance on 24 October. However, these threats were once again ignored.[56]

Two years later the task of countering their ravages was entrusted to John Tiptoft, earl of Worcester. On 20 March 1466, he was appointed as a commissioner to investigate reports that a substantial proportion of the rents and revenues in Caernarfonshire had not been paid since the accession of the king some five years earlier. No doubt the affairs of the county were greatly disturbed by the activities of the nearby Lancastrians. Later in the same year it was reported that a force under the command of Sir Richard Tunstall had seized control of Holt Castle and was rumoured to be present in the nearby town of Wrexham. It is unclear how the Lancastrians managed to advance so far eastwards and to carry out this exploit, but it evidently caused alarm throughout the area. The municipal authorities of Shrewsbury were so concerned by these activities and the malice the force supposedly bore towards the town that they hired a man to watch its movements. Tiptoft was therefore sent by the king to deal with the Lancastrian threat by 'certain commissions', with £200 later allocated for his expenses. His first objective was to secure control of

Denbigh Castle, which was threatened by the Lancastrians. He therefore travelled to the castle in early November with a force that included men from the towns of Shrewsbury and Ludlow. It was probably at around that time that the Lancastrians were evicted from Holt Castle. Tiptoft was afterwards sent by order of the king to advance towards Harlech, with his army including forty soldiers from Shrewsbury. Artillery was also sent from the Tower to Bristol by the master of the king's ordnance, John Wode, for the expedition. Yet, it appears that the wintery conditions and remoteness of Harlech was too much for him, as the campaign was soon abandoned, with Tiptoft sent to Ireland in the following year.[57]

A sustained effort to take this last remaining Lancastrian outpost only took place in response to the activities of Jasper Tudor. Jasper had spent some years in exile in France, where he had been recognised as a relative of king Louis XI and had become a member of the latter's household. In the summer of 1468, the French king furnished three ships with which to transport him from Honfleur in Normandy to Wales. Jasper was said to have landed near to Harlech with only fifty men and little money in late June. The French ships then returned to France, with one of them captured by Herbert's men during the voyage. Meanwhile, Jasper travelled across country towards the north-east of Wales. He was said to have held many judicial sessions in the name of Henry VI, with large numbers of men joining his army during the return journey. The target of his expedition was the town of Denbigh, possibly due to its association with the House of York. His army quickly captured and plundered the town, which they burnt, but seemingly not the castle. This exploit provoked a strong response from the Yorkists. Sir William Stanley rapidly marched from Chester with his forces to confront the invaders. However, by the time he had arrived at Denbigh they had already withdrawn westwards. Nevertheless, a garrison of twenty men under the command of James Manley, esquire, was installed at Chester Castle to ensure its safeguard.[58]

News of Jasper's incursion prompted the king to issue a commission of array to Herbert and Devereux on 3 July. They were authorised to raise their forces from the western counties of England and from Wales to confront the rebels. According to the author of the *Annales*, Herbert assembled an army as large as 10,000 men. This estimate was almost certainly an exaggeration, nevertheless he was later reimbursed the considerable sum of over £5,500 for his expenses during the campaign which suggests that he raised a sizeable force. Edward also indented with John Wode to assemble an ordnance company for the siege of Harlech on 20 July. This comprised a contingent of 67 gunners, smiths, carpenters and wheelwrights, together with 100 labourers and 600 soldiers and sailors. These men were to accompany the royal guns kept at Bristol, mostly probably stored in the royal castle there, which were to be transported by ship for the siege. Supplies were also provided for the ordnance company, which included flour, beer, meat, fish, candles, firewood, lead, iron and other items.[59]

In the meanwhile, the Yorkists had caught up with their opponents. Sir Richard Herbert, who appears to have commanded at least part of the army, was said to have defeated Jasper's forces in battle. The latter was forced to flee, with twenty prisoners taken during the fighting subsequently beheaded by the victors. Lord Herbert then pressed on towards Harlech, which he placed under siege. According to *Gregory's Chronicle*, the castle had been fortified and provisioned by those who 'loved King Harry', and was 'so strong that men say that it was impossible for any man to get it'. Yet, the siege was short, with the only notable Yorkist casualty being Philip Vaughan of Hay who was killed by gunshot. The defenders were dispirited by their recent defeat in battle and faced the prospect of being bombarded by the powerful artillery train of the besiegers. This prompted them to surrender under terms on 14 August. The author of the *Annales* relates that Dafydd, six named individuals who appear to have served as captains in the garrison and fifty other men were taken prisoner. Herbert then escorted them to London, where they were lodged in the Tower. Two of the captains were put on trial and after being convicted were executed at Tower Hill, but the others, who included amongst their number Sir Richard Tunstall, were pardoned. Therefore, by the autumn of 1468, the Lancastrians no longer controlled any territory in England or Wales, with Jersey in the Channel Islands recovered by a Yorkist fleet soon afterwards. A small number of exiles, including Queen Margaret, Prince Edward and Jasper Tudor, remained at large, but their cause was seemingly irrevocably lost.[60]

Chapter Five

The Wheel of Fortune

The Spoils of War

Edward IV through his resourcefulness and martial prowess had finally won the English Crown. Yet his triumph was only possible due to the faithful service of his supporters. These individuals would have to be suitably rewarded if he was to maintain his grip on the throne. All monarchs had to employ patronage to keep the nobility, or at least a significant proportion of it, content. For a king who had gained power through deposing his predecessor, this was even more important. If Henry VI could be deposed through military force, then so could his successor. Edward needed to ensure that the regions of the kingdom were governed by landowners who were invested in the survival of the Yorkist regime. He was also obliged to adequately provide for members of his family, notably his younger brothers, George and Richard, and his mother Cecily, the dowager duchess of York, as well as his other relatives. Fortunately for him, he had an abundance of titles, estates, offices and annuities to distribute. As king of England, he held the royal lands, the duchy of Lancaster, the principality of Wales and the duchy of Cornwall. Edward also acquired the proceeds which came from confiscations. Many male members of the nobility had stayed loyal to Henry VI, some of whom were killed, imprisoned or forced into exile during the struggle. Through this, valuable titles and estates were obtained, such as the earldoms of Pembroke and Northumberland. Castles, as major residential buildings that served as manorial and administrative centres, were prized assets, used to reward faithful supporters.[1]

The main beneficiary of Edward's patronage was his cousin, Richard Neville, earl of Warwick. Warwick had played a crucial role in the Yorkist victory and his rewards reflected his great service to his kinsman. The offices given to him included the chamberlainship of England, the constableship of Dover Castle, the wardenship of the west and east marches of Scotland, the captaincy of Calais, and the stewardship of various lordships in the duchy of Lancaster, as well as the constableships of Knaresborough and Pontefract. Warwick had previously been appointed to some of these positions during the latter years of the reign of Henry VI, but others were entirely new. He was also granted the lands of John, Lord Clifford, which included the castles and lordships of Appleby, Burgh, Brougham and Pendragon in Westmorland, and Skipton in Yorkshire. Later he also acquired the castle of Cockermouth in Westmoreland. Warwick's total income from the estates he owned, along with fees derived from offices and annuities was worth in excess of £10,000 per annum. This was a huge sum that far outstripped any of his peers. Warwick had become the wealthiest and most powerful magnate in the kingdom with significant military resources, who owned or controlled many of the principal castles of northern England. Such was his power and influence that the governor of Abbeville in northern France, in a letter sent to Louis XI in March 1464, which reported on affairs in England, joked that 'they have but two rulers – M. de Warwick and another, whose name I have forgotten'.[2]

Other members of the Neville family also benefitted from royal largesse. Warwick's brother, George, bishop of Exeter, was confirmed in his office as chancellor of England, and was later transferred to the archbishopric of York. Whereas their uncle, William, Lord Fauconberg, was made earl of Kent and appointed as steward of the royal household. Warwick's youngest brother, John, Lord Montagu, was rewarded for his victories at the battles of Hedgeley Moor and Hexham by being created as earl of Northumberland in 1464. In the same year, he was granted the Percy castles and lordships of Alnwick, Warkworth, Langley and Prudhoe in Northumberland and Wressle in Yorkshire. He was also appointed as warden of the east march of Scotland, which had been previously held by his older brother. This meant that much of northern England was effectively under the control of the Neville brothers, with Warwick dominant in the north-west and Montagu in the north-east.[3]

Edward was also generous in providing for members of his immediate family. His mother, Cecily, dowager duchess of York, was given a substantial settlement that made her one of the richest landowners in the kingdom. In June 1461, she was allocated extensive lands and annuities that were worth approximately £3,333 per annum. Her principal estates were the castle and manor of Fotheringhay in Northamptonshire, the lordship and castle of Clare in Suffolk, Bridgwater Castle in Somerset and Baynard's Castle in London. Edward's oldest surviving brother, George, was created as duke of Clarence, and given estates mostly situated in the West Country and Midlands. These grants included the castles of Old Wardour in Wiltshire, Somerton in Lincolnshire and Bolsover in Derbyshire in 1463, and two years later Castle Donnington in Leicestershire,

Peveril in Derbyshire and Tutbury in Staffordshire. By 1467, the annual value of his estates was around £3,400, making him the second wealthiest magnate after Warwick, which reflected his status as Edward's heir. By contrast, the king's youngest brother, Richard, was created as duke of Gloucester but received an endowment of far less value. His most valuable grant being Farleigh Hungerford Castle in Somerset in 1468, worth some £500 per year, which had been forfeited by Robert, Lord Hungerford. Richard also held the constableships of the castles of Gloucester in Gloucestershire and Corfe in Dorset. Yet, many of the estates originally allocated to him were eventually restored to their original Lancastrian owners, such as the lands of the earl of Oxford, or given to others, such as Richmond, which was transferred to his brother George.[4]

The king's decision to marry one of his subjects, as opposed to a foreign bride, meant that he not only had to provide for his new queen but also her family. In 1464, he secretly married Elizabeth Woodville, the widow of Sir John Grey of Groby, who had been killed at the Second Battle of St Albans whilst serving in the Lancastrian army. This was a love match, as opposed to a political alliance, as Elizabeth was of far lower rank than the king. It was perhaps partly for this reason that the value of the dower assigned to her, worth some £4,500 per year, was far less than had been received by her predecessors. The estates given to the queen included the castles of Hadleigh in Essex, Rockingham in Northamptonshire and Devizes in Wiltshire. Her father, Richard, was given the title of Earl Rivers and appointed as treasurer and constable of England. Elizabeth's siblings benefitted from advantageous marriages to suitable spouses, but otherwise received little from the king. Her eldest brother, Anthony, was the main exception, receiving the lordship of the Isle of Wight and the castle of Carisbrooke in 1466, followed by the constableship of Portchester in the following year.[5]

Edward's reign was remarkable for the number of new peerages he created, with seven men given the title of baron in 1461. The most exceptional of these individuals was William Herbert. His seminal role in the Yorkist takeover of Wales did not go unrewarded, with numerous estates and offices bestowed upon him by a grateful sovereign. These grants were initially concentrated in south Wales, where there was considerable scope for royal patronage. Jasper Tudor's earldom of Pembroke had been forfeited to the Crown, whereas the minorities of the earl of Shrewsbury and the dukes of Buckingham and Norfolk meant that their lands were held in wardship by the king's officials. Herbert was the main beneficiary of royal patronage in this region. For instance, he was appointed as steward of the castle and lordship of Brecon in the south-east, during the minority of Henry Stafford, duke of Buckingham, in September 1461. Some five months later, Herbert was granted the castles and lordships of Pembroke, Tenby, Walwyn's Castle and Cilgerran in Pembrokeshire, Llansteffan in Carmarthenshire and Caldicot in Monmouthshire. In addition to this, he was appointed to numerous offices, including the constableships of the Three Castles of Grosmont, Skenfrith and White Castle. New Marcher lordships were also created for Herbert. In June 1463, this consisted of Tretower and Crickhowell, which were removed from the earldom of March. Two years later, the lordship of Raglan was created for him, which was administered from his ancestral castle there. In addition to this, he was also granted estates in England, including the castles and lordships of Dunster in Somerset and Goodrich in Herefordshire.[6]

Herbert's sphere of influence was subsequently extended to north Wales. In 1463, he was appointed as the chief justice of the county of Merioneth and as constable of Harlech Castle. This region was still under the control of the Lancastrians, and was to remain so for a further five years, but these appointments signified that the king wanted him to take control of this area. Later in 1467, he was appointed as constable of Denbigh Castle, and in the following year received the same office for the castle of Conwy. The acquisition of these lands and titles meant that his gross income was worth more than £3,000 per annum by the mid-1460s, thereby making him one of the richest men in the kingdom. Herbert's elevation from the ranks of the gentry to becoming the foremost magnate in Wales was unparalleled. This was even more noteworthy due to his Welsh heritage. For the first time since the Edwardian conquest of Wales, a Welsh nobleman held a preeminent position in the country. It was for this reason that he was described as 'King Edward's master-lock' by the poet Lewys Glyn Cothi.[7]

Another royal favourite was William Hastings. He had been appointed as chamberlain in the summer of 1461, which meant that he controlled access to the king's person. Over time he received further offices, such as the receiver-generalship of the duchy of Cornwall and the chamberlainship of north Wales. Estates granted to Hastings included the castles and lordships of Belvoir and Folkingham in Lincolnshire. Humphrey Stafford was also favoured by the king and was the main recipient of royal patronage in the south-west of England. He was summoned to Parliament in 1461 as a baron and one year later was granted the forfeited lands of Thomas Courtenay, earl of Devon, which included the castles of Okehampton, Plympton and Tiverton. Stafford was also appointed as steward of all the castles and lordships belonging to the duchy of Cornwall, as well being granted the castle and borough of Lydford in Devon. These marks of royal favour culminated in his creation as earl of Devon in 1469. Patronage was also bestowed upon men of lower rank. These included John Donne, esquire, whose military service in Wales was rewarded with the constable-ships of Aberstwyth, Carmarthen and Kidwelly. Others included Alvred Cornburgh, esquire, appointed as constable of Restormel Castle in Corn-wall, and John Wode, esquire, as porter of the castle of Newcastle.[8]

Raglan Castle and Castle-Building in the 1460s

The most notable programme of castle-building in the 1460s was carried out by William Herbert. As we have already seen, his rise in power and status was stratospheric. To assert his authority in Wales he needed a suitable residence to display his wealth and prestige. In the 1460s, he decided to embark on a lavish building project to transform Raglan Castle, which he had inherited from his father, Sir William ap Thomas. None of the financial records for the building work survives but the finished product is impressive. Raglan is entered via a grand gatehouse flanked by two hexagonal towers. The castle has two courtyards, which are separated by the great hall. The outer one contained rooms for members of the household, as well as two large hexagonal towers, the Kitchen Tower and the Closet Tower, whereas the inner courtyard was primarily intended for accommodating the lord and high-status guests. The most striking part of Raglan is the moated great tower situated outside the circuit of the walls. It was a self-contained building with its own water supply and kitchen, accessed via a bridge and subsidiary tower from the main part of the castle. The splendour of this structure is apparent from a description of it by an observer from two centuries later. It was then known as the 'Yellow Tower of Gwent' and supposedly in terms of 'height, strength, and neatness, surpassed most, if not every other tower, in England or Wales'.[9]

By contrast, royal castle-building in the 1460s was on a modest scale, as the king already possessed many fine castles across the kingdom. What was more, the financial difficulties of the government and the need to allocate substantial funds to defeat Lancastrian rebellions meant that only limited money was available for construction work. The most substantial project was carried out at Hertford Castle in Hertfordshire. This focused on the construction of a new gatehouse to the inner ward of the castle, which was made mostly out of brick, although stonework was used for the machicolation. Over £200 was spent on the project in the first half of the 1460s, with the bricks made locally and laid by nine so-called

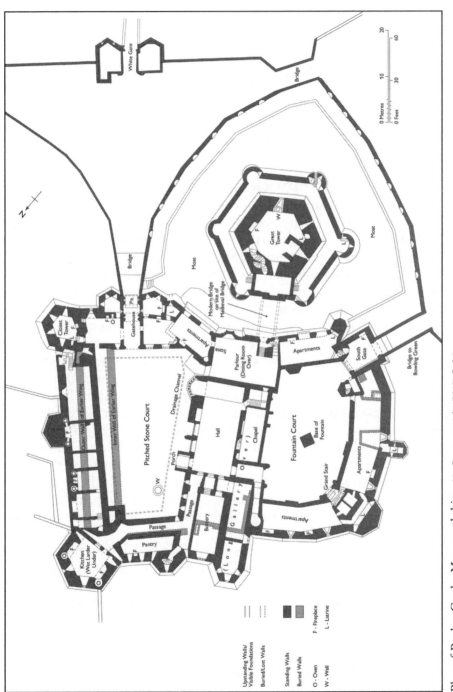

Plan of Raglan Castle, Monmouthshire. (© *Crown copyright (2019) Cadw*)

'breekmasons'. A mason was employed to carve the arms of the king on a stone that was fixed to the gatehouse. The stonework also included 'a white lion and a black bull with gilded horns', which was decorated by a painter. Work on the gatehouse was almost finished when it was transferred to the officials of Queen Elizabeth in 1465. Repairs were carried out to other royal castles, such as Bristol and the Tower of London. Works also took place at Fotheringhay Castle, which the king had granted to his mother Cecily, with masons, carpenters, sawyers and other workers paid to build chambers, latrines, turrets and a kitchen.[10]

Warwick's Bid for Power

The Lancastrians may have been defeated but Edward's hard-won peace was to be short-lived. Internal divisions between the members of the Yorkist aristocracy soon led to the resumption of conflict. This was chiefly due to the alienation of Warwick, who became progressively more resentful towards the policies of his cousin the king over the course of the 1460s. Warwick, as we have already seen, had benefitted enormously from the Yorkist victory. Yet, as noted by chroniclers, he was greedy and covetous. According to one account, 'his insatiable mind could not be content, and yet before him was there none in England of the half possessions that he had'. Furthermore, he did not have everything his own way. His attempts to expand his influence in south Wales, where he was the lord of Glamorgan and Abergavenny, through gaining control of the lands of the duke of Buckingham during the latter's minority, were unsuccessful. These estates were instead transferred to the custody of Herbert. This outcome contributed to the development of a rift between the two men. Similarly, some of the offices that he had been granted from the estates of the duchy of Lancaster, such as the stewardship of the honour of Leicester, were subsequently given to Hastings in 1461. These were comparatively minor grievances but some of the king's other decisions proved to be of greater consequence.[11]

Edward's reckless decision to marry Elizabeth Woodville in 1464 strained relations with Warwick. The latter had been engaged in negotiations with the French government earlier in the year. These discussions included the possibility of a marriage settlement between King Edward and a sister-in-law of Louis XI of France, Bona, daughter of the duke of Savoy. Edward's surprise announcement in a council meeting in September that he had already married in secret rendered these discussions futile. According to the Warkworth chronicler, 'after that rose great dissention ever more and more between the king and him'. This assessment may have been borne of hindsight. Nevertheless, the episode revealed that the king was willing to assert his independence against his powerful subject. It also led to a gradual separation of interests between the two men, who had hitherto been close allies. Warwick spent less time at court and did not attend Queen Elizabeth's coronation on 26 May 1465. Two years later, relations deteriorated yet further. The king relieved George Neville of the chancellorship and replaced him with Robert Stillington, the bishop of Bath and Wells. In response, the earl was said to have taken 'to him in fee as many knights, squires, and gentlemen as he might, to be strong'.[12]

Matters were made worse due to the capture of a Lancastrian agent in Wales. A messenger carrying letters from Queen Margaret to the garrison of Harlech was taken prisoner by Herbert and sent to the king in London. Under questioning he accused many of treachery, including Warwick who was said to secretly favour her cause. Given his role in defeating the Lancastrians this was a far-fetched accusation. Yet, Edward's suspicions were suitably roused for him to summon the earl to his presence to explain himself. Warwick refused to comply, and the king was instead forced to send the man to him at Sheriff Hutton Castle for interrogation. His testimony was ultimately deemed to be worthless. Nevertheless, the king's decision to recruit a force of 200 mounted yeomen archers to serve as his bodyguard suggests that he remained wary of betrayal. The final breach, however, occurred as a result of their disagreement over foreign policy. Warwick favoured an alliance with Louis XI, whereas Edward preferred coming to terms with his rival, Charles, duke of Burgundy. The latter was ostensibly a vassal of the French king, but in practice was the powerful ruler of a semi-autonomous territory, which included the wealthy and economically advanced Low Countries. Edward's stance was motivated by two factors. His desire to punish Louis for the support he had offered to the Lancastrian exiles and his intention to regain England's lost territories on the continent. These aims would be accomplished by an invasion of France, but in order to do so, he would require allies, due to French military superiority. A treaty was finally concluded in 1468, which was cemented by the marriage of Edward's sister, Margaret, to Charles in July. Warwick, as the proponent of an alliance with France, was left marginalised and angered by this outcome.[13]

By the beginning of 1469, Warwick had decided to rebel against the king. He could count on the support of his brothers in this venture, as well as Edward's own brother, the duke of Clarence. Clarence's defection was surprising given that he had been well treated by his sibling, who had provided him with extensive estates. It appears to have stemmed from the realisation that Edward's marriage to Elizabeth Woodville would soon lead to him losing his status as heir to the throne. Furthermore, his own marital prospects had been frustrated, with the king refusing to countenance a union with Warwick's eldest daughter, Isabel. Warwick also exploited popular discontent with Edward's rule. This was explained by the Warkworth chronicler who stated that the people had hoped that the new king's accession would lead to peace and prosperity. However, it had led to 'one battle after another, and much trouble and great loss of goods among the common people'. They had been afflicted with heavy taxation and had been forced to serve at their own cost in the king's armies.[14]

In late April 1469 a pro-Lancastrian rebellion broke out in Yorkshire led by an obscure individual known as Robin of Redesdale. This movement was short-lived as the rebels were soon defeated by the forces of Montagu. It was followed in quick succession by another rising, this time supposedly led by a man called Robin of Holderness that was also swiftly quelled. Yet another rebellion occurred in the same region in June of the same year. Unlike its predecessors, it was orchestrated by Warwick and his allies. The rebels were again ostensibly led by Robin of Redesdale. Their real leader was, in fact, Sir John Conyers of Hornby who served as steward of Warwick's honour of Richmond and as constable of Middleham Castle. It was intended to be part of a two-pronged assault on the king, with Conyers marching southwards with a strong force of northerners. Meanwhile, Warwick and Clarence were to sail from Calais and to land in southeastern England, where they expected support from the commons of Kent. The two men had cemented their alliance through Clarence's marriage to Isabel, in defiance of Edward's wishes. Before they set sail for England, they sent a manifesto, supposedly delivered to them by the 'king our sovereign lord's true subjects of diverse parts of this his realm of England'. The document claimed that the king had estranged the great lords of the blood from his council and had levied heavy charges on the people. Despite having 'as great livelihood and possessions ever had king of England', he had given these away to Rivers, Herbert, Stafford and others 'above their desserts and degrees'. It was accompanied by a letter from Warwick and Clarence, who stated that they would soon arrive in Canterbury to remonstrate with the king. A short time later they landed in Kent where their army rapidly swelled in size. However, the success of their allies elsewhere rendered their invasion superfluous.[15]

Edward had responded to news of the unrest in Yorkshire by moving northwards to confront the rebels in mid-June. He was unaware of

Warwick's treachery and his preparations for raising an army were lack-lustre. It was only when he arrived at Newark that he realised that the rebel forces were stronger than he imagined. Edward hurriedly withdraw southwards to Nottingham where he sent out urgent instructions for reinforcements to join him. This included the civic authorities of Coventry, to whom he directed a letter, dated 13 July, commanding them to immediately send men to his aid. Meanwhile, in response to the king's orders, Herbert and Stafford had assembled their forces, raised from Wales and the West Country respectively, and were marching to his assistance. However, the two commanders had a falling out at Banbury in Oxfordshire, allegedly over lodgings in the town, which led to a separation of their forces. This disagreement came at a particularly unfortunate time as they were unexpectedly attacked by the northern rebels. At the Battle of Edgecote, fought on 26 July, Herbert's forces were overwhelmed before their comrades could come to their assistance. In the aftermath of the battle, many of the king's favourites were executed, including Herbert, Rivers and Stafford. News of this outcome prompted Edward's soldiers to desert him and he was taken prisoner by George Neville.[16]

Warwick thereafter sought to rule through the captive king. He assumed Herbert's offices as chamberlain and chief justice of south Wales and appointed Sir John Langstrother, the prior of the hospital of St John in England, as treasurer. Instructions were also issued for Parliament to meet at York on 22 September. In the meanwhile, Edward was first taken to Warwick Castle for safekeeping where he had arrived by 8 August. However, he did not stay there for long. Concerns about the prospect that his supporters could attempt to free him, led to the king being moved to Middleham Castle later in the same month. According to one account, this was because Edward's 'faithful subjects in the South might be about to avenge the great insult inflicted upon the king'. Unlike Warwick, Middleham was in an area dominated by the Neville family, where he could therefore be held more securely. Yet, Warwick's grip on power was insecure. The capture of the king led to a breakdown in law and order across the kingdom. In the far north of England, a pro-Lancastrian rising was led by Sir Humphrey Neville of Brancepeth and his brother Charles, who had spent some years as outlaws. Warwick struggled to raise an army to quash the rebellion, as public proclamations to join the royal host were ignored by the king's subjects due to his imprisonment. These considerations prompted the earl to release Edward in late September. Warwick soon afterwards defeated the Lancastrian rebels, and their leaders were executed at York. Edward returned to the capital in October, accompanied by a strong array of lords. He had therefore regained power, but refrained from any immediate reprisals against Warwick or his supporters.[17]

Edward undoubtedly harboured resentment towards Warwick and Clarence. They had not only betrayed and imprisoned him but were also responsible for the deaths of his favourites, namely Herbert, Stafford and Earl Rivers. Nevertheless, he abstained from retaliating against them, either due to his desire to seek reconciliation, or for fear of provoking a dangerous confrontation. In late 1469, a general pardon was issued for insurrections and similar offences committed before 11 October. Edward also strengthened his personal connection to the Neville family through the betrothal of his daughter, Elizabeth, to George Neville, the eldest son of Montagu, who was raised to the rank of duke of Bedford. Furthermore, the king was keen to re-establish law and order in the localities. In Wales, where Herbert's death had led to the outbreak of unrest, he turned to his youngest brother, Richard, duke of Gloucester, to restore order. Gloucester was appointed as chief justice of north Wales on 7 November, and afterwards to various positions in the south of the country. On 16 December 1469, he was sent to the region to crush a rebellion led by two of the sons of Thomas ap Gruffydd, Morgan and Henry. They were said to have seized the royal castles of Carmarthen and Cardigan, which they used as bases to raid the surrounding areas. Gloucester was authorised to use force to besiege these castles and to grant pardons to those rebels willing to submit and swear oaths of allegiances to the king. He appears to have accomplished this task by the beginning of the next year.[18]

The Siege of Caister Castle

Another region affected by a breakdown in law and order following the king's captivity was Norfolk, where a property dispute over the ownership of Caister Castle led to a siege taking place. Caister had been constructed by Sir John Fastolf, a wealthy veteran of the Hundred Years War, between 1438 and 1446. The castle consists of two moated courtyards that were connected via drawbridges. It was principally constructed using brick, with the inner courtyard containing the main residential chambers as well as a five-storey great tower. Caister had numerous rooms including two great halls, one for the summer and another for the winter, twenty-eight residential chambers, an artillery house, chapel and service rooms. Fastolf in his old age became increasingly reliant upon his steward, John Paston. John was the head of an upwardly mobile family that had only recently entered into the ranks of the Norfolk gentry. His father, William, had made his fortune as a lawyer and eventually became a justice of common pleas. Fastolf lacked an obvious heir and planned to use his wealth to finance the foundation of a college at Caister, with seven priests or monks and seven poor men to pray for his soul and his family. Upon his death in 1459, John Paston claimed to be the sole witness of a will expressed orally, whereby he was made joint executor, together with Fastolf's chaplain, Thomas Howes, of all Fastolf's lands and possessions. Furthermore, his will supposedly specified that in return for the payment of £2,666, John could purchase his estates in Norfolk and Suffolk, which he duly did. Unsurprisingly, the suspect circumstances whereby he acquired Fastolf's inheritance was challenged by others who sought to gain control of the castle.[19]

One of these men was John Mowbray, fourth duke of Norfolk, a major landowner in East Anglia. His father, also called John, the third duke, had briefly occupied Caister in the summer of 1461, but died later that year. Following his death John Paston succeeded in regaining control of the castle. However, the fourth duke shared his father's interest in Caister and later sought to gain it for himself. In 1468, he paid £300 to some of the original executors of Fastolf's will to purchase the castle, alleging that the Paston family had acquired it illicitly. In the meantime, John Paston senior had died in 1466 and was succeeded by his eldest son, Sir John. The latter was determined to hold on to the castle despite pressure from the duke to relinquish it. This consisted of a campaign of harassment by Norfolk's affinity that included assaults committed against servants of the Paston family. Sir John therefore entrusted the safeguard of Caister to his younger brother, also called John. The latter was an experienced soldier who had taken part in military campaigns against the Lancastrians in the north of England and in Wales in the early 1460s. Concerns about the safety of Caister prompted Sir John to hire four soldiers for its defence in 1468. In a letter written to his brother he explained that these were 'proven men, and cunning in the war, and in feats of arms'. They were proficient in shooting both guns and crossbows, capable of devising artillery fortifications and could assist with keeping watch and ward.[20]

In 1469, the garrison was said to have comprised a group of twenty-six men in addition to John Paston. They consisted of servants of the Paston family, such as John Daubeney, esquire, and Osbern of Caister, but also a diverse range of other individuals. For instance, William Peny, described as a soldier from Calais, a Dutchman called Matthew, John Chapman, a soldier of the duke of Somerset, and a stranger called Raulyns. Remarkably, this group included one Thomas Stompys who was said to have been 'handless, and wished to shoot for a noble'. Some of these men undoubtedly had their own weaponry, but they could also draw upon the ample stockpile of equipment kept at Caister. Inventories of the 1450s and 1460s show that the castle was well-equipped with arms and armour. This ranged from body armour known as brigandines, helmets called sallets, gauntlets, crossbows, longbows and hand-to-hand weapons such as pole-axes and bills. An inventory compiled after the conclusion of the siege also shows that the defenders were heavily armed with ordnance. In all, they had nineteen guns of a variety of types, including short-barrelled fowlers and the longer ranged serpentines. They were deployed throughout the castle, in the gatehouses, towers and other rooms. This included two large fowlers in the inner gatehouse, a small fowler in the Bakehouse Gatehouse, four unspecified guns in Bedford's Tower, a small serpentine in Penys Tower and two small serpentines in the great tower. The provision of numerous gunports in the structure meant that these guns could be fired by their operators in safety. They were therefore well prepared for a siege.[21]

Norfolk decided to enforce his claim to Caister in the late summer of 1469. Taking advantage of the chaos caused by the capture of the king, he attempted to use military force to seize control of the castle. This was said to have begun with Sir John Heveningham sent to Caister in August to demand that the place be handed over to the duke. In reply, John stated that he held the castle on behalf of his brother and refused to comply. A week and a half later later, on 21 August, the duke appeared before Caister with a force said to have numbered 3,000 men and proceeded to lay siege to it. The besiegers included notable members of the gentry of East Anglia, such as Sir William Calthorpe, Sir Gilbert Debenham and Sir William Brandon. They were also equipped with artillery to bombard the castle. Nevertheless, the siege began with the attackers setting up a blockade to prevent any goods or people from entering the place. This was explained in a letter by Margaret Paston to her son, Sir John, dated 31 August. She had spoken to Heveningham in private at Norwich, despite him having been appointed as one of the captains to keep the watch about the castle. Furthermore, Margaret had also discussed with a 'faithful friend of ours' the possibility of Caister being handed over to 'indifferent men to keep the place'. They would then retain the profits of the manor on behalf of both parties until the dispute was determined by a legal judgment. Yet neither side was willing to compromise.[22]

Sir John rested his hopes upon the siege being ended through the intervention of the lords of the council, who were attempting to act on behalf of the king during his imprisonment. In the meanwhile, as he waited for their response, he sought to negotiate a truce with Norfolk through the auspices of Master Writtill, a servant of the duke of Clarence. Writtill had expressed concern about the safety of the defenders who were said to be running low on ammunition and provisions, but this explanation was rejected by Sir John in a letter dated 10 September. In his view, the lives of the garrison would only be jeopardised through their own 'recklessness ... which should be half impossible in my mind that they should so misuse so much stuff' in such a short time. Even if the duke of Norfolk offered him £1,000 he would refuse to relinquish Caister, if the defenders 'might in any wise keep it and save their lives'. He went on to convey his surprise that the duke had gained the assistance of both the sheriff and the justice of the peace for Norfolk in laying siege to Caister.[23]

Margaret, by contrast, was deeply concerned for the safety of her youngest son. In a letter dated 12 September, she admonished Sir John for his perceived inaction. She explained that 'your brother and his fellowship stand in great jeopardy at Caister', due to a shortage of provisions, gunpowder and arrows. Two of the defenders, Daubeney and Osbern Bernay, had been slain and many others had been injured. Caister had been 'sore broken with guns of the other party', so without swift assistance they would lose both their lives and the place. This would be the 'greatest rebuke to you that ever came to any gentleman, for every man in this county marvels greatly that you suffer them to be so long in great jeopardy without help or other remedy'. Writtill's intervention, far from calming matters, had only incited the duke, who was preparing for a great assault on the castle. His tenants had all been ordered to join his host at Caister and he had sent for guns from King's Lynn for the attack.[24] Three days later, Sir John penned a reply in which he addressed his mother's rebukes. He assured her that both Daubeney and Bernay were 'alive and merry' according to the latest information he had received. Sir John was confident that the truce would soon come into effect and that the lords would assist him in ending the siege. He also discussed the possibility of organising an expedition to rescue the defenders. This was his least preferred option, as it would be very expensive, and he was very short of money.[25]

Sir John subsequently wrote to his brother, on 18 September, asking him to remain firm in withstanding the siege. He was working hard to secure his relief, which would take place in fourteen nights at most and perhaps within seven days. Only if he failed to receive any further correspondence from him in that time, should he surrender under terms. Moreover, the duke's council had supposedly decided that none of the defenders would be harmed during the siege. Yet, he ended his letter by warning his brother to conserve his ammunition carefully, in case the attackers made an assault. Despite Sir John's optimism the situation of the garrison had become precarious. According to a later account, the besiegers had bombarded three sides of the castle with their guns. What was more, Daubeney had been killed by a quarrel from a crossbow, contrary to Sir John's assertions. This pressure led to the surrender of Caister on 27 September. The garrison were permitted to leave the castle with their lives and goods, which included their horses and armour, but were forced to abandon their guns, crossbows and quarrels. Following the surrender, John wrote to his brother to explain why he had yielded the castle. This was due to 'lack of victuals, gunpowder, men's hearts, lack of surety of rescue', which compelled him to seek terms. The Pastons were determined to regain Caister but with the duke's men firmly in control, their prospects appeared bleak. King Edward was unwilling to antagonise Norfolk, who was a faithful supporter, and did nothing to challenge his possession of the castle.[26]

The Readeption of Henry VI

Despite attempts at reconciliation, the peace between Edward and his relatives, Warwick and Clarence, was to prove to be short-lived. The latter remained discontented as their rebellion had failed to achieve their goal of increasing their influence over the king. Therefore, it was not long before they once again began to plot against their kinsman. Their opportunity came in the following year as a result of a private feud between two landowners in Lincolnshire. In early March, a group of men led by Richard, Lord Welles, his son, Sir Robert and Sir Thomas Dymoke attacked the manor of Sir Thomas Burgh, forcing the latter to flee. Upon receiving news of this outrage, Edward summoned the principal participants to come before him in Westminster to explain their actions. He also decided to travel in person to Lincolnshire to quell the unrest in the area. His approach was said to have sparked alarm in the county. It was feared that he intended to punish those men who had taken part in Robin of Redesdale's uprising in the previous year. A large force of rebels led by Sir Robert Welles took up arms and attacked the king's army near to Stamford on 12 March. Prior to the engagement, Lord Welles and Dymoke, who were with the king, were executed by royal command, with the rebels swiftly routed in the battle that followed.[27]

Sir Robert Welles was taken prisoner and before his execution implicated Warwick and Clarence. They were said to have been 'partners and chief provocateurs' of the rebellion in Lincolnshire, their intention being

(*left*) John Talbot, shown presenting a manuscript to Queen Margaret, seated next to Henry VI. *Poems and Romances* (Talbot Shrewsbury Book). BL, Royal 15 E VI, f. 2v.

(*Creative Commons CC0 1.0 Universal Public Domain Dedication*)

(*right*) Sir William Herbert and his wife, Anne Devereux, shown kneeling before a king (either Henry VI or Edward IV). John Lydgate, *Troy Book*, late fifteenth century. BL, Royal 18 D II, f. 6.

(*Creative Commons CC0 1.0 Universal Public Domain Dedication*)

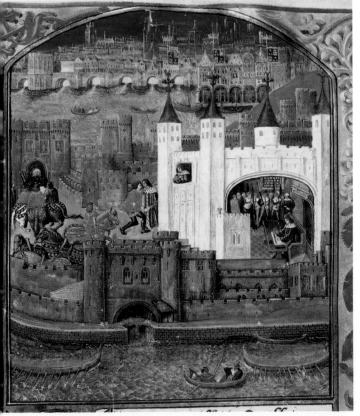

The Tower of London as depicted in a late fifteenth-century manuscript. Charles, duke of Orléans, *Pseudo-Heloise*. BL, Royal 16 F II, f. 73.

(*Creative Commons CC0 1.0 Universal Public Domain Dedication*)

Aerial view of Carreg Cennen Castle, Carmarthenshire. This rugged fortress has the distinction of being the only castle that was slighted during the Wars of the Roses. (© *Crown copyright (2019) Cadw*)

erial view of the town and castle of Denbigh, Denbighshire. Its strong defences posed a major
allenge to the Lancastrians when they laid siege to the place in 1460. (© *Crown copyright (2019) Cadw*)

erial view of Rhuddlan Castle, Denbighshire. This was one of the castles of north-east Wales that
as captured by the Yorkists in 1461. (© *Crown copyright (2019) Cadw*)

View of Harlech Castle, Gwynedd, from a distance. This isolated stronghold was the last Lancastrian fortress to fall to the Yorkists. (© *Crown copyright (2019) Cadw*)

The façade of Raglan Castle, Monmouthshire, which was extensively remodelled by William Herbert in the 1460s. (© *Crown copyright (2019) Cadw*)

View of Pembroke Castle, Pembrokeshire, from a distance. This was a stronghold of Jasper Tudor, earl of Pembroke, and the birthplace of Henry Tudor.

The facade of Warwick Castle, Warwickshire. This was one of the principal castles of Richard Neville, earl of Warwick, where Edward IV was briefly imprisoned in 1469.

External view of the inner ward of Ludlow Castle, Shropshire. This was the principal castle of Richard, duke of York, and the residence of his grandson, Edward V.

View of the main court of Caister Castle, Norfolk, with its impressive north-west tower on the right-hand side. A dispute over the ownership of the castle led to it being besieged in 1469.

External view of Chirk Castle, Wrexham. This was one of the castles of north-east Wales that was captured by the Yorkists in 1461.

View of Kenilworth Castle, Warwickshire, from a distance. This grand palatial castle served as the royalist headquarters for the campaigns of the 1450s.

View of the keep of Norham Castle, Northumberland. This strategic border fortress was subjected a major Scottish siege in 1463.

External view of the outer gatehouse and keep of Carlisle Castle, Cumbria. This strategic border fortress, described as the 'key to the west marches of England', was subjected to a major Scottish attack in 1461.

External view of Alnwick Castle, Northumberland. This was the seat of the Percy earls of Northumberland, and was frequently besieged in the 1460s.

View of Dunstanburgh Castle, Northumberland, from a distance. In the fifteenth century, the castle was surrounded by extensive water defences.

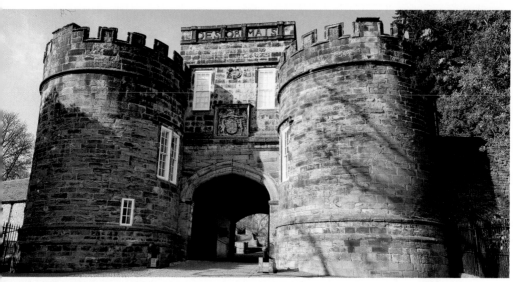

outer gatehouse of Skipton Castle, Yorkshire. This Clifford stronghold was besieged multiple
s during the 1460s.

External view of
Bodiam Castle, East
Sussex. This was one
of the few castles
that was held against
Richard III during
the rebellion of 1483.

rnal view of Sandal Castle, Yorkshire. The decision of Richard, duke of York, to travel to the
e in December 1460 led to his disastrous defeat at the Battle of Wakefield.

The gatehouse of Kirby Muxloe Castle, Leicestershire. The execution of its owner, William, Lord Hastings, in 1483, led to the abandonment of work on the castle, which was never finished.

gatehouse of Carisbrooke Castle, Isle of Wight. This strategic fortress was eventually captured he Yorkists after a long siege in 1461.

w of the castle and town walls of Conwy in north Wales, which was captured by the Yorkists ing their campaign of 1461.

Views of Bamburgh Castle, Northumberland, from the landside and the seaside. A royal fortress that was captured by assault by the Yorkists during a major siege in 1464. Its proximity to the coast is clearly visible.

to kill Edward and to place Clarence on the throne. In response, the king summoned the two men to his presence, who were instructed to disband the soldiers they had raised through commissions of array. However, they refused to do so without the offer of safe conducts and pardons, which Edward refused to countenance. Instead they attempted to raise forces in Lancashire, but the king's rapid advance prompted them to flee before him. They swiftly fled to Exeter in the south-west, where they took ship for Calais in early April. As they sailed eastwards, Warwick tried to recover his ship, the *Trinity*, which was being kept at the port of Southampton, but his men were defeated by the forces of Anthony Woodville. His attempt to gain entry to Calais was also unsuccessful, as the garrison, in compliance with orders they had received from the king, refused to admit him. Warwick and his companions instead took refuge in France.[28]

Following their flight overseas, orders were issued for their estates and castles across the kingdom to be confiscated. Their followers appear to have offered little resistance except in the north-west. Whilst in York, the king gave verbal instructions to Edward Story, bishop of Carlisle, for the inhabitants of Carlisle to seize control of the castle there. It was held for Warwick, who had hitherto served as warden of the west march of Scotland, by Richard Salkeld, who held the office of constable. The citizens were obliged to lay siege to the castle, which they eventually captured. On 7 May, Sir William Parr was appointed as the king's lieutenant for Carlisle Castle. Parr had formerly served Warwick and had played a part in the defeat of the royalist army at the Battle of Egecote. However, he defected in the spring of 1470, after delivering a message to the king on 19 March, in which the latter commanded him to join his service. Later in August, the king granted the wardenship of the west march to Gloucester.[29]

Edward's victory was marred by his failure to capture his principal opponents, who even as fugitives continued to pose a threat to him. Moreover, their arrival provided an opportunity for the French king to broker an extraordinary alliance between Warwick, Clarence and the Lancastrian exiles. Despite their personal enmity towards each other they agreed to unite against their common foe, Edward IV, to restore the captive Henry VI to the throne. They also received support from Louis, who provided ships and financial support for Warwick's invasion. Edward's principal countermeasure against this threat was to send fleets of ships to guard the Channel, with naval assistance also given by his brother-in-law, the duke of Burgundy. Yet, he was also forced to contend with unrest in the north of the kingdom. In the late summer, Henry, Lord FitzHugh, led a rebellion in Yorkshire, with further risings taking place in Cumberland.

Edward went north to quell these uprisings but during his absence his enemies invaded the realm. Warwick's forces made landfall at Plymouth and Dartmouth in Devon, where their ranks rapidly swelled in size, with their followers also taking up arms in Kent. Caught off-guard by this development, the king travelled towards London whilst ordering reinforcements to join him en route.[30]

He was expecting to be reinforced by a large contingent of men raised by Montagu, but this proved to be a major misjudgement. Montagu had thus far remained loyal to Edward, despite his brother's treachery. However, he was angered by the king's decision to restore Henry Percy to the earldom of Northumberland, thereby depriving him of that title. In recompense, Montagu was granted most of the estates of Humphrey Stafford, late earl of Devon, and raised to the rank of marquess. Yet, he regarded this compensation as wholly inadequate and a personal slight. From his base at Pontefract Castle he used the commissions of array issued to him to raise significant forces. When his soldiers were a mile away from the king's presence, he was said to have revealed to them his intention to fight against King Edward. According to the Warkworth chronicler, he likened the lands given to him as a '(mag)pies nest to maintain his estate with'. Edward, who was then at Doncaster, received warnings of Montagu's treachery just in time. Realising that he was heavily outnumbered by his opponents, he fled to King's Lynn in Norfolk, where he took ship for the Low Countries, with a small number of companions including Gloucester and Hastings.[31]

Meanwhile, the civic authorities of London were struggling to maintain law and order. Bands of men from Kent had descended on the capital, and these pillaged the suburbs and attacked the Dutch owners of beer houses. This prompted the citizens to deploy their guns to defend the gates and London Bridge. A royal garrison was also present in the city at the Tower under the command of John Tiptoft, earl of Worcester, the constable of England. Tiptoft was responsible for spending over £300 on strengthening the defences of the castle. This expenditure included the transportation of artillery from Bristol to the Tower, the purchase of bows, arrows, gunpowder and ammunition, and the wages of workers for improving the fortifications. A later document records that he carried out these measures at the behest of the king 'for the surety of our most dear wife the Queen our children and other our well beloved subjects then being within the same for their comfort and defence'. However, these preparations were thrown into disarray due to news of the king's flight. Queen Elizabeth, who was at the time heavily pregnant, decided to leave the Tower in secret with her young daughters and take refuge in the sanctuary of Westminster Abbey.[32]

The threat of attack by the men from Kent prompted the royalist soldiers in the Tower to surrender in return for the sparing of their lives. They were replaced by a force of Londoners who had been sent to take control of the castle by command of the common council of the city. Four days later, George Neville, the archbishop of York, arrived at London with an army. After being admitted into the city, he headed straight for the Tower, which was handed over to the custody of his men. There he found Henry VI who had languished as a prisoner for the past five years. According to the Warkworth chronicler, the conditions he had been kept in were not befitting of his rank and he was 'not so cleanly kept as should seem such a prince'. Henry was therefore moved to the chamber where Queen Elizabeth formerly resided. On the following day, Warwick, Clarence and their entourage entered the city. They removed Henry from the Tower and housed him in the bishop of London's residence at Fulham Palace.[33]

In the meanwhile, many of Edward's principal supporters were said to have taken refuge in sanctuaries in the city. However, Tiptoft was caught trying to escape. He was briefly imprisoned in the Tower, before being put on trial for treason before John de Vere, earl of Oxford, whose father and brother he had condemned to death as traitors more than eight years earlier. Tiptoft was deeply unpopular on account of his reputation for cruelty in performing his judicial duties as constable of England. The most notorious example of this took place in 1470 when he ordered the impalement of the bodies of twenty of Warwick's men after they were executed for treason. He was subsequently known as the 'butcher of England' for this reason. Therefore, few mourned his plight when he was convicted of treason and beheaded at Tower Hill. Prior to his death, he supposedly asked his executioner to behead him with three strokes in honour of the Trinity.[34]

The Return of the King

On 3 October, Henry went in a procession to Westminster Abbey, accompanied by Warwick, Oxford and other lords, where he was crowned. He was restored to the throne with his reign said to have begun on the day of Edward's flight. Yet, Henry was a shadow of the man he had once been. His health problems and long imprisonment meant that he was unable to exercise power for himself. Instead, the governance of the kingdom was effectively under the control of Warwick. The latter regained the offices he had previously held, such as the great chamberlainship of England and the captaincy of Calais. In addition to these, he also assumed the title of 'lieutenant to our sovereign lord, King Henry the Sixth'. Conscious of the threat posed by the supporters of King Edward, he took steps to secure the regions of the kingdom. Montagu was reinstated as warden of the east march of Scotland, whereas Jasper Tudor was sent to assert the new regime's authority in Wales. Commissions of array were issued for coastal defence and some of the former king's supporters, such as the duke of Norfolk, were incarcerated. However, despite Tiptoft's execution, there were few other reprisals against their opponents, with many officials left in post. A general pardon was also issued on 18 October, along with a directive to respect the inviolability of the sanctuaries.[35]

Edward had taken refuge in the territories of his brother-in-law, Charles, duke of Burgundy. The latter was at first embarrassed by the presence of his uninvited guest, but eventually agreed to provide financial assistance to him due to Warwick's pro-French stance. This support made it possible for Edward to mount an invasion of England in the following year, with a force of English exiles and a contingent of 300 Flemish hand-gunners. On 14 March, he landed at the coast of Holderness at Ravenspur in the East Riding of Yorkshire. At first, he struggled to attract many recruits in the north of England, only gaining admittance to the city of York through deception. This was through the claim that he only sought to recover the duchy of York as opposed to the Crown. Furthermore, as Edward travelled southwards through the West Riding of Yorkshire, he faced the threat of attack from Montagu, stationed at nearby Pontefract Castle. However, the latter allowed him to pass by without offering any resistance. According to the author of the *Arrivall of Edward IV*, this was in part because many of the inhabitants of the region were loyal to the Percy earl of Northumberland. The latter's decision to remain neutral therefore meant that they would not assemble. The other explanation was that Edward's men, though few in number, were well-equipped and motivated. Whatever his reasons, Montagu's failure to confront him had serious consequences. After reaching the Midlands, Edward's army rapidly swelled in size, with large numbers of men joining en route as he marched on London.[36]

In response, Warwick moved northwards from London to Coventry with his forces. He was soon confronted by Edward's army, but refused to meet with him in battle, instead preferring to keep his men safely behind the walls of the fortified city. Whilst this standoff was taking place, Edward was also said to have laid siege to the castles of Warwick and

Kenilworth, according to a newsletter written by a German merchant, Gerhard von Wesel. Warwick's refusal to meet Edward in battle meant that he surrendered the initiative, with the latter resuming his march on the capital. During the same time, Clarence decided to return to his brother's allegiance, with the forces he had raised from the west of England. This volte-face was motivated by his dissatisfaction with Warwick, who had failed to make him king, and with his treatment by the Readeption government of Henry VI. In the meantime, news of Edward's approach prompted the Lancastrians within London to put on a show of force. On 10 April, Henry VI proceeded through the city accompanied by George Neville, Ralph Boteler, Lord Sudeley and their entourages. Yet this display, far from impressing the inhabitants, did the exact opposite, as Henry's attendants were few in number and poorly dressed. According to the *Great Chronicle*, it 'was more like a play than the showing of a prince to win men's hearts'. The civic authorities therefore decided not to resist Edward's army, as it was too strong to withstand. On the same night, the imprisoned supporters of King Edward within the Tower, overpowered their guards and seized control of the castle.[37] ———

Edward entered the capital without encountering any opposition on 11 April. His first move was to go the palace of the bishop of London, where he arrested King Henry. Edward afterwards went to Westminster Abbey to see Elizabeth, where he met his son and heir, Edward, for the first time. Afterwards they spent the night at his mother's residence at Baynard's Castle. However, Edward's stay in London was to be brief. Warwick had responded to the defection of the Londoners by marching southwards from Coventry with his army. Edward prepared to confront his enemies in the field, leaving Elizabeth and his children at the Tower for safekeeping before leaving the city. He advanced northwards to confront Warwick, with the two armies meeting at Barnet, 10 miles north of London, on 14 April. The fighting was said to have taken place in thick fog. Despite Warwick's superiority in artillery and manpower, Edward's soldiers eventually prevailed, with Warwick and Montagu killed in battle. The king then returned to the capital in triumph, where he received a warm reception by the inhabitants. Subsequently, the bodies of Warwick and Montagu were put on public display in St Paul's Cathedral to prove that they were dead. Yet, Edward had little time to celebrate his victory as he was faced with a new danger from the west.[38]

On the same day as the Battle of Barnet, Queen Margaret landed at Weymouth in Dorset. She was accompanied by her son, Prince Edward, and other Lancastrian exiles. A short time later they were joined by

Edmund Beaufort, duke of Somerset, and John Courtenay, earl of Devon. These men came bearing commissions of array issued in the name of Henry VI, which they used to raise an army from the south-west of England. For instance, on 18 April, Courtenay wrote a letter from Tiverton in the name of Henry VI, Queen Margaret and Prince Edward, requesting that men be raised in their 'most warlike and fencible array'. In the meantime, Edward was also busy raising fresh forces to replace his losses at Barnet. Prior to confronting the Lancastrians, he celebrated St George's Day at Windsor Castle on 23 April. Edward then headed westwards travelling by way of Abingdon, Cirencester and Bath. At the same time, his opponents advanced northwards to Bristol, where they were said to have received reinforcements in men and artillery, before they moved towards Gloucester. The Lancastrians intended to cross the River Severn to join forces with Jasper Tudor, who had been recruiting in Wales. Yet their passage to the west was blocked. Edward had sent instructions to Richard Beauchamp to hold the town and castle of Gloucester against the Lancastrians. Beauchamp prepared the defences of the settlement and refused to grant them entry, even when threatened with attack. The Lancastrians therefore moved north to Tewkesbury to find another crossing place. However, before they could cross over, Edward's army intercepted them on 4 May. The Lancastrians took up a strong defensive position but were provoked into launching an attack due to the superior firepower of their enemies. Their lack of discipline cost them dearly as they were defeated and routed.[39]

The Siege of London

Edward's victory proved to be decisive due to the deaths of his principal enemies. Amongst those slain during the fighting itself were Prince Edward and the earl of Devon. Others, including Somerset, escaped from the battlefield but were subsequently captured and executed. This heavy death toll decimated the Lancastrian aristocracy, leaving few men of royal or noble blood left to oppose Edward's triumph. Yet, in the immediate aftermath of the battle, the king had still to take control of the kingdom. Reports reached him that rebels in the north were gathering their forces for a confrontation. Edward therefore travelled eastwards to Coventry to prepare for an expedition to northern England. This proved to be unnecessary as news of his victory prompted the rebels there to capitulate. However, whilst at Coventry, he received intelligence that the city of London was under threat from an army and fleet commanded by Thomas Neville, otherwise known as the Bastard of Fauconberg.[40]

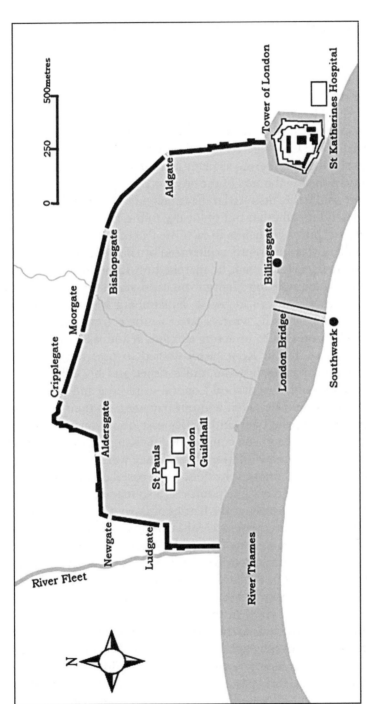

Plan of London. (*Drawn by Scott Hall,* © *Dan Spencer*)

Fauconberg was a member of the Neville family, being an illegitimate son of William Neville, Lord Fauconberg. He adhered to the cause of his cousin, the earl of Warwick, and had previously taken part in naval expeditions in 1462 and 1470. Fauconberg was responsible for acts of piracy in the Channel, which included the seizure of Portuguese ships in March 1471. He subsequently went to Kent in late April to raise men for the Lancastrian cause. Further contingents comprised men from Essex, soldiers from the Calais garrison and sailors from his fleet. This army was later described as numbering as many as 20,000 men. The *Arrivall* claimed that many of the inhabitants of the city were also sympathetic to his cause. They were said to be 'disposed to have helped to have such mischief rather than to defend it', whether out of loyalty to the Lancastrian cause or from the desire to 'put their hands in rich men's coffers'.[41]

Fauconberg was apparently undeterred by the news of Warwick's defeat and death at Barnet. Instead, he marched on London with the professed intention of rescuing King Henry from captivity in the Tower and defeating the 'usurper' Edward in battle. Fauconberg was at Sittingbourne in Kent on 8 May, when he wrote a letter to the commonalty of the city of London. He professed to be acting as 'captain and leader of our liege lord king Henry's people in Kent', who wished to pass through the city to 'revenge his quarrel against the said usurper and his adherents'. Claims that his men intended to despoil London were false and he promised that no provisions would be taken without payment. In their response, dated the following day, the civic authorities cast doubt on this pledge. They explained that they had been commanded by King Edward to keep the city and to prevent any unlawful assemblies. They were sceptical of his ability to enforce discipline amongst his followers, based on the past behaviour of similar armies in the city. The point was also made, rather forcefully, that news of the king's victories at the battles of Barnet and Tewkesbury meant that Fauconberg's enterprise was futile. Warwick and Prince Edward, in whose names he claimed to be acting, were undoubtedly dead. They therefore implored him not to be 'deceived by simply sayings and feigned tales', but to 'accept and obey the king' to whom God had given 'great victories'. Yet, this appeal was to no avail. Two days later, on 11 May, Fauconberg's army arrived in the vicinity of London.[42]

In anticipation of their arrival, the civic authorities had carefully prepared the defences of the city. The mayor, John Stockton, assumed overall command of the defenders, with aldermen from different parts of London entrusted with overseeing the defence of their wards. Men-at-arms and other soldiers were allocated to guard the walls and gates, as well as the banks of the River Thames from Baynard's Castle to the Tower, with guns and other weaponry distributed from the Guildhall. One site of special importance was London Bridge, as it was the principal entrance to the city from the south. The bridge was a large stone structure with a gatehouse at each end and incorporated nineteen arches, together with a drawbridge in the middle. The latter could be raised by pulleys joined to its own gatehouse, to allow the passage of ships or to prevent entry to the city, which was also protected by a portcullis. Responsibility for its defence was assigned to two aldermen, George Ireland of Cordwainer Ward and Thomas Stalbrook of Bridge Ward, who were accompanied by 'other good men of the city'. They were equipped with guns, gunpowder, bows and arrows sent from the arsenal at the Guildhall. Twelve sacks of stone and wool were hung over the raised drawbridge, as well as canvas soaked in vinegar, to protect it from gunshot and wildfire. Three holes were made in the same structure by two carpenters, so that the defenders could return fire, with the guns supervised and operated by men assigned to the task by day and night. Six men were employed to keep a lookout from the draw-bridge tower and to control the drawbridge, with a careful watch also kept on the attackers and their movements by means of men called spies.[43]

The Londoners could also rely upon the support of the royal garrison of the Tower, who were led by Anthony Woodville and Henry Bourchier, earl of Essex. Prior to his departure from the city, the king had appointed Richard Haute, a member of the gentry of Kent, as lieutenant of the Tower. To ensure its safeguard, Haute recruited 100 soldiers, who had formerly served in the Calais garrison, on 21 April. This force was supported by the retinues of members of the royal household, such as those of Robert Radcliff, esquire, Sir William Peche and Sir John Fogge, who were present at the Tower. These soldiers were supplied with military equipment, including 200 bows, over 16,000 arrows and 9 crossbows provided by bowyers, fletchers and crossbowmen working in the Tower. A team of twenty-five gunners was also employed to supervise the guns kept in the Tower and furnished with large quantities of gunpowder and lead shot for bullets. Carpenters and labourers carried out improvements to the defences. These works included the construction of specialised artillery fortifications known as bulwarks on the shoreline and wharf of the Tower. Bulwarks were small forts typically built using materials such as stone-work, bricks or wood for deploying guns. However, time constraints meant that they were instead made by filling empty pipes, used for storing wine, with sand and gravel to provide protection from gunshot. A continuous watch was also maintained in the Tower by day and night, with lamps and torches purchased for the garrison.[44]

These measures meant that the defenders were well prepared to resist a siege. This was fortunate as Fauconberg's forces attacked on 12 May. Edward's rapid approach meant that there was no time for a formal siege, with the rebels instead needing to launch an immediate assault. The accounts of the wardens of London Bridge subsequently recorded that the attackers 'arrayed and armed in warlike manner ... with banners and pennons displayed ... falsely and traitorously besieged the same City as if they were in a land of war'. The besiegers focused their efforts on gaining entry via London Bridge, with a fierce assault made against the defenders. It was repulsed but not before the attackers set fire to the outer gate, as well as the beer houses in the vicinity of the hospital of St Katharine just outside the city walls. This setback prompted Fauconberg to adopt another strategy. On the following day, he attempted to bypass the city by marching westwards with his forces to Kingston upon Thames, leaving his ships behind at the dock by the hospital of St Katharine. Yet, they were frustrated by the actions of Anthony Woodville. He sent ships known as barges to transport soldiers from the Tower to Kingston and they blocked the passage of the rebels. The latter, who were already concerned about the prospect of being trapped between Edward's army and the city, withdrew to their original positions outside of London.[45]

The next day, a great assault was launched against the city, with the attackers assailing multiple places simultaneously in an attempt to overwhelm the defenders. To cover their offensive, they set up batteries of guns taken from their ships. These were placed both along the southern shoreline of the River Thames, facing the city, as well as on the eastern side of London. Yet the defenders responded in kind, with the *Arrivall* stating that they 'made so sharp shot against them, that they dared not abide in any place along the waterside, and so were driven from their own ordnance'.[46] Part of the rebel army attacked London Bridge, with fourteen tenements set on fire during the fighting, but they were driven back by the firepower of the defenders. However, the attackers had more success on the eastern side of the city, where they launched assaults against both Bishopsgate and Aldgate. The *Great Chronicle* states that the men of Essex furiously assailed both gates and succeeded in overrunning the bulwark outside Aldgate. They drove the Londoners back through the gate and pursued them so quickly that five or seven men gained entry. Yet these rebels were killed, either by being crushed by the portcullis that was dropped onto them, or by the defenders. There was then a 'mighty shot of handguns and sharp shot of arrows which did more harm to the portcullis and to the stonework than to any enemies on either side'. It was at this critical stage in the fighting that the defenders decided to counterattack.[47]

The defence of Aldgate was led by Robert Basset, the alderman for the ward, and Thomas Urswick, the recorder of the city. The *Great Chronicle* states that they ordered that the portcullis be raised in the name of God and St George and sallied forth with the defenders. This action was coordinated with the garrison of the Tower by prior arrangement. According to the *Arrivall*, Anthony Woodville collected a force of 400 to 500 men who issued out of the postern gate of the castle. This force fell upon the flank of the rebels outside the Aldgate, assailing them with arrows and melee weapons in hand-to-hand fighting. Taken by surprise, the rebels were routed and pursued as far as the waterside. The mayor, aldermen and the defenders in the other sectors of the city then issued forth and drove off the attackers, many of whom were said to have been killed or taken prisoner. Those rebels to the east of the city fled to their boats, with the survivors crossing to the other side of the Thames.[48]

Fauconberg and his men regrouped at nearby Blackheath. There they remained for three days, but the imminent arrival of King Edward prompted them to flee. The *Arrivall* states that the soldiers from Calais made their way back to the territory, the sailors to their ships and the men of Kent to their own county. A short time later, on 21 May, Edward entered the capital accompanied by a large entourage. He clearly appreciated the faithful service of the Londoners as in recognition of their loyalty, he bestowed knighthoods upon the mayor, the recorder and ten aldermen of the city. Edward's next step was to eliminate his rival, Henry VI, who despite his ill health and captivity remained a source of opposition to his rule. Henry was therefore murdered by his command on the same night that he returned to London. The official account, as provided by the author of the *Arrivall*, states that he died of despair and melancholy after learning of the death of his son and the defeat of his partisans, but this is scarcely creditable. His body was put on public display in St Paul's Cathedral the following evening, before being taken by river to Chertsey Abbey the next morning.[49]

Edward then led his army into Kent to punish the rebels. Fauconberg was said to have strongly garrisoned Sandwich with his remaining soldiers and sailors, and to have retained a sizeable fleet. Yet, as soon as he learnt of the king's approach, he surrendered and agreed to return to Edward's allegiance. Commissions of enquiry were set up to try rebels in Kent and Essex, with some men pardoned after paying fines, whereas others, such as the mayor of Canterbury, Nicholas Faunt, were executed. According to the *Great Chronicle* those 'as were rich were hanged by the purse, and others that were poor were hanged by the neck'. The liberties of the Cinque Ports were temporarily rescinded and only restored after the payment of hefty fines. Measures were also taken to secure key fortifications. Sir John Scott was placed in command of Sandwich with 200 men, whereas Thomas Seyntleger was allocated 100 men for the defence of the town and castle of Rochester. Having ensured that Kent was pacified, Edward then made his way back to the capital. The *Crowland Chronicle* relates that he 'returned a conqueror of renown and a monarch whose praises resounded everywhere throughout the land for so many remarkable successes so quickly and so smoothly achieved'.[50]

The last remaining area of Lancastrian resistance was in Wales. As we have already seen, Jasper Tudor had been sent to the region to raise support for the cause of Henry VI. He was in the process of marching eastwards to join forces with the Lancastrian army, when he received news of the Battle of Tewkesbury. This prompted him to withdraw to the safety of Chepstow Castle in Monmouthshire. The chronicler John Hardyng relates that he briefly took refuge there whilst 'lamenting greatly both his own fate, and also the ill fortune that King Henry had'. He was still at Chepstow when he was attacked by the forces of Robert Vaughan, who had been sent against him by command of Edward IV. It was said that Vaughan hoped to capture Jasper by 'some treachery or guile' but was himself taken prisoner and beheaded. Jasper then decided to retreat to his old stronghold of Pembroke Castle in the south-west of Wales. Meanwhile, William Herbert, earl of Pembroke, son and heir of the previous earl, had been sent to south Wales by command of the king's council. He was instructed to capture rebels and traitors and to regain control of castles they had occupied. Herbert was afterwards paid 500 marks (£333 6*s.* 8*d.*) for his expenses in subduing Lancastrian resistance in the area.[51]

Jasper was subsequently besieged by the forces of Morgan ap Thomas (a grandson of Gruffydd ap Nicholas). According to Polydore Vergil, Morgan's men were said to have employed ditches and trenches to prevent the escape of the beleaguered defenders. A seventeenth-century account claims that he 'so strongly besieged the said castle . . . that they were driven to this hard choice, either to perish through famine, or else to put themselves into such hands from whom they could expect for little mercy or favour'. Yet, they were rescued by Thomas's brother, David, who raised a force with which to drive off his sibling's army. However, their situation remained precarious. Jasper therefore decided to set sail for France from

Tenby, taking along with him his nephew, Henry. The latter had resided at Raglan Castle for some years in the household of the Herbert family. Bad weather instead forced their ship to land at le Conquet in Brittany, where they received the protection of Duke Francis. Despite attempts by Edward to persuade the duke to hand them over to his custody, this failed to occur. At the time this outcome appeared to be inconsequential. Henry's claim to the throne was tenuous and Edward was firmly in control, but it would prove to be of great significance some years later.[52]

Chapter Six

The Yorkist Supremacy

The Siege of St Michael's Mount

Edward emerged victorious from the campaigns of 1471, with almost all his enemies not only defeated, but also destroyed. Deaths in battle and executions had all but extinguished the Lancastrian lineage. The demise of King Henry and Prince Edward of Westminster meant that there were no viable alternatives to his rule. Jasper and Henry Tudor were out of his grasp, but few other adherents of their cause remained at large. Chief amongst their number was John de Vere, earl of Oxford. After the Battle of Barnet, he had fled first to Scotland then to France, where he resided as a guest of Louis XI. He received assistance from the French king and had a small number of companions with him, including his three brothers George, Thomas and Richard, as well as William, Lord Beaumont. In 1473, Oxford set sail from Dieppe in Normandy and landed with a small force near to St Osyth in Essex on 28 May. Yet, he failed to garner local support, and hurriedly re-embarked after receiving news that an army led by Henry Bourchier, earl of Essex, was marching against him. On 5 June, Edward IV wrote to the sheriff of Devon concerning the 'great rumours of the landing of our rebel and traitor John late earl of Oxford' in his county. He commanded him to prevent any assemblies for any reason, instead he was to 'sit still and be quiet' unless further instructions were sent.[1]

These rumours proved to be well-founded. After committing various acts of piracy at sea, Oxford then descended on the Cornish coast and seized control of St Michael's Mount on 30 September. This is a small tidal island in Mount's Bay in the south-west of the county. It had been the site of both a priory and a castle since the twelfth century. In 1473, it was owned by Syon Abbey, a monastery of the Bridgettine Order. Oxford's arrival was unexpected, and he appears to have had little difficulty in capturing the island. He was only accompanied by a small force, said to be eighty men strong, but the natural defences of the place made it an imposing fortress. The Warkworth chronicler went so far as to claim that the castle was so strong that 'twenty men may keep it against all the world', if they had sufficient provisions.[2]

Oxford's seizure of the island was a bold move. He had few men with him and could easily be isolated. His decision was motivated by the expectation of receiving support from the region and sparking a wider uprising against King Edward. Two years earlier, the Lancastrians had gained many recruits from the south-west, including Cornwall, and he evidently hoped to encourage the inhabitants to join his cause. At least some of the locals appear to have been sympathetic. According to Warkworth, after taking the mount he and his men went into Cornwall where they 'had right good cheer of the commons'. However, this failed to materialise into any practical assistance when faced with the Yorkist response. Edward entrusted the task of recovering the island to prominent landowners in Cornwall. On 27 October, instructions were given to Sir John Arundell, Henry Bodrugan, John Fortescu and others to array the men of the county and to recover the island. Warkworth claims that Bodrugan, as the 'chief ruler of Cornwall', was placed in command of the besiegers. Yet, he was said to have carried out this task in a wholly unsatisfactory manner. Rather than press the siege with any vigour he frequently engaged in negotiations with the defenders, who he even allowed to resupply themselves with provisions. The king therefore relieved Bodrugan of his command and replaced him with Fortescue on 7 December.[3]

Fortescue's appointment led to a renewed attempt to take the castle. A naval force that included 4 royal ships, the *Caricon*, *Christopher of Calais*, *Mary of Calais* and *Garce*, crewed by 260 sailors, was allocated to him as well as 300 soldiers and artillery. Warkworth states that the siege began in earnest on 12 December, with both sides engaging in frequent skirmishes. The besiegers had superior numbers and firepower but struggled to make much headway, due to the strong defences of the fortress, and suffered some losses. However, the morale of the defenders was low. This was exploited during some temporary truces, when men from both sides spoke to each other. The king and council had secretly sent messengers offering to pardon and reward members of the garrison who were willing to defect. This stratagem undermined Oxford's authority and forced him into negotiations to surrender. Otherwise, it was said, 'his own men would have brought him out' of the mount. Oxford was reluctant to do so but had little other choice. The failure of the French to provide naval assistance meant that he was cut off and isolated. Furthermore, it was reported that he had been wounded in the face by an arrow. Oxford therefore was said to have sued for pardon of his life alone, with his goods and possessions left to the king's mercy. He was subsequently sent to the Pale of Calais and imprisoned at Hammes Castle. Fortescue took control of the island on

15 February. There he supposedly found large quantities of provisions that would have supplied the garrison until mid-summer.[4]

Winners and Losers

Oxford's capture marked the end of serious opposition to Edward's rule. Thereafter he no longer had to contend with the threat of major rebellions or sedition, although there were periodic outbreaks of disorder, such as in Wales. Long-running disputes were also resolved. One of these concerned the ownership of Hornby Castle in Lancashire. It had previously belonged to Sir Thomas Harrington, who was killed, along with his eldest son, John, at the Battle of Wakefield in December 1460. Thomas's youngest son, Sir James, subsequently took control of Hornby. His claim was disputed by Thomas, Lord Stanley, who was granted the wardship of John's two daughters, Anne and Elizabeth, in 1466. Two years later, a commission declared that the latter were the rightful heirs to the Harrington inheritance. Yet, James refused to relinquish custody of Hornby. In the spring of 1471, Stanley attempted to gain control of it using force. He gathered his forces and was provided with a large gun called *Mile End* from Bristol by the government of Warwick. However, it is unknown whether a siege took place or not. If it did it was unsuccessful, as James still held the castle four years later. At this point, Edward intervened and forced Harrington to hand over control of Hornby to Stanley.[5]

The king's authority had been greatly strengthened by the demise of the Neville brothers, Warwick and Montague. They no longer posed a threat to him and the forfeiture of their estates to the Crown meant that he once again had significant resources of patronage available to him. This he employed to bolster the power of his favoured supporters in the regions. The brothers William and John Parr, knights, were given the lordships and castles of Appleby, Pendragon, Brougham and Brough in Westmorland. Other supporters received grants of offices. For instance, William FitzAlan, earl of Arundel, was appointed as constable of Dover Castle in Kent, with John, Lord Berners, and his son, Thomas, receiving the same office for Windsor Castle in Berkshire.[6]

The main beneficiary of royal patronage was the king's youngest brother, Richard, duke of Gloucester. Gloucester was chosen to replace Warwick as the leading magnate in the north of England. He was restored to the previous offices he had previously held, such as the wardenship of the west marches of Scotland and the constableship of England. In 1471, he was also appointed as chief steward of the duchy of Lancaster in Lancashire and keeper of the royal forests north of the River Trent. This was in addition to being granted Warwick's former northern estates, which included the castles of Middleham and Sheriff Hutton in Yorkshire, Penrith in Cumberland and Oxford's castle of Hedingham in Essex. Gloucester subsequently acquired the castles of Scarborough and Skipton in Yorkshire, as well as Castle Barnard in County Durham, and Abergavenny in Monmouthshire. Later in 1478, he exchanged estates in the south, including Corfe in Dorset, Farleigh Hungerford in Wiltshire and Sudeley in Gloucestershire, for Richmond and Helmsley in Yorkshire. Gloucester thereby became the wealthiest and most powerful man in the kingdom after the king himself.[7]

His importance was further enhanced due to the misfortunes of two other leading magnates, William Herbert, earl of Pembroke, and his own brother, George, duke of Clarence. Clarence was initially forgiven by the king for his treachery, with his lands and titles restored to him. He was even given the castles and lordships of Okehampton and Plympton in Devon, Old Wardour in Wiltshire, Helmsley and Richmond in Yorkshire, and Queenborough Castle in Kent. However, his rapprochement with the king did not last as Edward became increasingly exacerbated by Clarence's high-handed behaviour. The latter had attempted to claim the entire Warwick inheritance though his wife Isabel. This brought him into conflict with Gloucester, who sought a division of these estates, by arranging his marriage to Warwick's other daughter, Anne. The dispute became so hostile that the king was forced to intervene to impose a settlement upon them to share the inheritance. Over time the relationship between Edward and Clarence deteriorated further, which culminated in the latter's arrest and imprisonment in the Tower of London in June 1477. He was put on trial before Parliament in January of the following year, and after being found guilty of treason was executed, supposedly by being drowned in a butt of malmsey wine.[8]

William Herbert, earl of Pembroke, inherited his father's extensive estates and preeminent position in Wales. Yet, he struggled to maintain law and order in that country. In 1478, Pembroke Castle was seized by three bastard sons of the first earl of Pembroke and two bastard sons of Roger Vaughan. Commissions of array were issued against them, but they were subsequently pardoned at the request of Queen Elizabeth. These difficulties contributed to the king's decision to force him to surrender his earldom of Pembroke in 1479. In recompense, he received the far less valuable title of earl of Huntingdon and some estates in the south-west of England. Herbert's influence in Wales was replaced by that of the king's eldest son, Prince Edward. The latter had been created as prince of Wales and earl of Cornwall in 1471, but during his minority a council was appointed for the administration of the principality. Over the course of the 1470s this council came to assume an increasingly important role in overseeing the judicial and administrative governance of not merely the principality, but also the Welsh Marches and the border counties of England.[9]

Prince Edward and the council were frequently resident at Ludlow Castle from 1473 onwards. In the same year ordinances for the governance of his household were composed. These specified that his maternal uncle, Anthony Woodville, Earl Rivers, should be his governor, whereas John Alcock, bishop of Rochester, would be president of the council and his teacher. They also regulated Prince Edward's daily routine and the management of his household, whilst at Ludlow and elsewhere. He was to rise every morning at an hour suitable to his age and to hear Mass in his chapel, before having breakfast. Between that time and his dinner, he was to be engaged in 'virtuous learning'. At his dinner, Edward would be served by men of rank wearing livery, with his mealtime companions to be occupied in reading before him 'noble stories' suitable for a prince to know. Furthermore, they were to communicate virtuous, honourable and religious sentiments in his presence and to avoid uttering anything that could lead to vice. After his meal in 'eschewing of idleness' he should be engaged in learning and other appropriate activities before hearing evensong and then retiring to his chamber by 8 o'clock. He was to be accompanied by attendants all night who were to 'make him merry and joyous towards his bed', with a watch maintained to ensure his safeguard. It was also stated that the prince was to be brought up with the sons of noble lords and gentleman in his household, who would be educated in grammar, music and other activities. His security arrangements were also taken seriously. The porters were to be diligent in carrying out their duties and to ensure that visitors left their weapons with them at the gatehouse. From the beginning of May to the end of September the gates of his residence were to be opened between 5 and 6 o'clock in the morning and closed at 10 o'clock at night, with shorter opening times in the other months of the year.[10]

The Court of Edward IV and the King's Works

Edward's second reign was more prosperous and secure than his early years. He was therefore free to demonstrate his power by flaunting the wealth and splendour of his court to both his own subjects and foreign visitors alike. This is apparent from an eyewitness description by an

English herald of the reception of the Burgundian courtier and diplomat, Louis de Gruuthuse, at Windsor Castle in 1472. Edward had resided as Gruuthuse's guest during his time in exile in the Low Countries in 1470–1 and wished to show his gratitude. The king therefore rewarded him with the title of earl of Winchester and an annuity when Gruuthuse next visited England as part of an embassy. Prior to attending Parliament, where he received these honours, he was entertained at Windsor Castle. Upon his arrival in the quadrant of the castle, he was received by William, Lord Hastings, with many other lords and nobles who took him to the king's presence. After having a conversation with the king and queen, he was then taken to the chambers that had been prepared for him. These were richly decorated with fine clothes of Arras and with beds of estate. There he supped with Hastings and Sir John Parr, together with their respective servants. Hastings then accompanied him to the king's chamber, who took them both to the queen's chamber. There they found Queen Elizabeth with her ladies and gentlewomen engaged in games and dancing. King Edward then danced with his eldest daughter, Elizabeth, before they all retired to their chambers to sleep.[11]

On the following morning, Edward and Gruuthuse listened to 'our lady's mass' in the royal chapel, which was 'melodiously sung'. They then went to the 'little park' where the king gifted him a horse and crossbow, before having dinner in the lodge. Afterwards they hunted deer in the park with dogs and killed six bucks. As night was beginning to fall, the king showed him his garden and 'vineyard of pleasure', before returning to the castle. They then heard evensong in their own chambers and afterwards went to the queen's chamber, where she had thrown a grand banquet. This was attended by many lords and ladies of the court. At 9 o'clock, Gruuthuse was taken by the king, queen and her ladies to new chambers in the 'pleasance'. These were furnished with hanging silk and linen cloth, carpets, fine sheets for his bed and pillows 'of the queen's own ordinance'. Gruuthuse was then left to partake in a bath, along with Hastings, after which they and their companions ate and drank delicacies, before retiring to bed. The next day the party left Windsor for Westminster Palace. We do not know Gruuthuse's feelings about his brief stay at Windsor, but it seems reasonable to assume that he was suitably impressed.[12]

The revenues of the English state were further augmented after 1475 by a pension provided by Louis IX. In that year, Edward IV had invaded France with a large and well-equipped army with the avowed aim of re-conquering England's ancestral territories on the continent. However, the failure of his allies, the dukes of Burgundy and Brittany, to provide meaningful assistance prompted him to come to terms with the French king. In return for concluding a seven-year-long truce, the latter agreed to pay Edward a one-off sum of £15,000 and then a further £10,000 per year. This was partly invested in building projects at castles and palaces, as well as the purchase of fine clothing, jewels, furnishings and books. The *Crowland Chronicle* relates that 'in the building of castles, colleges and other notable places … not one of his ancestors could match his remarkable achievements'.[13]

One of Edward's most substantial building projects was at Nottingham Castle, one of his favourite residences, where major works were carried out in the second half of the 1470s. Between 1476 and 1480 some £3,000 was spent on repairs and erecting new structures overseen by Gervase Clifton, esquire, master of the king's works at the castle. The workforce employed on-site consisted of masons, carpenters, stone carvers, joiners, sawyers, glaziers, painters, plumbers, plasters and labourers. Materials purchased included iron for making window bars, hinges and hooks for doors, as well as lead and glass for glazing windows and slate for making roof tiles. The Tudor antiquarian John Leland some years later wrote that 'Edward the fourth began a right sumptuous piece of stone work, of the which he clearly finished one excellent goodly tower of three storeys, and brought up the other part likewise from the foundations with stone and marvellous fair windows'.[14]

Unfortunately, this tower and the other structures built at Nottingham during his reign no longer survive. By contrast, the product of another major construction project, St George's Chapel at Windsor Castle, still exists. This building replaced an earlier thirteenth-century structure on the same site. It was conceived on a grand scale more akin to a cathedral as opposed to chapel, intended to display the magnificence of the Yorkist dynasty. Work began in 1473, under the supervision of Richard Beauchamp, bishop of Salisbury, with more than £6,500 spent alone between 1478 and 1483, which at the time was a substantial sum. The chapel represents one of the finest examples of Perpendicular Gothic architecture in England, which, although unfinished by his death, was eventually completed by his successors. Building work was also carried out at other castles, such as the Tower, the defences of which were strengthened through the construction of a bulwark at its entrance.[15]

The repair and maintenance of royal castles was also an important issue for the king's officials. This is apparent from the surveys carried out to inspect the condition of these buildings, some of which still survive. For instance, in May 1476, a 'progress' of the king's council in the duchy of Lancaster took place in Yorkshire. These councillors met at York on 16 May, and over the next three weeks visited the ducal castles and lordships of Pickering, Knaresborough, Pontefract and Tickhill. These officials attended the judicial sessions being held in those places, but also observed the condition of the castles and made recommendations for necessary repairs. Their suggestions were relatively modest for Pickering. This included repairing the west end of the chapel, the houses between the west side of the great hall and the kitchen, the bakehouse and part of the north side of the curtain wall. Repairs were also required at Knaresborough, with the great tower, referred to as the 'donjon', to be repaired 'in all things'. In particular, the lead covering the great chamber over the hall was to be new cast and laid on again 'with all diligence', with new doors and windows required for the same room. The roofs of other towers in the castle, such as the 'round tower', also needed to be mended, with dilapidated structures, including the 'old kitchen' to be pulled down and the materials reused.[16]

By contrast, more substantial repairs were required at Pontefract. This included repairs to various towers, houses and the chapel, as well as the lead drainage pipes on the walls. The lead covering of these structures also needed to be cleaned and scoured to prevent water damage. Their report also mentions 'the tower new begun which is fallen down'. This was to remain in its ruined state until the 'king's pleasure be known'. The final castle visited by the members of the council was Tickhill. They reported that the chapel and other houses needed to be mended, with shingle to be used for the great hall. Work was also required for repairing the battlements of the castle, which needed to be set fast with lime and sand, otherwise they would 'else fall down and break'. Finally, a chamber located on the wall of the same entrance to the great tower was so 'feeble that it may not long stand'. It was therefore demolished with any suitable salvageable timber to be kept in a dry place, for use in future building work.[17]

Ashby de la Zouch and Kirby Muxloe

Construction work was not restricted to royal castles during Edward's second reign. Building projects were also carried out by magnates or members of the gentry to improve or refurbish their residences. The most notable examples of this can be seen with Ashby de la Zouch and Kirby Muxloe in Leicestershire. These were originally manorial buildings that were transformed into castles. This was due to the ambitions of their owner, William, Lord Hastings, to establish a lordship for himself in

Leicestershire. Hastings was a close friend of the king, who had distinguished himself in royal service over the years, both on the battlefield and in diplomatic missions. He had received many rewards including being raised to the baronage, the office of chamberlain, the constableship of Nottingham Castle and the lieutenancy of Calais. In addition to this, he had also been granted numerous offices in the duchy of Lancaster, particularly in the Midlands, a region where many of his estates were located. Hastings therefore acquired the means to carry out substantial construction projects. On 17 April 1474, he was granted a licence to crenellate his manors of Ashby de la Zouch, Bagworth, Thornton and Kirby in Leicestershire, and his castle of Slingsby in Yorkshire. This document also specified that he could enclose as many as 9,000 acres of land in those estates, with permission to erect fences called deer leaps for keeping deer in his parks, and the right to hunt game.[18]

Hastings initiated building projects at all of these properties but focused his efforts on Ashby de la Zouch and Kirby Muxloe. Work on the former began in 1472–3, with a relatively small number of carpenters, masons and other professionals employed on the site. Over time the scale of the construction work grew in intensity, with Hastings later said to have gone so far as to order the removal of lead from his other castle of Belvoir for the works. Ashby de la Zouch was conceived as a rectangular shaped enclosure flanked by four towers, which incorporated older structures. The principal surviving remains from this period are two towers, the Kitchen Tower and the Great Tower. The latter has four storeys and is 23m tall, which is adjoined by a seven-storey high turret. It was entered at ground-floor level via a small doorway protected by a portcullis, with the kitchen on the first floor, whereas the upper floors contained a great chamber and withdrawing rooms. The tower was topped by machicolation and corner turrets. It was clearly intended to impress, being built out of expensive cut stone and decorated throughout with the coat of arms of the Hastings family and symbols of the Yorkist dynasty. By contrast, the Kitchen Tower is much smaller, with only two storeys. This building, as its name suggests, was intended as a place for cooking and preparing food and incorporates a large kitchen.[19]

Construction work at Kirby Muxloe started six years later in 1480. It has a similar rectangular design to Ashby de la Zouch, which also incorporates part of the original manor house. However, unlike the other castle, it was primarily constructed using brick as opposed to stone and was encircled by a moat. The survival of the financial accounts means that the activities of its builders can be traced in detail from October 1480. Work began in that month with wood, sand and straw brought to the brickhouse near to the site. Six labourers were employed: four of whom were tasked with digging out the moat, whereas the other two assisted the gardener in clearing trees from the garden of the old manor house. The intensity of the work gradually increased in early 1481 with a corresponding growth in the size of the workforce. Foundations were laid for walls, and a bridge for the moat was constructed. Bricks were supplied by the brick-maker, whereas both rough and free stone were transported to the site from nearby quarries. The project received fresh impetus due to the arrival of the master mason, John Couper, from Tattershall in May. In this era, master masons were not merely responsible for overseeing masonry work, but also the overall design and construction of stone and brick buildings.[20]

Throughout the summer, masons, bricklayers, carpenters, labourers and ditchers were hard at work on the site. By September, the moat had been completed and scaffolding prepared for the two 'middle' towers on the south-east and north-west corners of the site, with progress made on the construction of the walls of the inner court. To ensure that the partly built structures were not damaged by the elements, they were covered with stubble over the winter. Work resumed in earnest in the spring of 1482, with the foundations of the middle towers laid out in March and for the gatehouse by early June. Carpenters were also employed on making floors for the middle towers, with a bakehouse and forge under construction in July. In the following January, the centering for the vault over the gatehouse entrance was made. Over the next few months, further work was carried out on the same structure, which included the vaulting, battlements and upper floors. Therefore, by the early summer of 1483, the workforce had made good progress, with the west tower finished, some of the other towers fully roofed and the gatehouse partly completed. Yet, construction at Kirby Muxloe, as well as Ashby de la Zouch, was all but brought to an end following Hastings execution in the same year.[21]

War with Scotland

Anglo-Scottish relations underwent a dramatic improvement in October 1474. This was due to the decision of James III, king of Scots, to agree to a marriage alliance proposed by Edward IV between their infant children. The former's son, also called James, was to marry the latter's third daughter, Cecily. Edward provided a dowry of 20,000 crowns, to be paid over the course of seventeen years, and there was to be a long-term truce until 1519. Yet, the English alliance was unpopular in Scotland, with cross-border raiding by the Scots leading to the resumption of warfare in 1480. James's failure to prevent breaches of the truce led to Edward issuing an ultimatum. Unless these demands were met, the English would 'make against the said Scots rigorous and cruel war'. James was to surrender the disputed border settlements of Berwick, Roxburgh and Coldingham, to give homage to Edward as his overlord and to surrender custody of Prince James prior to his marriage to Cecily. These terms were wholly unacceptable, with hostilities breaking out a short time later. Archibald Douglas, earl of Angus, led a force across the border into Northumberland, which burnt the town of Bamburgh.[22]

Edward appointed Gloucester as his lieutenant-general with authority to raise an army from the northern counties of England on 12 May. Six days later, orders were given for artillery to be transported from Nottingham Castle to Norham Castle for the defence of the latter. Commissions of array were subsequently issued on 20 June for the assembling of men from the counties of Yorkshire, Cumberland, Westmoreland and Northumberland. One of the commissioners was Henry Percy, earl of Northumberland, who wrote from his castle of Wressle on 7 September, to Robert Plumpton, esquire, with instructions to appear at Topcliffe in Yorkshire, with 'all such persons as you may make in their most defensible array'. Gloucester led a raid into Scotland with his forces, but otherwise remained on the defensive, with garrisons maintained in the border castles. This was due to the decision by the king to defer any active campaigning until the following year.[23]

In March 1481, Edward explained in a letter to Pope Sixtus IV that he intended to lead an army in person into Scotland to punish the Scots for having 'drawn their hostile swords on us and our realm'. Magnates including Anthony Woodville, Earl Rivers, and Thomas, Lord Stanley, agreed to raise substantial contingents for the royal host, with large quantities of provisions procured and despatched to the soldiers in the north. A powerful naval force had also been assembled under the command of John, Lord Howard. This fleet attacked the east coast of Scotland, burnt the town of Blackness and captured many ships. On land, the Scots raided across the border, whereas the English unsuccessfully laid siege to Berwick. However, despite the substantial costs incurred in these military preparations, the campaign was ultimately abortive due to Edward's indecisiveness, which resulted in his failure to arrive in the north before the end of the campaigning season. Another consequence was a shortage of food, due to the presence of large numbers of soldiers in the border garrisons over the winter of 1481–2. This necessitated the procurement of further quantities of foodstuffs, including wheat, barley, rye and oats.[24]

In the following year, Edward instead decided to delegate command of military operations to Gloucester. By the summer, the latter had assembled a formidable force of 20,000 men for the invasion of Scotland. The first target of the expedition was Berwick. This settlement had been under Scottish control for the past twenty-one years and the government of James III had spent large sums of money on its defence. The fortifications of the settlement had been repaired and improved, furnished with artillery and garrisoned with a force of 500 men. Yet, the size of the English army prompted the inhabitants to hurriedly capitulate, although the defenders of the castle remained defiant. Gloucester left a small force behind to besiege the castle, before proceeding to march through southern Scotland, burning towns and villages. James III had raised an army to meet the English in the field, but he was taken prisoner by some of his own subjects, who were angry with his style of rulership, and incarcerated in Edinburgh Castle. This development led to a collapse in Scottish resistance.[25]

A short time later, Gloucester entered the city of Edinburgh without encountering opposition. He soon left, however, after inconclusive negotiations with James's captors. Gloucester returned to Berwick, where he disbanded most of his army, but kept a force of 1,700 to continue the siege of the castle on 11 August. The English artillery caused significant damage to the defences of the fortress, but the defenders put up a staunch resistance. It was only after 'some slaughter and bloodshed' that they eventually surrendered on 24 August.[26] The capture of Berwick marked the end of the war, with a short truce agreed between the two belligerents. Edward had therefore finally gained full control of the kingdom of England. However, this was a relatively modest return for the great costs incurred during the war. The *Crowland Chronicle* has a scathing assessment of the conflict, characterising it as a 'trifling gain, or perhaps more accurately, loss', as large sums had to be subsequently spent on its defence against the Scots. However, the net result was the final recovery of Berwick, which remains part of England to this day.[27]

Chapter Seven

The Final Struggle

The Usurpation of Richard III

Edward IV unexpectedly died after a short illness on 9 April at the age of 40 at Westminster Palace. The French writer Philippe de Commynes attributed it to his unhealthy lifestyle, due to his fondness for food and drink, whereas Dominic Mancini, an Italian visitor to England, claimed that it resulted from a chill caught whilst on a boat trip. Regardless of the reason, his unanticipated demise caused a problem, as his son and heir, Prince Edward, was only 12 years and therefore a minor. At a meeting of the royal council held in late April, it was decided that Edward V's coronation should take place on 4 May. However, there were concerns that the young king's maternal relatives, the Woodvilles, would seek to take control of the government through force. According to the *Crowland Chronicle*, William, Lord Hastings, threatened to withdraw to Calais, where he was lieutenant, if Edward was accompanied by an army. This argument was accepted by the council, with the king's uncle, Anthony Woodville, Earl Rivers, instructed to limit his retinue to 2,000 men. On 24 April, Edward V and his entourage left Ludlow for London, but were intercepted en route at Stony Stratford in Buckinghamshire by Richard, duke of Gloucester, and Henry Stafford, duke of Buckingham.[1]

Mancini claims that this meeting took place at the suggestion of the dukes, who initially greeted Rivers warmly at a dinner held in Northampton on the evening of 29 April. Yet, on the following morning, Rivers was suddenly arrested by their men and taken into custody. The dukes then proceeded to Stony Stratford where they dismissed the king's men and seized his treasurer, Sir Thomas Vaughan, his half-brother, Richard Grey, and Sir Richard Haute. In justification for their actions, they alleged that the Woodvilles and their supporters had contributed to the late king's death, had sought to deny Gloucester the office of regent and to kill him. Edward boldly tried to refute these claims, but, as he was effectively at their mercy, had no choice but to go along with their actions. Rivers, Vaughan, Grey and Haute were subsequently taken to Pontefract Castle where they were imprisoned. News of these events quickly reached the capital. Queen Elizabeth fled to sanctuary at Westminster Abbey with her daughters and youngest son, Richard, duke of York. The Woodvilles sought to raise an army to rescue the king, but their failure to gain support prompted their leaders, including Sir Edward Woodville, to flee abroad.[2]

Gloucester and Buckingham arrived at London with the king on 4 May. Six days later, the royal council postponed the date of the coronation until late June and confirmed Gloucester in his office as Protector of the Realm, who thereafter took control of the governance of the kingdom. One of his priorities was to reward his supporters. He lavished plentiful rewards on Buckingham, who received an unprecedented series of grants of offices and lands in Wales and the Marches. In all, he was given the constable-ships and stewardships of fifty-three lordships and castles, as well as becoming chamberlain and chief justice of both north and south Wales. These grants not only had considerable monetary value, but also gave Buckingham command of the garrisons stationed in the principal royal castles. Furthermore, he was given authority to raise soldiers and to send them where needed as he thought expedient. Buckingham was thereby given even more extensive powers in Wales than had previously been held by Herbert some years earlier. By contrast, more modest rewards were given to others, such as Henry Percy, earl of Northumberland, who was appointed as captain of Berwick with its garrison of 600 men.[3]

Gloucester's powers were limited, however, by the influence of the royal council. Despite appointing him as Protector, they refused to countenance the execution of Rivers or any of the other prisoners held at Pontefract Castle without a trial. By early June, he had decided to send for reinforcements from the north of England to crush his opponents. In a letter to the city of York, dated 10 June, Gloucester requested assistance 'against the queen, her blood adherents and affinity, which have intended and daily doeth intend, to murder and utterly destroy us and our cousin, the duke of Buckingham, and the old royal blood of this realm'. Yet, his next move was entirely unexpected. Three days later he summoned a meeting of the council at the Tower of London. According to Mancini, after the councillors had entered the inner chamber of the castle, Gloucester cried out that they intended to attack him. The soldiers he had stationed nearby then rushed in with Buckingham and arrested them. Hastings was killed on the spot, whereas John Morton, bishop of Ely, Thomas Rotherham, archbishop of York, and Thomas, Lord Stanley, were imprisoned, although the latter was soon released. Other accounts vary, with the *Great Chronicle* stating that Hastings was taken to a green outside the chapel and beheaded on a block of wood.[4]

Gloucester's justification for this outrage was said to have been widely disbelieved at the time. Instead, it was interpreted as a pre-emptive strike against the only men powerful enough to stand in his way. His next step was to secure custody of Richard, duke of York, ostensibly as his presence was required at the coronation of Edward V. Cardinal Thomas Bourchier, archbishop of Canterbury, was sent inside Westminster Abbey to persuade Queen Elizabeth to give up her son. His words were backed by the threat of violence, with the sanctuary having been surrounded by armed men. This persuaded her to submit to his demands. The young prince was then sent to join his brother in the Tower, under the supervision of a specially appointed guard. Mancini writes that the attendants of Edward V were then removed from him, with the two boys 'withdrawn into the inner apartments of the Tower proper, and day by day began to be seen more rarely behind the bars and windows, till at length they ceased to appear altogether'.[5]

On 22 June, Dr Ralph Shaw delivered a sermon at Paul's Cross in which he espoused Gloucester's claim to the throne. Three days later, Buckingham advanced the same arguments to a gathering of lords and gentlemen. Mancini claims that Gloucester's supporters at first argued that Edward IV was illegitimate, as he was born of an extramarital affair by their mother, Cecily. Yet, this embarrassing argument, if it was ever adopted, was soon abandoned. Instead, it was claimed that Edward's marriage to Elizabeth Woodville was invalid, as the late king had previously entered into a pre-contractual agreement to marry a woman named Eleanor Butler. Therefore, both Edward V and Richard of York were bastards conceived out of wedlock who were ineligible to inherit the throne. Gloucester's only other main dynastic rival was his nephew, Edward, earl of Warwick, the son of his brother Clarence. Edward's claim to the succession was passed over and he was sent to London to be kept in the household of Gloucester's wife. Orders were also sent to John Neville, constable of Pontefract Castle, who commanded a garrison of thirty men, to execute Rivers, Vaughan, Grey and Haute. According to the *Crowland Chronicle*, they were beheaded without even the semblance of being put on trial.[6]

Buckingham's Rebellion

Gloucester's coronation as King Richard III took place at Westminster Abbey on 6 July. Afterwards he embarked on a tour of the kingdom to assert his authority. Richard had thus far faced little challenge to his seizure of power, but this was soon to change. The *Crowland Chronicle* states that the people of southern England began to 'murmur greatly, to form assembles and to organise associations' for the purpose of rescuing the two sons of Edward IV. Remarkably, given his role in Richard's rise to power and the rewards showered upon him, Buckingham decided to join the rebels. According to the same author, he regretted his previous actions and agreed to become 'captain-in-chief in this affair'. At the instigation of his erstwhile prisoner, the bishop of Ely, he sent a message to Henry Tudor, then an exile in Brittany, to ask him to accept the throne. The latter's claim to be king was tenuous, as it derived from his mother, Margaret Beaufort, a great-granddaughter of John of Gaunt, fourth son of Edward III, yet Henry was now the only viable alternative to Richard. This was because a rumour had circulated that 'King Edward's sons, by some unknown manner of violent destruction, had met their fate'. The rebels had widespread support throughout the south of England, including many former members of Edward IV's household. Henry also received the support of Duke Francis II of Brittany, who provided a fleet of five ships and a small force of soldiers for his invasion. Yet, the rebellion proved to be a fiasco.[7]

The rebels in Kent began their uprising on 10 October by attempting to march on London. However, they were prevented from doing so by John Howard, who had recently been made duke of Norfolk by Richard III. Howard placed a force to guard the crossing of the River Thames at Gravesend in north-west Kent and took control of the capital. He sent for reinforcements from his estates in East Anglia and hurriedly sent a messenger to warn the king of the rebellion. The rebels thereby lost the initiative, as the men of Kent had risen before their co-conspirators in Wales or the south-west of England were ready. Buckingham from his seat at Brecon Castle struggled to raise an army from his tenants. Vergil states that he was 'a sore and hard dealing man' who had brought his Welsh soldiers 'to the field against their wills, and without any lust to fight for him, rather by rigorous commandment than for money'. Storms and flooding hampered his ability to cross the River Severn into England and many of his men deserted him.[8]

Meanwhile, Richard had tasked Sir Thomas Vaughan of Tretower and others with containing the duke. Vaughan was said to have 'kept a most diligent watch over all the surrounding countryside' around Brecon, whilst Humphrey Stafford posted guards at the crossings into England and destroyed bridges. Buckingham managed to reach Shropshire but with the number of his followers rapidly dwindling went into hiding. Vaughan took Brecon Castle, seemingly without any difficulty, which his men then plundered. The duke was soon betrayed by one of his own servants, Ralph

Banastre, and was sent to the king's presence in Salisbury. Richard had arrived in the city a short time before with a sizeable army. Buckingham asked to speak to the king but his request was refused and he was beheaded. News of these developments greatly disheartened the rebels who had assembled in the south-west of England. Richard's rapid approach towards Exeter prompted their leaders, including Edward Courtenay and Peter Courtenay, bishop of Exeter, to flee overseas. Henry Tudor's invasion also failed to materialise, as his small fleet was dispersed by a storm and he returned to Brittany.[9]

The last remaining pocket of insurrection was in East Sussex, where a prominent member of the local gentry, Sir Thomas Lewknor, held his castle of Bodiam in the name of Henry Tudor. Bodiam is a small moated courtyard castle dating from the late fourteenth century, which had been founded by Sir Edward Dallingridge. It has a rectangular shape, which is flanked by round towers at its corners, and has two square mural towers on its west and east sides. The castle was approached via a right-angled timber bridge that came to a barbican and then a twin-towered gatehouse; with a postern gate on its opposite side. On 8 November, Richard issued orders for Thomas Howard, earl of Surrey (the son of the duke of Norfolk), Sir John Broke of Cobham, Sir Thomas Echingham and others to besiege Bodiam. However, given the failure of the rebellion elsewhere, it appears unlikely that a siege took place. Instead, the garrison most probably surrendered without offering any resistance, as it was soon in the hands of Richard's forces.[10]

Henry Tudor

Richard had won an easy victory against the rebels who had been quickly defeated. Yet, it showed the strength of opposition to Richard in southern England. Approximately a hundred named individuals were attainted in the Parliament of January 1484. A small minority were subsequently pardoned, but many others joined Henry Tudor in exile. Richard was therefore forced to rely increasingly on his northern supporters, who were given extensive grants of offices and lands in southern England. The *Crowland Chronicle* states these were distributed 'amongst his northerners whom he had planted in every part of his dominions, to the shame of all the southern people'. Beneficiaries of forfeited estates included Sir Thomas Mauleverer who received Plympton Castle in Devon, and Sir Thomas Everingham who gained the castles of Barnstaple and Torrington in the same county. Offices were also given to northerners, with John, Lord Scrope, appointed as constable of Exeter Castle, Sir John Saville as lieutenant and captain of

Carisbrooke Castle and the Isle of Wight, and John Hoton as constable of Southampton Castle.[11]

Another area of concern was Wales, where a potentially dangerous power vacuum had emerged. This derived from the removal in quick succession of the council of Edward V from Ludlow Castle and the execution of Buckingham. Richard's solution was to distribute grants of offices and lands to multiple trusted supporters, as opposed to vesting vice-regal authority upon one magnate. Sir William Stanley was appointed as justiciar of north Wales and as constable of the castles of Caernarfon, Flint and Rhuddlan. The constableships of the other royal castles of the region, namely Beaumaris, Conwy and Harlech, were given respectively to Sir Richard Hudleston, Sir Richard Tunstall and Sir Roger Kenaston. In the south, William Herbert, earl of Huntingdon, was made justiciar, whereas Richard William, esquire, received the constableships of the castles of Cilgerran, Haverford West, Tenby and Pembroke. The decision was also taken to reinforce the garrison of Harlech Castle, which was increased in size from twenty to eighty men. A force of twelve men was also installed in Denbigh Castle. This measure was taken due to the ever-present threat of invasion by Henry Tudor.[12]

Henry had safely returned to Brittany after the debacle of the 1483 rebellion, where he continued to enjoy the protection of Duke Francis. He was also accompanied by a sizeable band of English exiles and was in regular correspondence with sympathisers in England. Henry publicly proclaimed his intention to win the throne on Christmas Day 1483 in the grand setting of Rennes Cathedral. Once he had done so, he promised to marry Elizabeth Woodville, daughter of Edward IV, and received the homage of his English supporters who were present. Richard was acutely aware of the threat posed to him by Henry. His attempts to win over the duke of Brittany through bribery failed, so he instead resolved to employ military force against him. English merchants were instructed to target Breton shipping, with the king's ships also used against them. This military pressure encouraged the Bretons to reach an accommodation with Richard. In the summer of 1484, at which time the aging duke was incapacitated, his treasurer, Peter Landois, agree to hand over Henry. However, the latter received warning of his scheme just in time and succeeded in fleeing to France.[13]

Henry and his companions were provided with a warm reception by the regency government of Charles VIII. The latter also agreed to support him in his endeavour to gain the English throne. This was a significant reversal for Richard as, unlike with Brittany, he lacked the means to exert pressure on a state as powerful as the kingdom of France. This was compounded by the news that John de Vere, earl of Oxford, had escaped from Hammes Castle in the Pale of Calais. Oxford had been imprisoned there since 1474, following his surrender at St Michael's Mount. By the end of 1484, he had succeeded in subverting his jailor, James Blount, lieutenant of the castle, who not only released him but also joined Henry's cause. After their departure the fortress was besieged by a pro-Ricardian contingent of the Calais garrison led by John, Lord Dynham. The attackers were accompanied by a sizeable artillery train with large quantities of gunpowder. Yet, the siege was soon broken by a force led by Oxford, which gave an opportunity for the defenders to leave the castle. According to Vergil, Henry was so delighted to learn of his escape that 'he was ravished with joy' due to his 'great nobility and knowledge in the wars'. Richard had also suffered a personal and dynastic setback, with the death of his son and heir, Edward, at Middleham Castle on 9 April 1484. This weakened his position as he was left with no immediate heir. Yet, Henry was initially unable to exploit the situation, as French support took time to materialise.[14]

Richard sought to counter an invasion through carrying out extensive military preparations. On 7 December 1484, he issued a proclamation calling upon his subjects 'to be ready in their most defensible array', which was reissued in June of the following year. Francis, Viscount Lovell, was placed in command of a fleet based at Southampton to watch the Channel. Richard also revived a courier system devised during the recent Scottish war of assigning one courier every 20 miles for the quick delivery of messages and had a network of spies in England and in France. However, these measures were expensive, as noted by the *Crowland Chronicle*, which steadily diminished his financial reserves. Furthermore, uncertainty about where or when Henry would strike forced him to spread his forces thinly. It was for this reason that he decided to base himself in Nottingham. The town was in a central location, which would allow him to react to threats from different directions. It also had a royal castle, where Richard and his brother Edward IV had carried out major building works to convert it into a comfortable residence. It meant, however, that he lacked the ability to quickly move against any invaders after they made landfall.[15]

By the summer of 1485, the provision of assistance by the French government meant that Henry's long-anticipated invasion of England was now possible. He was provided with money, ships and a substantial contingent of French, Scottish and Breton soldiers. Henry's army also comprised a sizeable company of English exiles. His venture was co-ordinated with his supporters in England and Wales, with whom he had exchanged frequent messages. This included notable figures such as Thomas, Lord Stanley, and Rhys ap Thomas, who agreed to join forces with him when he returned to the kingdom. Henry set sail from Harfleur in Normandy at the end of July and made landfall at Milford Haven in Pembrokeshire on 7 August. Milford appears to have been chosen due to its remote location, where his arrival would be unexpected by Richard or his supporters. Henry then moved northwards to Cardigan before marching eastwards across central Wales through difficult terrain, thereby bypassing the garrisons of the castles in the north and south of the country. Initially, he gained few recruits until Rhys ap Thomas joined forces with him on 12 August. Five days later the border town of Shrewsbury opened its gate to his army, and he entered England.[16]

Richard responded to news of Henry's landing by sending urgent instructions for men to join his host. On 19 August, he left Nottingham and moved southwards to Leicester, before advancing westwards to confront the invader. During his march he was reinforced by contingents led by the duke of Norfolk and the earl of Northumberland. Richard's army was almost certainly larger than Henry's but he did not have an overwhelming advantage. The speed of the campaign meant that further reinforcements were still en route, whereas the Tudor army comprised many experienced French soldiers. Both sides were therefore evenly matched. On 22 August, the two armies met in battle near Leicester. The fighting was hard-fought with the outcome apparently decided by the decision of Sir William Stanley to intervene with his forces midway through the battle, having hitherto remained neutral a short distance away from the action. According to Vergil, Richard made a bold attempt to kill his rival on the field through a cavalry charge, which came close to success, before Stanley's intervention turned the tide. This led to Richard being 'killed fighting manfully in the thickest press of his enemies', and the rout of the Yorkist army. Henry was acclaimed as king by his soldiers, with Lord Stanley placing Richard's crown, which was recovered from the field, on his head.[17]

The End of the Wars

Henry had won a decisive victory at Bosworth. His claim to the throne was validated through success in battle, with Richard's death leaving few credible Yorkist alternatives. The strongest candidate was Edward, earl of Warwick, who was transferred to the Tower for safekeeping, whereas other contenders, such as John de la Pole, earl of Lincoln, made their peace with Henry. This meant that his assumption of power initially met with no opposition. On 30 October 1485, his coronation as King Henry VII took place at Westminster Abbey. A few months later he fulfilled the promise he had made at Rennes Cathedral by marrying Elizabeth Wood-ville on 18 January 1486. One of his principal objectives was to reward his faithful supporters who had made his unlikely victory possible. Before doing so, it was necessary to reverse acts of attainder that had been passed against many of them. This duly took place in his first parliament, which was held from November 1485 until March 1486.[18]

The main beneficiary of these rewards was his uncle, Jasper Tudor, whose service had been invaluable to his accession to the throne. He regained his earldom of Pembroke and was created as duke of Bedford. Jasper was also granted all the castles and lordships in Glamorgan, Haverfordwest, and Abergavenny, and appointed as justice of south Wales and constable of the castles of Monmouth, Skenfrith, Grosmont and White Castle in Monmouthshire. Other Lancastrian exiles were restored to their ancestral lands and titles. A major beneficiary of this was Sir Edward Courtenay, who received the earldom of Devon, which came with the castles of Okekampton, Tiverton and Plympton. Whereas Hugh Luttrell regained his family's castle of Dunster in Somerset. The king's stepfather, Lord Stanley, was created as earl of Derby, whereas the latter's younger brother, Sir William, was appointed as constable of Caernarfon Castle and as chief justice of north Wales. Other recipients of grants of offices included Sir Rhys ap Thomas, who received the constableship of Brecon Castle, and Sir Ralph Bigod, who received the same office for the castle of Sheriff Hutton.[19]

Henry's patronage derived in part from lands obtained through confiscations. He deliberately dated the start of his reign to 21 August, the day before the Battle of Bosworth, thereby designating all those who fought in Richard's army as traitors. This policy bred resentment particularly in the north of England, where many of the late king's followers were unwilling to accept the outcome of Bosworth. Two of these men were Francis, Lord Lovell, and Humphrey Stafford, who had escaped from the battlefield at Bosworth and taken refuge in sanctuary at Colchester. In the spring of 1486, they left sanctuary and sought to raise a rebellion against the king, with Lovell active in Yorkshire and Stafford in Worcestershire. However, their revolt quickly collapsed as they failed to attract support. Loyalists were also active in the region, with John Dawney holding Sheriff Hutton Castle for the king. Stafford was captured and executed, whereas Lovell fled overseas. Meanwhile, Sir Thomas Vaughan of Tretower took up arms in east Wales, with risings at Brecon, Tretower and Hay. However, the actions of Sir Rhys ap Thomas succeeded in containing the rebels. He led the defence of the region, with Brecon Castle held by his deputy, William Fisher. Fisher commanded a force of 140 men for 7 weeks, with repairs carried out to the drawbridge and gunpowder purchased for the castle's arsenal. The failure of the rebels to capture Brecon contributed to the rapid collapse of the uprising.[20]

A far more serious threat emerged in the following year. Lovell had escaped to the court of Margaret of York, dowager duchess of Burgundy, the sister of Edward IV and Richard III. In March 1487, he was joined by John de la Pole, earl of Lincoln. Lincoln had been well treated by Henry, despite his adherence to Richard, but nevertheless turned against him. Margaret provided them with financial and military assistance, which included a contingent of German soldiers. Henry was kept aware of these developments and, anticipating a landing on the east coast of England, ordered watches to be kept and garrisons to be placed in key fortifications. On 20 April, he wrote to the civic authorities of York ordering them to prepare the defence of the city. They replied with a request for assistance as their fortifications were dilapidated and they lacked armaments. What was more, the castle was in a ruinous condition as the old structure had been demolished by order of Richard III, who intended to rebuild it, but it had yet to be replaced. In response, the king instructed William Tunstall, the constable of Scarborough Castle, to send twelve serpentines to the city. Yet, the latter was unable or unwilling to comply with this order, as he claimed that he did not have even four serpentines in the castle's arsenal. However, a short time later, on 15 May, the king assured the citizens that they no longer faced the imminent prospect of being attacked. This was because news had arrived that Lovell and Lincoln had instead travelled to Ireland.[21]

Unbeknownst to Henry, this was because they had gone to Dublin to attend the coronation of a boy named Lambert Simnel. Simnel at the instigation of a priest, Richard Simons, professed to be Edward, earl of Warwick, and was taken to Ireland in late 1486. Much of the Irish nobility were hostile to Henry's rule and they decided to support his cause. On 24 May 1487, he was crowned as King Edward VI at Christ Church Cathedral in Dublin. Soon afterwards a combined Irish-German invasion force set sail from Ireland and landed in Furness in Lancashire on 4 June. They moved rapidly eastwards towards Yorkshire where they expected to receive reinforcements. Henry was at Kenilworth Castle when he received news of the invasion. He at once set about raising an army to confront the invaders. In the meanwhile, the rebels soon reached the vicinity of York, but the refusal of the civic authorities to grant admittance prompted them to instead move southwards. They were pursued by a royalist force led by Henry, Lord Clifford, but succeeded in routing their attackers. A detachment of the Yorkist army commanded by John, Lord Scrope of Bolton, and Thomas, Lord Scrope of Masham, then returned to the city. They attempted to storm the defences but were beaten off by the inhabitants on 12 June.[22]

Henry advanced north with his rapidly assembled army, via Coventry and Leicester, before heading to Newark. On 16 June, he encountered the rebels nearby at East Stoke. According to Vergil, the Yorkist commander, Lincoln, went onto the offensive. The rebels were said to have fought fiercely, but they were outnumbered, and the poorly armoured Irish were particularly vulnerable to arrows. Eventually the royalists prevailed, with many of the Yorkists killed, including most of their leaders. Simnel was taken prisoner, but on account of his youth was pardoned by the king and was put to work in the royal kitchens. Stoke proved to be the last battle of the Wars of the Roses. The Tudor dynasty continued to be threatened by Yorkist pretenders for some years to come, notably Perkin Warbeck and Edmund de la Pole, duke of Suffolk. They received intermittent support from foreign hostile powers who wished to put pressure on the English government. Yet, none of these pretenders could muster sufficient domestic support to threaten Henry VII or his son Henry VIII on the battlefield.[23]

Conclusion

Castles played a significant role in the military campaigns of the Wars of the Roses. There is firm evidence that at least thirty-six sieges took place between the years 1455 and 1487 (see Appendix B). These varied markedly in their intensity, scale and duration. Major sieges include Denbigh and the Tower of London (1460), Norham (1463) and Bamburgh (1464). These were significant military actions, which had an impact on wider events. Sizeable numbers of men and artillery were involved, and they were fiercely contested. By contrast, other sieges were more minor affairs. Examples of this type include Thorpe Waterville and Chirk (1461), and Carlisle (1471). These were more localised actions which involved relatively small numbers of combatants. They also varied in their length of duration, which ranged from just three days for the siege of London (1471) to approximately six months for Carisbrooke (1460–1).

The typical tactic used in most sieges was for the attackers to isolate and blockade castles. Defenders were often forced to surrender under terms when their provisions ran low, unless there was a realistic prospect of being rescued by a friendly army. For instance, the Lancastrian defenders of Thorpe Waterville surrendered in these circumstances in 1461. Determined attempts by besiegers to storm the defences of castles were comparatively unusual. The capture of Bamburgh in 1464 was one of the rare exceptions where a castle was carried by storm. In other instances, assaults seem to have been made to put pressure on garrisons to yield, such as by the Yorkists at the siege of Alnwick in the summer of 1462. Similarly, artillery was sometimes used to intimidate garrisons, for example at Chirk in 1461. In some cases, the threat alone of using gunpowder weapons appears to have been employed. The army of Richard Neville, earl of Warwick, had a powerful artillery train in the winter of 1462, but it was seemingly unused at the sieges of Alnwick, Bamburgh and Dunstanburgh. This was in part due to a reluctance to damage fortifications. The deliberate destruction of Carreg Cennen in 1462 was very much an aberration. Instead, as mentioned in the most detailed account of the siege of Bamburgh in 1464, there was a desire to capture castles that were undamaged by gunfire.

On a few occasions, sieges led to battles taking place. The Scottish sieges of Carlisle in 1461 and Norham in 1463 were only broken due to the arrival of Yorkist armies, which led to the attackers being routed. Whereas at Alnwick in January 1463, the Yorkists lifted the siege due to the imminent arrival of an army of Scots, who threatened, but ultimately did not, offer battle. The attempt of Richard, duke of York, to relieve the precarious situation of his garrison at Sandal Castle ultimately led to the Battle of Wakefield taking place on 30 December 1460. Defeat in battle often led to garrisons surrendering after short sieges, if they did not capitulate outright. In 1468, the rout of the Lancastrian army in the field prompted the defenders of Harlech to yield after a short siege, despite the strong defences of the castle. Similarly, news of the outcome of battles frequently prompted beleaguered garrisons to surrender under terms, as with the defenders of the Tower of London in 1460.

Some of the aforementioned sieges may seem unrelated to the Wars of the Roses, at least directly. The attack on Caister in 1469 resulted from a dispute over the ownership of the castle between the Paston family and John Mowbray, duke of Norfolk. Whereas the siege of Roxburgh by the Scots in 1460 was an international conflict. Yet, even these actions were linked to the military and political situation in England. In both cases, the aggressors sought to take advantage of the weakness of the English government. Whether that was the captivity of Edward IV in 1469, or Henry VI in 1460. Similarly, attacks on castles during the private wars of the 1450s, such as with Powderham in 1455, contributed to national instability and ultimately to the outbreak of civil war.

Gaps in the surviving evidence means that it is often unclear whether sieges took place or not. In 1469, for instance, Edward IV ordered his brother, Richard, duke of Gloucester, to besiege the rebel-held castles of Cardigan and Carmarthen. Later in 1483, the latter, having ascended to the throne as Richard III, issued instructions to his supporters to capture Bodiam. In both cases it is unknown if any resistance was offered by their garrisons or if they simply surrendered. Similarly, the circumstances by which castles were occupied by the opposing sides at certain times are sometimes unclear. For example, by the winter of 1461–2 the Lancastrians had taken control of Alnwick, despite the fortress having been garrisoned by a Yorkist force of 100 men. Whether the latter surrendered immediately or if it was taken after a siege is not recorded. In other cases, it is unclear if attempts were even made to seize castles. In 1471, Thomas, Lord Stanley was provided with artillery for laying siege to Hornby held by Sir James Harrington, but the latter was still in possession of the castle three years later. In all there is evidence to suggest that a further sixteen sieges may have taken place (see Appendix B).

Yet, this is almost certainly an underestimate. Given the loss of many sources from the period it is probable that more sieges did take place. Particularly as some campaigns, such as the Yorkist invasion of Wales in 1461–2, are poorly documented. What is more, some sieges are only known from incidental references. For instance, the siege of Skipton Castle in May 1461 is only known from a single entry referring to the payment of money to Yorkist soldiers serving in the besieging army. This is recorded as an extraordinary item of expenditure in the financial accounts of the lordship of Knaresborough for 1461–2. The survival of the document itself is largely due to the lordship being part of the duchy of Lancaster, whose records have been well preserved. If it had been otherwise then the siege would have been entirely unknown.

This situation also applies to other military activities associated with castles. At least sixty-five castles in England and Wales were garrisoned at various times during the Wars of the Roses (see Appendix C), although the real figure is probably higher. Most of these garrisons were only present for short periods of time. This typically occurred when castles were threatened with attack, for instance at Pontefract in 1464, Chester in 1468, Gloucester in 1471 and Brecon in 1486. Garrisons were also installed following the occupation of newly conquered areas, such as by the Lancastrians in the Welsh Marches in 1460, or by the Yorkists in Pembrokeshire in the following year. Similarly, fears of rebellion or foreign invasion also prompted the garrisoning of castles, for instance at Wallingford and Corfe in southern England by the government of Edward IV in 1461. Sustained hostilities meant that garrisons were sometimes maintained for lengthy periods of time. Notably in the north of England in the early 1460s. Lancastrian control over much of Northumberland meant that certain castles, such as Newcastle upon Tyne and Tynemouth, needed to be kept in a defensible state by the Yorkists throughout 1461 to 1464.

Permanently garrisoned castles were comparatively rare. The only garrisons that were continually kept in existence were major royal fortresses located in Wales or on the Anglo-Scottish border. Their strategic importance meant that it was considered necessary to defend them despite the costs involved. The number of soldiers stationed in these castles was sometimes maintained at a consistent number, such as at Aberstwyth, which only ever consisted of one man-at-arms and twelve archers, but others fluctuated markedly in size. For instance, at Beaumaris, where the garrison for the town and castle varied between twenty-four and forty-eight men for much of the period. Efforts were also made to supply soldiers serving in garrisons with provisions and military equipment. For example, victuals including malt and barley were frequently transported by ship from East Anglia to Newcastle in the early 1460s, whereas 42 bows and 9,600 arrows were purchased for a force of 20 men at Pontefract in 1464. Repairs were frequently carried out to castles when threatened with attack. Building work was often focused on improving fortifications, such as at Tynemouth in the early 1460s, with the ditch scoured and cleansed, the walls repaired and large wooden shields called pavises provided for protecting the defenders. At other places, such as at Pembroke in 1461–2, work was instead carried out on repairing the residential quarters for the soldiers.

Some castles were used as headquarters by commanders during military campaigns. These tended to be the principal castles owned by specific magnates, which had the advantage of being secure bases, that also had suitable accommodation for lords and their households. This included both major and minor operations. In 1459, the Yorkist lords planned their rebellion against Henry VI from their main strongholds: Richard, duke of York, from Ludlow and Richard Neville, earl of Salisbury, from Middleham. Similarly, Kenilworth was used as a base for royalist operations throughout the 1450s and up until 1460. Occupied castles were occasionally used in this way, with Warwick basing himself at Warkworth whilst overseeing the sieges of nearby Alnwick, Bamburgh and Dunstanburgh in late 1462. Small-scale operations were also conducted from fortresses. William, Lord Herbert, sent a contingent of 200 men from Raglan to take Carreg Cennen in 1462, whereas John, Lord Howard, operated from Holt in 1463–4 with a force of 1,200 men.

How effective was the military performance of castles during the Wars of the Roses? On a superficial level they appear to have been relatively ineffectual. Most sieges resulted in garrisons surrendering under terms, with lengthy sieges comparatively rare. Only on a few occasions were defenders able to successfully hold out against attackers. On other occasions, such as Pembroke in 1461, garrisons even capitulated without offering any resistance, despite being able to rely on strong fortifications and ample provisions. Why was this the case? The defences of castles were rarely breached by artillery and very few were taken through assault. In some instances, this was because garrisons surrendered before this could occur. However, fortifications were capable of withstanding gunfire. This included major fortresses, such as Norham in 1463, but also places that were little more than fortified manor houses, such as Powderham in 1455.

Instead, it seems that poor morale and a lack of provisions often prompted defenders to yield. This typically occurred when there was little prospect of being rescued by a friendly army. The prolonged resistance put up by a small number of garrisons in these circumstances is therefore remarkable, notably at Denbigh in 1460, following the Yorkist debacle at Ludford Bridge, and Carisbrooke in 1460–1, after the Lancastrian defeat at the Battle of Northampton. Furthermore, the widespread garrisoning of castles implies that commanders regarded them as being useful. Therefore, they could be, and sometimes were, effectively used in warfare.

Yet, castles were clearly more important in certain phases of the Wars of the Roses as opposed to others. This is particularly apparent during warfare in the 1450s and 1460s. There were numerous sieges, with control of castles playing a key role in many of the campaigns, noticeably in Wales in 1461–2 and the north of England in 1461–4. This is in stark contrast to the latter stages of the Wars of the Roses. There were few sieges during the campaigns of 1469–71 and 1485, with military operations focused almost entirely on battles. This was because castles were more useful in certain types of warfare as opposed to others. The conflicts that made up the Wars of the Roses were different in their nature and duration. Castles were most valuable in sustained periods of warfare that involved controlling and contesting territory. This meant that they were less useful in dynastic conflicts of a short duration that were decided on the battlefield. The era of the Wars of the Roses was unusual for the number and frequency with which battles took place. It is for this reason that castles played a minor role in certain phases, as opposed to any diminution in their intrinsic military value.

Furthermore, their importance was not merely limited to their use in warfare. The ownership of castles continued to be highly prized by the landowning elite. This was not just due to their economic value, as estate centres, but also because of their symbolic significance. They were a visual demonstration of the wealth and power of their possessors. It was therefore unsurprising that members of the aristocracy actively sought to acquire castles, which sometimes brought them into conflict with other landowners. Disputes over the ownership of castles contributed to the development of feuds between the magnates, particularly in the 1440s and 1450s. These disagreements in turn contributed to the outbreak of civil war. For instance, Percy attempts to regain their ancestral castle of Wressle brought them into conflict with the Neville earls of Salisbury and Warwick. The use of violence to resolve disputes over these buildings also occurred in the reign of Edward IV, notably during periods of crisis, such as at Caister in 1469.

Castles were also an important source of patronage to the monarchy. Kings were expected to reward their supporters with grants of lands and titles, which included castles and offices, such as constableships. The acquisition of power, whether through the accession of new kings, such as Edward IV, or by men who appropriated royal authority, such as Richard, duke of York, was typically accompanied by the widespread distribution of resources. They often had the means to do so, at least in part, through the seizure of estates confiscated from rebels. These grants also helped to secure royal influence in different parts of the kingdom. This can be seen with Edward IV who made a concerted effort to build up the power of his favourites in the localities. William Herbert essentially became the king's viceroy in Wales, whereas the Neville brothers were initially dominant in the north of England, and thereafter Edward's brother, Richard, duke of Gloucester. Castle-building continued to be carried out, albeit on a comparatively minor scale. The construction of new castles, such as by William, Lord Hastings, at Kirby Muxloe, was rare. Nevertheless, major programmes of works were carried out on existing sites, such as by William, Lord Herbert, at Raglan and Edward IV at Nottingham. Efforts were also made to repair these structures and to keep them in good condition. The decline of the castle has therefore been exaggerated, at least in relation to the Wars of the Roses.

Appendix A

Brief Biographies of Key Figures

BASTARD OF FAUCONBERG, Thomas Neville (d. 1471). He was an illegitimate son of William Neville, earl of Kent (d. 1463). In 1471, Fauconberg led an army against the city of London in the name of Henry VI, but after a three-day siege was routed by the defenders.[1]

BONVILLE, William, first Baron Bonville (1392–1461). William was an important landowner in south-west England, who became involved in a bitter rivalry with Thomas **Courtenay**, earl of Devon, throughout the 1440s and 1450s. He was besieged in Taunton Castle by the latter in 1450, and later fought a pitched battle against him at Clyst Bridge five years later. Bonville was executed following the Lancastrian victory at the Second Battle of St Albans in 1461.[2]

BOURCHIER, Henry, first earl of Essex (*c.* 1408–83). He inherited the title of Baron Bourchier in 1433 and was later rewarded for his military service in France by being elevated to the rank of viscount. Bourchier was related to two prominent magnates, his half-brother, Humphrey Stafford, duke of **Buckingham**, and his brother-in-law, Richard, duke of **York**, having married the latter's sister, Anne, in 1426. He joined the Yorkist cause in 1460 and was created earl of Essex by his nephew **Edward IV** in the following year. In 1471, he played an important role in the defence of London against the forces of the **Bastard of Fauconberg**.[3]

BUCKINGHAM, Henry Stafford, second duke of (1455–83). He was the grandson and heir of Humphrey Stafford, first duke of **Buckingham** (d. 1460), his own father, also called Humphrey, having died in 1458. Buckingham played an important part in the accession of Richard, duke of Gloucester, to the throne in 1483. Yet, he soon turned against **Richard III** and was executed for his involvement in a failed rebellion against him later that year.[4]

BUCKINGHAM, Humphrey Stafford, first duke of (1402–60). Buckingham was one of the wealthiest magnates in the kingdom, with widespread estates throughout England and Wales. He had extensive military experience from serving in France during the later stages of the Hundred Years

War. Buckingham remained loyal to **Henry VI** and was wounded fighting in his service at the First Battle of St Albans in 1455. He later commanded the royal army at the Battle of Northampton in 1460 and was killed during the combat.[5]

BUTLER, James, first earl of Wiltshire and fifth earl of Ormond (1420–61). Butler was a major landowner in southern Ireland who also held many estates throughout England. He became aligned with the Lancastrian faction in the 1450s but developed a reputation for cowardice for his conduct in warfare, such as at the battles of First St Albans and Mortimer's Cross. Later in 1461, following the Battle of Towton, he was captured and executed by the Yorkists.[6]

CADE, Jack (d. 1450). A rebel leader known as the 'Captain of Kent' who briefly seized control of London before being killed in 1450.[7]

CECILY, duchess of York (1415–95). She was a daughter of Ralph Neville, first earl of Westmorland (d. 1425), who married Richard, duke of **York**, in 1429. Cecily gave birth to twelve children, two of whom became kings as **Edward IV** and **Richard III**.[8]

CHARLES THE BOLD, duke of Burgundy (1433–77). He was the powerful ruler of a semi-autonomous territory, which included the wealthy and economically advanced Low Countries. His rivalry with the French king, **Louis XI**, led him to allying himself with **Edward IV**, which included marrying the latter's sister, Margaret.[9]

CLARENCE, George, duke of (1449–78). George was created as duke of Clarence by his older brother, **Edward IV**, in 1461, who granted him extensive estates. However, he later rebelled against the latter, in alliance with his cousin, Richard Neville, earl of **Warwick**. This led to Edward IV being forced to flee the realm and the restoration of **Henry VI** in 1470. In the following year, the former invaded England and regained power. Clarence reconciled himself with his brother prior to the Battle of Barnet and returned to his allegiance. Yet, the two men later fell out once again. This led to Clarence being put on trial for treason, with his execution taking place in the Tower of London in February 1478.[10]

CLIFFORD, John, ninth Baron Clifford (1435–61). He was the son and heir of his father, Thomas, eighth baron **Clifford**, who was killed at the First Battle of St Albans. Clifford was given the lordship of Penrith in December 1459, which had been forfeited by Richard Neville, earl of **Salisbury**. Even after the Yorkist victory at the Battle of Northampton in the following year, he refused to surrender the castle to Salisbury. Clifford subsequently fought on the Lancastrian side at the battles of Wakefield and St Albans, before being slain at Ferrybridge.[11]

CLIFFORD, Thomas, eighth Baron Clifford (*c.* 1414–55). Clifford was a prominent landowner in northern England who held the baronies of Westmorland and Skipton in Craven. He was an ally of the Percy family, who shared his enmity towards Richard Neville, earl of **Salisbury**. Clifford was killed fighting on the Lancastrian side at the First Battle of St Albans in 1455.[12]

COURTENAY, Thomas, thirteenth earl of Devon (1414–58). The son and heir of Hugh Courtenay, twelfth earl of Devon (d. 1422). His rivalry with another prominent landowner in the south-west of England, William, Lord **Bonville**, led to the outbreak of a private war in 1450, which culminated in the siege of Taunton Castle. He joined forces with Richard, duke of **York**, for his campaigns of 1452 and 1455. In the latter year, he laid siege to Powderham Castle, owned by his cousin, Sir Philip Courtenay, and fought a pitched battle with the forces of Bonville at Clyst Bridge. Courtenay subsequently reverted to the allegiance of **Henry VI** prior to his death by natural causes at Abingdon Abbey in 1458.[13]

COURTENAY, Thomas, fourteenth earl of Devon (1432–61). Eldest son of the thirteenth **Courtenay** earl of Devon, who was a prominent supporter of the Lancastrian cause and fought on their side at the battles of Wakefield and Second St Albans. He was injured at the Battle of Towton and a short time later was executed at York on 3 April 1461.[14]

CROMWELL, Ralph, third Baron Cromwell (1393–1456). A prominent landowner in the Midlands, who served as treasurer of England from 1433–43. Cromwell became involved in a violent dispute with his neighbour, William **Tailboys**, in 1449, and in the following year played a part in the impeachment of the king's favourite, William de la Pole, duke of **Suffolk**.[15]

DEVEREUX, Walter, first Baron Ferrers of Chartley (*c.* 1432–85). He was the son and heir of Sir Walter Devereux (1411–59), a prominent landowner in Herefordshire and a retainer of Richard, duke of **York**. Devereux fought on the Yorkist side at the Battle of Towton and was knighted by **Edward IV**. The latter raised him to the baronage later that year by granting him his deceased father-in-law's title of Baron Ferrers of Chartley. Devereux subsequently played a prominent role in asserting Yorkist authority in Wales in the following years. He was later killed fighting for **Richard III** at the Battle of Bosworth in 1485.[16]

EDMUND TUDOR, earl of Richmond (*c.* 1430–56). He was the eldest son of a Welsh gentleman, **Owen Tudor** (*c.* 1400–61), and Catherine of Valois (1401–37), widow of Henry V. Edmund was therefore the half-brother of **Henry VI**. The latter granted him the title of earl of Richmond in 1452 and knighted him early in the following year. Edmund was sent to assert royal authority in Wales in 1455 but was captured at Carmarthen Castle in the following year by **William Herbert** and Sir Walter Devereux. Edmund was soon released, but a short time later died of the plague. His widow, Margaret Beaufort, subsequently gave birth to his son, Henry, who became King **Henry VII** in 1485.[17]

EDWARD IV, king of England (1442–83). He was the eldest son of Richard, duke of **York**, and **Cecily**, duchess of York, who acquired his father's title of earl of March in around 1445. Edward's victories at the battles of Mortimer's Cross and Towton in 1461, allowed him to gain the throne. The alienation of his principal supporter, Richard Neville, earl of **Warwick**, led to his deposition and flight overseas to the territories of his brother-in-law, **Charles the Bold**, duke of Burgundy, in 1470. Edward invaded the realm in the following year with Burgundian support and re-gained power after defeating his enemies at the battles of Barnet and Tewkesbury. He later died unexpectedly of an illness in 1483.[18]

EDWARD OF WESTMINSTER, prince of Wales (1453–71). He was the only son and heir of **Henry VI** and **Margaret of Anjou**. The over-throw of his father by the Yorkists meant that Edward spent much of his life as an exile in Scotland and France. He was later killed either during or immediately after the Battle of Tewkesbury in 1471.[19]

EGREMONT, Thomas Percy, first Baron Egremont (1422–60). He was a younger son of Henry Percy, second earl of **Northumberland** (d. 1455), who was granted the title of Baron Egremont by **Henry VI** in 1449. His family's bitter rivalry with the Nevilles meant that Egremont was frequently involved in disturbances in the north of England throughout the 1450s. He was later killed fighting on the Lancastrian side at the Battle of Northampton in 1460.[20]

ELIZABETH WOODVILLE, queen of England (*c.* 1437–92). Elizabeth was a daughter of Richard **Woodville** (later first Earl Rivers) and Jaquetta de Luxembourg, dowager duchess of Bedford. Her first husband, Sir John Grey, was killed fighting on the Lancastrian side at the Second Battle of St Albans in 1461, but three years later she married **Edward IV** in secret. Her children by her second marriage included two sons, who later became Edward V and Richard, duke of York, and five daughters, one of whom, also called Elizabeth, later married **Henry VII**.[21]

EXETER, Henry Holland, second duke of (1430–75). He was a relative of King **Henry VI** as his grandmother Elizabeth (d. 1425) was a sister to Henry IV. Exeter also had strong links to the Yorkists, through his marriage in 1445 to Anne, the eldest daughter of Richard, duke of **York**. He fought on the Lancastrian side in many of the campaigns of the 1460s and was badly wounded fighting in Warwick's army at the Battle of Barnet in 1471. Exeter was spared by his brother-in-law, **Edward IV**, but four years later drowned at sea, possibly through foul play, whilst returning from the expedition to France.[22]

FASTOLF, Sir John (1380–1459). Fastolf came from a minor Norfolk gentry family, who made an advantageous match with Millicent, daughter to Robert, Lord Tiptoft, in 1409. His successful military service in France during the Hundred Years War brought him great wealth, which he invested in the construction of Caister Castle in Norfolk.[23]

GREY, Edmund, first earl of Kent (1416–90). He succeeded his grandfather, Reynold Grey, to the barony of Ruthin in 1440. Grey was frequently present at the royal councils of **Henry VI** in the later 1450s, but his defection to the Yorkists played a crucial role in their victory at the Battle of Northampton in 1460. He was later created as earl of Kent by **Edward IV** in 1465, soon after the marriage of his oldest son, Anthony, to the king's sister-in-law, Joan Woodville.[24]

HARRINGTON, Sir James (d. 1485). Harrington came from a prominent gentry family of Lancashire, which adhered to the Yorkist cause. He became embroiled in a bitter custody dispute over the ownership of Hornby Castle, which he held against Thomas, Lord **Stanley**. He later died in 1485, most probably at the Battle of Bosworth.[25]

HASTINGS, William, first Baron Hastings (*c.* 1430–83). Hastings became a close friend of **Edward IV**, who served his royal master loyally on military campaigns and on diplomatic missions. The king granted him the title of Baron Hastings in 1461 and he later held the office of chamberlain of England and the lieutenancy of Calais. Later in 1483, following the death of Edward IV, he was unexpectedly arrested and executed without trial by Richard, duke of Gloucester, at the Tower of London.[26]

HENRY VI, king of England (1421–71). Henry became king at a young age following the death of his father, Henry V, in 1422. He was the husband of **Margaret of Anjou** and father to **Edward of Westminster**. His health problems and style of government contributed to the outbreak of civil war in the 1450s. He was captured by the Yorkists at the Battle of Northampton in 1460 but was freed by his supporters at the Second Battle of St Albans in 1461. The victory of **Edward IV** at the Battle of Towton later that year meant that he was forced to flee into exile in Scotland. He was eventually captured by the Yorkists in 1465, having spent some time in Northumberland. Henry was briefly freed from captivity by Richard Neville, earl of **Warwick**, five years later, who ostensibly restored him to power. Yet, following Edward's triumphant return to England he was murdered in the Tower in 1471.[27]

HENRY VII, king of England, also known as Henry Tudor (1457–1509). He was the only child of **Edmund Tudor**, earl of Richmond, and Margaret Beaufort. Following his father's death in 1456, he was first brought up by his uncle, **Jasper Tudor**, earl of Pembroke, and then afterwards by William **Herbert** at Raglan Castle. Following the overthrow of **Edward IV** in 1470, he was reunited with his uncle, Jasper, who took him into exile in Brittany after the Lancastrian defeat in 1471. Henry later received French military assistance for an invasion of England. In 1485, he invaded the realm and became king after defeating **Richard III** at the Battle of Bosworth.[28]

HERBERT, William, first earl of Pembroke (*c.* 1423–69). A prominent member of the gentry of south Wales and the Marches, who secured spectacular advancement through his service to the Yorkist cause. He was a retainer of Richard, duke of **York**, who was knighted by **Henry VI** in 1452. Four years later, he and his associate, Sir Walter Devereux, led an army into Wales and arrested the king's half-brother, **Edmund Tudor**, earl of Richmond. Herbert was raised to the baronage by **Edward IV** in 1461 and played a seminal role in the Yorkist conquest of Wales. In recognition of his services, the king granted him the earldom of Pembroke in 1468, which made him the premier magnate in Wales. However, only a year later, he was later captured and executed following the Battle of Edgecote.[29]

HERBERT, William, second earl of Pembroke (1455–90). He was the son and heir of William **Herbert**, first earl of Pembroke. Herbert inherited his father's earldom of Pembroke in 1469 but was forced to exchange it for the earldom of Huntingdon by Edward IV in 1479.[30]

HOWARD, John, first duke of Norfolk (d. 1485). He was a prominent landowner in East Anglia and a relative of John **Mowbray**, fourth duke of Norfolk. Howard fought for **Edward IV** at the Battle of Towton in 1461 and was knighted after his coronation. Subsequently he served in military campaigns against the Lancastrians in the north of England and in Wales in the 1460. Howard was later raised to the baronage by the king in 1470. In 1483, **Richard III** granted him the title of duke of Norfolk, and he was killed fighting on his side at the Battle of Bosworth two years later.[31]

HUNGERFORD, Robert, third Baron Hungerford (*c*. 1423–64). He was summoned to Parliament as Baron Moleyns in 1445 and fourteen years later inherited his father's title as Baron Hungerford. He stayed loyal to **Henry VI** upon the outbreak of civil war and held the Tower of London with Thomas, Lord **Scales**, in his name in 1460. Hungerford was later captured following the Battle of Hexham and was executed at Newcastle on 18 May 1464.[32]

JAMES III, king of Scots (1452–88). He was the eldest son of James II, king of Scots (d. 1460), and Mary of Gueldres (d. 1463). The death of his father at the siege of Roxburgh Castle in 1460 meant that he ascended to the throne at a young age. During his minority, the Scots offered military assistance to the Lancastrians but later came to terms with the Yorkist king, **Edward IV**. James pursued a policy of peace with England, but nevertheless war broke out in 1480, which resulted in the English recovery of Berwick-upon-Tweed two years later.[33]

JASPER TUDOR, duke of Bedford (*c*. 1431–95). He was the second eldest son of **Owen Tudor** and younger brother of **Edmund Tudor**. His half-brother, **Henry VI**, granted him the title of earl of Pembroke in 1452. Following the death of his brother Edmund in 1456, Jasper played a leading role in maintaining royal influence in Wales until 1461, when he was defeated at the Battle of Mortimer's Cross. He thereafter fought against the Yorkists in the north of England and Wales throughout the 1460s. Jasper returned to the realm following the restoration of Henry VI to power in 1470. Yet, only a year later, he was forced to flee to Brittany, along with his nephew, due to the triumphant return of **Edward IV**. Following the victory of **Henry VII** at the Battle of Bosworth in 1485, he was created as duke of Bedford.[34]

LOUIS XI, king of France (1423–83). In 1461 Louis succeeded his father, Charles VII, as king of France. He provided both financial and military assistance to Lancastrian exiles in the 1460s and early 1470s. Louis later came to terms with **Edward IV** with the Treaty of Picquigny concluded in 1475.[35]

MARGARET, queen of England (1430–82). She was a daughter of René, duke of Anjou, and Isabelle of Lorraine. Margaret married **Henry VI** and was crowned as queen of England in 1445. She played a prominent role in promoting the Lancastrian cause following the outbreak of civil war with the Yorkists. Margaret secured Scottish and French military assistance for campaigns in the north of England in the early 1460s but was ultimately defeated. She was captured by the Yorkists following the Battle of Tewkesbury in 1471 and was imprisoned in the Tower of London. In 1475, her ransom was paid by the king of France, **Louis XI**, and she was released into his custody.[36]

MONTAGU, John Neville, marquess of (*c.* 1431–71). He was the third son of Richard Neville, earl of **Salisbury**, and younger brother to Richard Neville, earl of **Warwick**. Montagu was knighted by **Henry VI** in 1453, but later joined his relatives in rebelling against the king. Together with his brother Warwick, he played a prominent role in suppressing Lancastrian rebellions in northern England in the early 1460s. **Edward IV** rewarded him through granting him the title of Baron Montagu in 1461, the earldom of Northumberland in 1464 and the marquess of Montagu in 1470. However, he became alienated from the king and played an important part in his overthrow. Montagu was subsequently defeated and killed, along with Warwick, at the Battle of Barnet in 1471.[37]

MOWBRAY, John, third duke of Norfolk (1415–61). He was a prominent landowner in East Anglia who was an opponent of the king's favourite, William de la Pole, duke of **Suffolk**. Mowbray initially remained loyal to **Henry VI**, but after the Battle of Northampton in 1460, he defected to the Yorkists, and fought on their side at the battles of Second St Albans and Towton in 1461.[38]

MOWBRAY, John, fourth duke of Norfolk (1444–76). He was the son and heir of John **Mowbray**, third duke of Norfolk. In 1451, **Henry VI** granted him the title of earl of Surrey and Warrene, and ten years later he inherited the dukedom of Norfolk from his father. Mowbray was a consistent supporter of **Edward IV** throughout his lifetime. He participated in military campaigns against Lancastrian rebels in the north of England and in Wales in the 1460s, and later fought in the Yorkist army at the Battle of Tewkesbury in 1471.[39]

NEVILLE, George, archbishop of York (1432–76). He was the fourth son of Richard Neville, earl of **Salisbury**, and a younger brother of Richard Neville, earl of **Warwick**, and John Neville, marquess of **Montagu**. Neville became bishop of Exeter in 1458 and seven years later archbishop of York. He was appointed as chancellor of England by **Edward IV** in

1461 but was removed from office six years later. During the Readeption of **Henry VI**, the chancellorship was restored to him, but he was imprisoned following the restoration of Edward in 1471.[40]

NEVILLE, Sir Humphrey (*c.* 1439–69). He was the eldest son of Sir Thomas Neville and the nephew of Ralph Neville, earl of **Westmorland** (d. 1484). Neville fought on the Lancastrian side during the Wars of the Roses. He was captured by the Yorkists in 1461 and imprisoned in the Tower of London, but succeeded in escaping two years later. Neville re-joined the Lancastrians in 1464 and went on the run after their defeat the Battle of Hexham. He remained at large until 1469, when he was captured and executed by the forces of **Edward IV** and Richard Neville, earl of **Warwick**.[41]

NORTHUMBERLAND, Henry Percy, second earl of (1394–1455). He was the son and heir of Henry 'Hotspur' Percy, who was in turn the eldest son of Henry Percy, first earl of Northumberland. The rebellion and forfeiture of these men meant that he spent most of the early years of his life in Scotland. He was permitted to return to England by Henry V who restored the earldom to him in 1416. Northumberland succeeded in regaining much of his family's influence in the north of England but later became involved in a fierce rivalry with Richard Neville, earl of **Salisbury**, and the latter's son, Richard Neville, earl of **Warwick**. He was killed fighting on the Lancastrian side at the First Battle of St Albans in 1455.[42]

NORTHUMBERLAND, Henry Percy, third earl of (1421–61). He was the son and heir of Henry Percy, second earl of **Northumberland** (d. 1455). Northumberland was a prominent supporter of **Henry VI** during the Wars of the Roses. He rallied resistance against the Yorkists after their victory at the Battle of Northampton in 1460, which resulted in the capture of the king. Northumberland played a prominent role in leading the Lancastrians to victory at the battles of Wakefield and Second St Albans but was later killed at the Battle of Towton.[43]

NORTHUMBERLAND, Henry Percy, fourth earl of (*c.* 1449–89). He was the son and heir of Henry Percy, third earl of **Northumberland** (d. 1461). Following the death of his father at the Battle of Towton, he suffered the forfeiture of his lands, but was later restored to his earldom by **Edward IV** in 1470. The latter was forced to flee overseas a short time later but invaded the realm in the following year. Northumberland's decision to remain neutral during the campaign proved to be crucial in the success of Edward in regaining his throne. Later in 1483, he supported the takeover of power by Richard, duke of Gloucester. Northumberland accompanied **Richard III** to the Battle of Bosworth two years later but failed to intervene with his forces. He was subsequently pardoned by the new king, **Henry VII**, and organised the defence of York against the forces of Lambert Simnel in 1487.[44]

PERCY, Sir Ralph (1425–64). He was a younger son of Henry Percy, second earl of **Northumberland** (d. 1455). Percy was active on the Lancastrian side in the Wars of the Roses and held the important castle of Dunstanburgh in Northumberland. He surrendered the castle after a siege to the Yorkists and swore allegiance to **Edward IV** in 1462. Yet, he soon defected back to the cause of **Henry VI** and was killed at the Battle of Hexham in 1464.[45]

RICHARD III, king of England (1452–85). He was the youngest son of Richard, duke of **York**, and **Cecily**, duchess of York, who survived infancy, and a younger brother of **Edward IV** and George, duke of **Clarence**. Edward IV granted him the title of duke of Gloucester and knighted him in 1461. Unlike his brother, Clarence, he remained loyal to Edward IV, and went into exile with him when the latter was overthrown in 1470. Following Edward's restoration to power a year later, he became a leading magnate in the north of England. Gloucester acted as the king's lieutenant during the war with Scotland from 1480–2 and recaptured Berwick-upon-Tweed. Following Edward's death in 1483, he imprisoned his nephews, Edward V and Richard, duke of York, and was crowned king as Richard III. Two years later he was defeated and killed at the Battle of Bosworth.[46]

SALISBURY, Richard Neville, fifth earl of (1400–60). He was the eldest son of Ralph Neville, first earl of Westmorland, by his second marriage, and therefore a half-brother of Ralph Neville, second earl of **Westmorland**. Salisbury's children included Richard Neville, earl of **Warwick**, John Neville, Marquess **Montagu**, and George **Neville**, archbishop of York. He was one of the wealthiest magnates in the north of England, who inherited his title as earl of Salisbury from his father-in-law, Thomas Montagu, in 1428, and was a rival of the Percy family. Salisbury was a close ally of Richard, duke of **York**, and joined forces with him at the First Battle of St Albans in 1455. Four years later, he was forced to flee overseas following a stand-off with the royal army at Ludford Bridge. Early in the following year, Salisbury was one of the Yorkist lords who invaded England. The Lancastrians were defeated at the Battle of Northampton and **Henry VI** was captured. Salisbury accompanied York on his expedition to the north of England in late December 1460 and was killed with him at the Battle of Wakefield.[47]

SCALES, Thomas, seventh Baron Scales (1399–1460). He inherited the title of Baron Scales following the death of his older brother, Robert, in 1419. Scales had extensive military service in France during the Hundred Years War. He helped defend the Tower of London against the rebels of Jack **Cade** in 1450 and remained loyal to **Henry VI** upon the outbreak of civil war with the Yorkists. In 1460, he led the defence of the Tower against the Yorkists but was killed after trying to flee the castle.[48]

SOMERSET, Edmund Beaufort, first duke of (*c.* 1406–55). A royal favourite of his cousin **Henry VI**, who granted him the title of duke in 1448. Somerset was blamed for the rapid English expulsion from Normandy over the following two years. He thereby incurred the enmity of Richard, duke of **York**, and was killed fighting on the Lancastrian side at the First Battle of St Albans in 1455.[49]

SOMERSET, Edmund Beaufort, third duke of (*c.* 1438–71). He was the second eldest son of Edmund, first duke of **Somerset**, who was placed in command of Carisbrooke Castle in the Isle of Wight in 1460. Following the capture of the castle by the Yorkists in the following year, he was imprisoned in the Tower of London. He re-joined the Lancastrian side following his release in 1463, but after their defeat at the Battle of Hexham, in 1464, fled into exile in France. In 1471, Somerset returned to England during the Readeption of **Henry VI**, but was executed after being removed from sanctuary following the Yorkist victory at the Battle of Tewkesbury.[50]

SOMERSET, Henry Beaufort, second duke of (1436–64). He was the eldest son of Edmund, first duke of **Somerset**, who succeeded to the dukedom following the death of his father at the First Battle of St Albans in 1455, where he himself was badly wounded. Somerset was a prominent Lancastrian commander during the military campaigns of 1460–1, who fled into exile in Scotland following their defeat at the Battle of Towton. He later participated in **Margaret of Anjou's** expedition to Northumberland, where he was placed in command of Bamburgh Garrison. On 26 December 1462 he surrendered the castle to the Yorkist besiegers and pledged his allegiance to **Edward IV**. Despite the efforts of the latter to win him over, he soon reverted to the Lancastrian cause. Somerset was later executed following the Yorkist victory at the Battle of Hexham on 15 May 1464.[51]

STAFFORD, Humphrey, earl of Devon (*c.* 1439–69). He was a notable member of the Somerset and Dorset gentry, who fought for **Edward IV** at the Battle of Towton in 1461. Stafford was knighted at the king's coronation and a short time later was raised to the baronage as Lord Stafford of Southwick. The grant of most of the forfeited estates of the Courtenay earls of Devon was followed by his elevation to the earldom of Devon in 1469. Only a short time later, however, he was captured and executed following the Battle of Edgecote.[52]

STANLEY, Thomas, first earl of Derby (*c*. 1433–1504). He was the eldest son of Thomas Stanley, first Baron Stanley (d. 1459) and older brother to Sir William **Stanley** (d. 1495). Stanley avoided participating in the battles of Blores Heath (1459) and Northampton (1460) but following the victory of **Edward IV** at Towton (1461) openly supported the new king. He served in military campaigns against the Lancastrians in the north of England in the 1460s. Stanley supported the Readeption government of **Henry VI** but was pardoned by Edward IV following the latter's restoration to power in 1471. Stanley assembled an army in 1485 but refrained from joining forces with either **Richard III** or Henry Tudor. The intervention of his younger brother, Sir William Stanley, proved to be crucial to the victory of the latter at the Battle of Bosworth. On 27 October 1485, his son-in-law, the newly crowned **Henry VII**, granted him the title of earl of Derby.[53]

STANLEY, Sir William (*c*. 1435–95). He was a younger son of Thomas Stanley, first Baron Stanley (d. 1459) and younger brother to Thomas **Stanley**, first earl of Derby (d. 1504). Stanley was active on the Yorkist side during the Wars of the Roses and served in military campaigns against the Lancastrians in Wales and the north of England in the 1460s. He later played a seminal role in the victory of Henry Tudor at the Battle of Bosworth in 1485. In recognition of his services, the newly crowned **Henry VII** appointed him as chamberlain of the king's household later that year.[54]

SUFFOLK, William de la Pole, first duke of (1396–1450). He inherited his older brother's title of earl of Suffolk in 1415. Suffolk was a favourite of **Henry VI**, who played a prominent role in his government and was raised to the rank of duke in 1448. Suffolk's unpopularity meant that he was sent into exile and was murdered at sea two years later.[55]

TAILBOYS, Sir William (*c*. 1416–64). He was a notable landowner in Lincolnshire who became involved in a fierce rivalry with Ralph, Lord **Cromwell**, in 1449. Tailboys was active in fighting for the Lancastrian cause during the campaigns of the 1450s and 1460s and was captured and executed following the Battle of Hexham in 1464.[56]

TIPTOFT, John, first earl of Worcester (1427–70). He inherited his father's title as Baron Tiptoft in 1443 and was later created as earl of Worcester in 1449. Tiptoft's first marriage to Cecily (d. 1450), daughter of Richard Neville, earl of **Salisbury**, helped cement his links to the Yorkists. He went to Italy in 1458 and did not return to England until September 1461. The new king, **Edward IV**, was favourably disposed towards him and bestowed grants including the office of constable of England. Tiptoft served in military campaigns against the Lancastrians in the north of England and Wales in the 1460s. He acquired a reputation for cruelty due to his decision to add the punishment of impalement to men found guilty of treason in 1470. Following the flight of Edward IV later that year, he was captured, put on trial and executed.[57]

TUDOR, Sir Owen (*c.* 1400–61). He was the second husband of Catherine of Valois, the widow of Henry V, and the father of **Edmund Tudor** and **Jasper Tudor**. Owen was captured and executed following the Battle of Mortimer's Cross in 1461.[58]

VAUGHAN, Sir Roger (d. 1471). He was from a notable gentry family that mostly held estates in east Wales and Herefordshire. Vaughan played an important part in asserting Yorkist authority in Wales in the 1460s but was defeated and executed by **Jasper Tudor** at Chepstow in 1471.[59]

WARWICK, Richard Neville, sixteenth earl of (1428–71). He was the eldest son and heir of Richard Neville, earl of **Salisbury**, and older brother of John Neville, Marquess **Montagu**, and George **Neville**, archbishop of York. In 1445, he was knighted by **Henry VI** and four years later was granted the title of heir of Warwick. Warwick was a prominent Yorkist commander during the Wars of the Roses who skilfully exploited his position as captain of the Calais garrison. He fought at the battles of Northampton, Second St Albans and Towton, and so contributed to the triumph of **Edward IV** in 1461. Together with his brother Montagu, he was tasked with suppressing Lancastrian rebellions in northern England in the early 1460s. Warwick received numerous rewards from the new king and became the dominant magnate in the north of England. However, he became alienated from Edward and succeeded in overthrowing him in 1470. In the following year, the latter invaded England with Burgundian assistance, and Warwick was subsequently defeated and killed at the Battle of Barnet.[60]

WESTMORLAND, Ralph Neville, second earl of (*c.* 1407–84). He was the son and heir of Ralph Neville, first earl of Westmorland (d. 1425), one of the most important magnates in the north of England. Westmorland was a rival of his half-brother, Richard Neville, earl of **Salisbury**, but his ill health meant that he played little part in the Wars of the Roses.[61]

WOODVILLE, Anthony, second Earl Rivers (d. 1483). He was the eldest son and heir of Richard **Woodville**, first Earl Rivers. His prospects were greatly improved by the marriage of his sister, **Elizabeth Woodville**, to **Edward IV** in 1464, which made him the king's brother-in-law. Following the death of his father, he inherited his title of Earl Rivers in 1469. He played an important part in the defence of London against the rebels of the **Bastard of Fauconberg** of 1471 and was the tutor to his nephew Prince Edward (the future Edward V). Woodville was later arrested by order of Richard, duke of Gloucester, in 1483, and after being imprisoned in Pontefract Castle was executed without trial.[62]

WOODVILLE, Richard, first Earl Rivers (d. 1469). Richard came from the ranks of the Northamptonshire gentry, who gained military experience serving in France during the Hundred Years War. His status was greatly enhanced through his marriage to Jaquetta de Luxembourg, dowager duchess of Bedford. This led to his creation as Baron Rivers in 1448 and his election as a knight of the Garter two years later. He initially remained loyal to **Henry VI** and was captured by the Yorkists in Sandwich in 1460, but after the Battle of Towton submitted to **Edward IV**. The marriage of his daughter, **Elizabeth Woodville**, to the Yorkist king in 1464 led to him being raised to the rank of earl. He was later captured and executed by supporters of Richard Neville, earl of **Warwick**, following the Battle of Edgecote in 1469.[63]

YORK, Richard, third duke of (1411–60). He was a wealthy magnate who had a strong claim to the English throne. He served the Crown as lieutenant of France in the Hundred Years War, but following the French conquest of Normandy in 1450, became alienated from the government of **Henry VI**. In 1455, with his relatives and allies, Richard Neville, earl of **Salisbury**, and Richard Neville, earl of **Warwick**, he attacked the royal court at the First Battle of St Albans. York briefly became Lord Protector for a second time following the battle, with a reconciliation taking place between the two factions at a 'Loveday' in 1458. Yet, civil war broke out a year later, which resulted in the flight overseas of York and his allies after the debacle of Ludford Bridge. The Yorkists invaded the realm in 1460, with Henry VI captured at the Battle of Northampton. York attempted to claim the throne but was rebuffed in Parliament by the Lords. He was subsequently killed later that year at the Battle of Wakefield.[64]

Appendix B

Recorded and Possible Sieges, 1455–87

Aberystwyth, Cardiganshire

Possible sieges: Late summer 1456 – A Yorkist force led by Sir William Herbert and Sir Walter Devereux, said to number 2,000 men, occupied the castle, but it is unclear if a siege took place.[1]

Alnwick, Northumberland

Recorded sieges: (1) July–August 1462 – Yorkist besiegers led by William, Lord Hastings, and Sir Ralph Grey, with the Lancastrian defenders commanded by Sir William Tailboys. Siege began in July, with the garrison having surrendered by the end of the month or the beginning of August.[2] (2) Late October/November 1462 – Lancastrian besiegers compelled the Yorkist defenders to surrender after the latter ran out of provisions.[3] (3) December 1462–January 1463 – Yorkist besiegers led by William Neville, earl of Kent, and Anthony Woodville, Lord Scales. According to one source, they had a force of 10,000 men under their command, as opposed to 300 defenders. Most of the garrison escaped on 5 January, with the remainder surrendering under terms a short time later.[4]

Possible sieges: (1) Summer 1461 – Alnwick was occupied by the Yorkists by 13 September 1461, when Sir William Bowes held it with a garrison of 100 men. It is unclear if this occurred after a siege.[5] (2) Winter of 1461–2 – The Lancastrians recovered the castle during the winter of 1461–2. Bowes received wages for his garrison from 13 September to 30 November, which suggests that it may have occurred by the latter date. It is unrecorded whether a siege took place.[6] (3) May 1463 – Sir Ralph Grey, who held the constableship, defected to the Lancastrians and used deception to imprison the captain, Sir John Astley, and to seize control of the castle. It is unclear if a siege or any fighting took place.[7]

Bamburgh, Northumberland

Recorded sieges: (1) December 1462 – The siege began in early December, with the Yorkist besiegers led by John Neville, Lord Montague, and Robert, Lord Ogle. According to one source, they had a force of 10,000 men under their command, as opposed to 300 defenders led by Henry Beaufort, duke of Somerset, Jasper Tudor, earl of Pembroke, Thomas, Lord Roos, and Sir Ralph Percy. The garrison surrendered under terms on 26 December.[8] (2) Summer 1464 – Yorkist besiegers led by Richard Neville, earl of Warwick, and John Neville, earl of Northumberland, with the defenders led by Sir Ralph Grey. According to the most detailed account of the siege, the castle was eventually taken by storm.[9]

Possible sieges: October–November 1462 – The Lancastrians seized control of the castle after Queen Margaret's invasion force made landfall in Northumberland on 25 October. It is unclear if this took place after a siege.[10]

Berwick-upon-Tweed, Northumberland

Recorded sieges: (1) 1455 – A Scottish army briefly besieged Berwick, before the imminent arrival of an English relief force prompted the siege to be abandoned.[11] (2) July–August 1482 – An English army led by Richard, duke of Gloucester, began the siege of Berwick in July. The Scottish defenders, who were 500-strong, eventually surrendered under terms in August.[12]

Bodiam, East Sussex

Possible sieges: Winter 1483 – On 8 November 1483, Richard III issued orders for Thomas Howard, earl of Surrey, Sir John Broke of Cobham, Sir Thomas Echingham and others to besiege Bodiam. It is unclear if the garrison led by Sir Thomas Lewknor offered any resistance.[13]

Caister, Norfolk

Recorded sieges: 21 August–27 September 1469 – An army led by John Mowbray, duke of Norfolk, supposedly 3,000-men strong, laid siege to the castle on 21 August 1469. The defenders were said to number twenty-six men and were led by John Paston, who surrendered under terms on 27 September.[14]

Cardigan, Cardiganshire

Possible sieges: December 1469 – Richard, duke of Gloucester, was ordered to besiege Cardigan, held by Morgan and Henry ap Thomas, on 16 December. It is unclear if a siege took place.[15]

Carisbrooke, Isle of Wight

Recorded sieges: December 1460–June 1461 – Yorkist besiegers consisted of at least 125 men led by Geoffrey Gate, whereas the Lancastrian defenders led by Edmund Beaufort were approximately 60-men strong. The attackers eventually gained control of the castle in June, but it is unclear if it was taken by storm or if the garrison surrendered.[16]

Carlisle, Cumberland

Recorded sieges: (1) Probably May/June 1461 – Yorkist besiegers led by Richard Salkeld seized control of Lancastrian-held Carlisle in the late spring or early summer of 1461.[17] (2) June 1461 – A combined Scottish-Lancastrian army laid siege to the city and castle in June 1461. Carlisle was held for the Yorkists by Richard Salkeld and the civic authorities. The siege was eventually broken by a Yorkist army commanded by John, Lord Montagu, who routed the attackers.[18] (3) Spring 1470 – The citizens of Carlisle besieged the castle at the command of Edward IV, which was held for Richard Neville, earl of Warwick, by Richard Salkeld. It is unclear if it was captured through being stormed or if the garrison surrendered.[19]

Carmarthen, Carmarthenshire

Recorded sieges: Late summer 1456 – A Yorkist force led by Sir William Herbert and Sir Walter Devereux, said to number 2,000 men, captured the castle and imprisoned Edmund Tudor, earl of Richmond.[20]

Possible sieges: (1) 1455 – Gruffydd ap Nicholas was said to have seized control of the castle from its custodians in a petition dating from late 1455. It is unclear if a siege took place.[21] (2) By the summer of 1456 – Edmund Tudor, earl of Richmond, seized control of the castle from Gruffydd ap Nicholas. It is unclear if a siege took place.[22] (3) December 1469 – Richard, duke of Gloucester, was ordered to besiege Carmarthen, held by Morgan and Henry ap Thomas, on 16 December. It is unclear if a siege took place.[23]

Chirk, the lordship of Chirk

Recorded sieges: August 1461 – Yorkist besiegers led by Sir William Stanley captured the castle after a siege in August 1461.[24]

Conwy, Caernarfonshire

Recorded sieges: Winter 1461 – An undated petition (*c.* 1467–73) by Sir Robert Bold records that he captured Conwy at the king's command at an unspecified date. The context suggests that it occurred in the winter of 1461 when the Yorkists took control of the castles of north Wales, except for Harlech. This document states that an unnamed Lancastrian captain was slain during the fighting, presumably when the castle was stormed.[25]

Denbigh, the lordship of Denbigh

Recorded sieges: February–March 1460 – Lancastrian besiegers led by Jasper Tudor, earl of Pembroke, captured Yorkist-held Denbigh. It is unclear whether it was stormed or if the garrison surrendered under terms.[26]

Dunstanburgh, Northumberland

Recorded sieges: December 1462 – The siege began in early December, with the Yorkist besiegers led by John Tiptoft, earl of Worcester, and Sir Ralph Grey. According to one source, they had a force of 10,000 men under their command, as opposed to 120 defenders led by Sir Richard Tunstall and Thomas, Lord Fyndern. Serving under the latter were Thomas Carre, the captain, and Thomas Clenell, as the constable of the castle. The garrison surrendered under terms on 27 December.[27]

Possible sieges: October–November 1462: The Lancastrians seized control of the castle after Queen Margaret's invasion force made landfall in Northumberland on 25 October. It is unclear if this took place after a siege.[28]

Harlech, Merionethshire

Recorded sieges: August 1468 – Yorkist besiegers led by William, Lord Herbert, with the Lancastrian defenders commanded by Dafydd ab Ieuan ab Einion surrendering under terms on 14 August 1468.[29]

Hornby, Lancashire

Possible sieges: Spring 1471 – Instructions were given for artillery to be sent to Thomas, Lord Stanley for the siege of Hornby, which was held against him by Sir James Harrington. Yet, it is unclear if a siege took place.[30]

Kenilworth, Warwickshire

Possible sieges: Spring 1471 – The newsletter of Gerhard von Wesel claims that Edward laid siege to the castle prior to the Battle of Barnet in 1471. Yet, this claim is not verified by any other source.[31]

Kirkoswald, Cumberland

Recorded sieges: *c.* 1462 – Yorkist besiegers captured the Lancastrian-held castle in *c.* 1462. This siege is only known through a reference to the military service of Sir Thomas Lamplugh. It is probable that it took place at a similar time to the siege of nearby Naworth Castle, which occurred in July 1462.[32]

Naworth, Cumberland

Recorded sieges: July 1462 – Yorkist besiegers led by John Neville, Lord Montagu, with the Lancastrian defenders led by Sir Humphrey Dacre. The latter eventually surrendered under terms later that month.[33]

Possible sieges: Winter of 1461–2 – The Lancastrians gained control of the castle during the winter of 1461–2. It is unrecorded whether a siege took place.[34]

Norham, Norhamshire

Recorded sieges: (1) July 1463 – Scottish-Lancastrian besiegers, whose leaders included Henry VI, Queen Margaret and Pierre de Brézé, laid siege to the castle in July. After an eighteen-day siege, the Yorkist defenders were rescued by an army led by Richard Neville, earl of Warwick, and John Neville, Lord Montagu, with the attackers routed.[35] (2) Winter of 1463–4 – The Lancastrians succeeded in seizing control of the Yorkist-held castle in the winter of 1463–4. Given the fact that the castle was garrisoned this almost certainly would have taken place following a siege.[36]

Pembroke, Pembrokeshire

Recorded sieges: Late spring 1471 – Yorkist besiegers led by Morgan ap Thomas, with the Lancastrian defenders led by Jasper Tudor, earl of Pembroke. The siege was eventually broken by a relief force commanded by Thomas's brother, David, who raised a force with which to drive off his sibling's army.[37]

Powderham, Devon

Recorded sieges: 3 November–December 1455 – Besiegers led by Thomas Courtenay, earl of Devon, with a force said to have numbered 1,000 men, whereas the defenders were commanded by the owner of the castle, Sir Philip Courtenay. The siege was eventually lifted in December due to the intervention of Richard, duke of York.[38]

Rhuddlan, Flintshire

Recorded sieges: November 1461 – Sir William Stanley commanded a force of 464 men at the siege of Rhuddlan, with the Lancastrian defenders, led by Nicholas Wyrall, surrendering under terms after 13 days.[39]

Roxburgh, Roxburghshire

Recorded sieges: (1) Early 1456 – A Scottish army briefly besieged the castle in early 1456, before the imminent arrival of an English relief force prompted the siege to be abandoned.[40] (2) 20 July–3 August 1460 – A Scottish army led by James II, king of Scots, laid siege to the castle on 20 July 1460. James was killed during the siege, but the garrison eventually surrendered Roxburgh, which was then slighted.[41]

St Michael's Mount, Cornwall

Recorded sieges: Late October/November 1473–15 February 1474 – Yorkist besiegers led by Sir John Arundell, Henry Bodrugan and John Fortescu, which numbered at least 300 men. The Lancastrian defenders led by John de Vere, earl of Oxford, consisted of a force of between 80 and 400 men, who eventually surrendered under terms on 15 February 1474.[42]

Skipton, Yorkshire

Recorded sieges: (1) May 1461 – Yorkist besiegers laid siege to the Lancastrian-held castle in May 1461, which they had gained control of by the end of the month.[43] (2) Winter of 1463–4 – Lancastrian besiegers succeeded in seizing control of the Yorkist-held castle in the winter of 1463–4.[44] (3) Spring 1464 – Yorkist besiegers led by Thomas, Lord Stanley, and Sir William Stanley, captured Lancastrian-held Skipton Castle after a siege in the spring of 1464.[45]

Thorpe Waterville, Northamptonshire

Recorded sieges: March–April 1461 – Yorkist besiegers led by Sir John Wenlock began the siege in March, with the Lancastrian defenders having surrendered by 4 April.[46]

Tower of London

Recorded sieges: (1) July 1460 – Yorkist besiegers led by Thomas Neville, earl of Salisbury, and the civic authorities of London began the siege of the Tower on 2 or 3 July. The Lancastrian defenders led by Thomas, Lord Scales, and Robert, Lord Hungerford, surrendered under terms on 19 July.[47] (2) 10 April 1471 – The imprisoned supporters of Edward IV overpowered their Lancastrian guards and seized control of the castle.[48] (3) 12–14 May 1471 – Lancastrian besiegers led by Thomas Neville, otherwise known as the Bastard of Fauconberg. The defence of the city was led by the corporation of London, supported by a royal garrison stationed in the Tower led by Anthony Woodville, Earl Rivers, and Henry Bourchier, earl of Essex. After a three-day siege the attackers were driven off by the defenders.[49]

Wark, Northumberland

Recorded sieges: August 1460 – Scottish besiegers captured English-held Wark Castle, which they afterwards slighted.[50]

Warwick, Warwickshire

Possible sieges: Spring 1471 – The newsletter of Gerhard von Wesel claims that Edward laid siege to the castle prior to the Battle of Barnet in 1471. Yet, this claim is not verified by any other source.[51]

Warkworth, Northumberland

Possible sieges: (1) October/November 1462 – The Lancastrians seized control of the castle after Queen Margaret's invasion force made landfall in Northumberland on 25 October. It is unclear if this took place after a siege.[52] (2) December 1462 – The Yorkists occupied Warkworth in December, which Richard Neville, earl of Warwick, used as his campaign headquarters for the sieges of the nearby castles of Alnwick, Bamburgh and Dunstanburgh. It is unclear if this took place after a siege.[53]

Recorded Garrisons, 1455–87

Aberystwyth, Cardiganshire

Date range: 1455–87*
Details: Aberystwyth was held by a permanent garrison of one man at arms and twelve archers throughout the period. Note that the financial records only survive up until 1482 but it seems probable that the garrison continued to be maintained after that date.[1]

Alnwick, Northumberland

Date range: 1461–4
Details: 13 September–30 November 1461, held by a Yorkist garrison commanded by Sir William Bowes consisting of a force of 100 men.[2] Winter 1461–August 1462, held by a Lancastrian garrison commanded by Sir William Tailboys.[3] August–October/November 1462, held by a Yorkist garrison.[4] October/November 1462–6 January 1463, held by a Lancastrian garrison said to number 300 men.[5] 6 January–May 1463, held by a Yorkist garrison commanded by Sir Ralph Grey and Sir John Astley. This was until Grey defected to the Lancastrians in May 1463.[6] May 1463–Summer 1464, held by a Lancastrian garrison.[7]

Bamburgh, Northumberland

Date range: 1455, 1462–4
Details: 1455, held by a Lancastrian garrison of forty men commanded by a lieutenant serving under John Heron of Ford.[8] October/November–26 December 1462, held by a Lancastrian garrison of 300 men commanded by Henry Beaufort, duke of Somerset, Jasper Tudor, earl of Pembroke, Thomas, Lord Roos, and Sir Ralph Percy.[9] 26 December 1462–March 1463, held by a Yorkist garrison commanded by Sir Ralph Percy, until the latter defected to the Lancastrians in March 1463.[10] March 1463–summer 1464, held by a Lancastrian garrison commanded by Sir Ralph Percy, and afterwards by Sir Ralph Grey.[11]

Beaumaris, Anglesey

Date range: 1455–87*

Details: Beaumaris was held by a permanent garrison throughout the period, but the number of soldiers fluctuated markedly. The accounts of 1453–4 show that twenty soldiers were stationed there. Following the takeover of Beaumaris by the Yorkists in late 1461, the garrison was increased to a force of twenty-four soldiers for the castle and twenty-four soldiers for the town. This force was halved in size in 1468, after the Yorkist capture of Harlech. There is a gap in the surviving records between 1470 and 1483, but it most probably remained garrisoned during this time. In the latter year, the garrison was recorded as having consisted of twenty-four men, which had been doubled in size to forty-eight men. Two years later, it was recorded as consisting of twenty-four men.[12]

Berwick-upon-Tweed, Northumberland

Date range: 1455–87

Details: 1455–61, held by an English garrison serving under the command of the warden of the east march towards Scotland until 25 April 1461.[13] 1461–82, held by a Scottish garrison. In 1482, it consisted of a force of 500 men, which surrendered to an English army on 24 August.[14] 1482–7, held by an English garrison serving under the command of the warden of the east march towards Scotland. In 1483, this consisted of a force of 600 men led by Henry Percy, earl of Northumberland.[15]

Bodiam, East Sussex

Date range: 1483

Details: October–November 1483, held by a garrison led by Sir Thomas Lewknor in the name of Henry Tudor.[16]

Brecon, the lordship of Brecon

Date range: 1486

Details: 1486, held by a Tudor garrison of 140 men commanded by William Fisher.[17]

Bristol, Gloucestershire

Date range: 1460

Details: Winter 1460, the mayor and common council of Bristol were instructed by Richard, duke of York, to garrison the castle against the Lancastrians.[18]

Buckenham, Norfolk

Date range: 1461
Details: Held by a force of fifty men led by Alice Knyvet in the name of her husband John.[19]

Bywell, Northumberland

Date range: 1463–4
Details: Winter 1463/4–May 1464, held by a Lancastrian garrison.[20]

Caernarfon, Caernarfonshire

Date range: 1455, 1461–87*
Details: Caernarfon was garrisoned for much of the period with the number of soldiers fluctuating over time. The accounts of 1453–4 record that a contingent of twenty-five soldiers were stationed there, but these men had been disbanded by 1458. Following the Yorkist takeover of Caernarfon, a garrison of twenty-four soldiers for the castle and twelve soldiers for the town was installed. There is a gap in the surviving records between 1470 and 1483, but it most probably remained garrisoned during this time, with the accounts for 1483–7 recording that a garrison of the same size was still being maintained.[21]

Caister, Norfolk

Date range: 1469
Details: 1469, held by a garrison of twenty-six men led by John Paston.[22]

Cardigan, Cardiganshire

Date range: 1455, 1469
Details: 1455, held by the forces of Gruffydd ap Nicholas.[23] Late 1469, held by the forces of Morgan and Henry ap Thomas.[24]

Carisbrooke, Isle of Wight

Date range: 1455–65
Details: 1455–61, held by a Lancastrian garrison. In 1452, it consisted of a force of ten men-at-arms and ten archers, which was increased to ten men-at-arms and thirty archers five years later. The garrison was further augmented by the twenty men of the retinue of Edmund Beaufort, prior to its surrender to the Yorkists.[25] 1461–5, held by a Yorkist garrison of ten men-at-arms and twenty archers led by Geoffrey Gate.[26]

Carlisle, Cumberland

Date range: 1455–87
Details: Carlisle was held by a permanent garrison serving under the command of the warden of the west march towards Scotland.[27]

Carmarthen, Carmarthenshire

Date range: 1455–6, 1461–2
Details: 1455, held by the forces of Gruffydd ap Nicholas.[28] Summer 1456, held by the forces of Edmund Tudor, earl of Richmond.[29] Late summer 1456, held by a Yorkist force led by Sir William Herbert and Sir Walter Devereux.[30] October 1461–January 1462, held by a Yorkist garrison from 14 October 1461–24 January 1462. This originally consisted of eighty-four men, which was reduced to fifty-six on 7 November, thirty-eight on 30 November and thirty-four on 16 January, before being disbanded eight days later.[31] Late 1469, held by the forces of Morgan and Henry ap Thomas.[32]

Carreg Cennen, the lordship of Is Cennen

Date range: 1455, 1459–60, 1462
Details: 1455, held by the forces of Gruffydd ap Nicholas.[33] Summer 1459–60, held by a Lancastrian garrison led by John Reyner.[34] Until April 1462, held by a Lancastrian garrison led by Thomas and Owen ap Gruffydd until the end of April 1462.[35] 1 May–18 August 1462, held by a Yorkist garrison of nine men from 1 May–18 August 1462, after which the castle was slighted.[36]

Castle Rising, Norfolk

Date range: 1456, 1461
Details: 1456, held by a Lancastrian garrison led by Thomas, Lord Scales.[37] Early 1461, held by a Lancastrian garrison until the castle was taken over by a Yorkist force. It is unclear when this took place, but on 7 February 1461 the escheator for Norfolk and Suffolk, Richard Cropwell, received orders to take Castle Rising and to install a garrison there.[38]

Chester, Cheshire

Date range: 1468
Details: 1468, held by a Yorkist garrison of twenty men led by James Manley, esquire, in July 1468.[39]

Chirk, the lordship of Chirk

Date range: 1461
Details: 1461, held by a Lancastrian garrison until the surrender of the castle in September 1461.[40]

Clifford, Herefordshire

Date range: 1460
Details: From the late spring or summer of 1460, held by a Lancastrian garrison.[41]

Cockermouth, Cumberland

Date range: 1461–2
Details: December 1461–September 1462, held by a Yorkist garrison of eighty men led by Sir John Hudleston.[42]

Conwy, Caernarfonshire

Date range: 1455, 1461–87*
Details: Conwy was garrisoned for much of the period with the number of soldiers fluctuating over time. The accounts of 1453–4 record that a contingent of twenty-four soldiers was stationed there, but these men had been disbanded by 1458. Three years later, in 1461, it was held by a Lancastrian force of unknown size, before it was captured by the Yorkists. Following the takeover of Conwy, a garrison of twenty-four soldiers for the castle and twenty-four soldiers for the town were installed. This force was halved in size in 1468, after the Yorkist capture of Harlech. There is a gap in the surviving records between 1470 and 1483, but it was probably still maintained, as the accounts for the period 1483–7 record that a garrison of twenty-four men was retained for the castle and town.[43]

Corfe, Dorset

Date range: 1461–2
Details: July–December 1461, held by a Yorkist garrison of thirty men led by William Rastryk for twenty-two weeks.[44] December 1462, held by a Yorkist garrison of unspecified size led by William Rastryk.[45]

Denbigh, the lordship of Denbigh

Date range: 1460–1, 1483
Details: 1460, held by a Yorkist garrison until the spring of 1460.[46] 1460–1, held by a Lancastrian garrison led by Roger Puleston until at least

July 1461. It is unclear when the Yorkists gained control of the castle and if they garrisoned it afterwards.[47] 1483, held by a Yorkist garrison of twelve men led by Thomas Salesbury.[48]

Dunstanburgh, Northumberland

Date range: 1462–4, 1470
Details: October/November–27 December 1462, held by a Lancastrian garrison of 120 defenders commanded by Sir Richard Tunstall and Thomas, Lord Fyndern. Serving under the latter were Thomas Carre, the captain, and Thomas Clenell, as the constable of the castle.[49] 27 December 1462–March 1463, held by a Yorkist garrison commanded by Sir Ralph Percy, until the latter defected to the Lancastrians in March 1463.[50] March 1463–summer 1464, held by a Lancastrian garrison commanded by Sir Ralph Percy.[51] 1470, held by a Yorkist garrison serving under the orders of Henry Percy, earl of Northumberland.[52]

Durham, County Durham

Date range: 1459, 1464
Details: 1459, the north gate of the castle was held for the bishop of Durham, Lawrence Booth, by its keeper, Ade Frithbank, with two men from 14–16 November. For the last two days, the garrison was reinforced by Thomas Claxton, esquire, with fifteen of his men.[53] 1464, held by a Yorkist garrison. This is only known from a reference to a payment to Reginald Newton who was serving as one of the king's soldiers in the garrison.[54]

Flint, Flintshire

Date range: 1456
Details: 1456, held by a Lancastrian garrison of eight men.[55]

Gloucester, Gloucestershire

Date range: 1471
Details: 1471, held by a Yorkist garrison led by Richard Beauchamp.[56]

Harlech, Merionethshire

Date range: 1455–68, 1483–7
Details: 1455–9, held by a Lancastrian garrison of twenty-four men.[57] 1460–8, held by a Lancastrian garrison of unspecified size led by Dafydd ab Ieuan ab Einion until 14 August 1468.[58] 1483–4, held by a Yorkist garrison of twenty soldiers, which was reinforced by a contingent of sixty

men from 5 March–29 September 1484.[59] 1485–7, held by a Tudor garrison of twenty-four men.[60]

Hexham, Tower of, Northumberland

Date range: 1463–4
Details: Winter 1463/4–May 1464, held by a Lancastrian garrison.[61]

Holt, the lordship of Bromfield and Yale

Date range: 1463–4, 1466
Details: 1463–4, held by a Yorkist garrison.[62] 1466, held by a Lancastrian garrison led by Sir Richard Tunstall.[63]

Hornby, Lancashire

Date range: 1471–5
Details: 1471–5, held by a garrison led by Sir James Harrington.[64]

Kenilworth, Warwickshire

Date range: 1460–1
Details: 1460–1, held by a Yorkist garrison led by Thomas Huggeford and William Vale.[65]

Kidwelly, the lordship of Kidwelly

Date range: 1455, 1459–60
Details: 1455, held by the forces of Gruffydd ap Nicholas.[66] 1459–60, held by a Lancastrian garrison led by Sir Walter Skull.[67]

Kirkoswald, Cumberland

Date range: *c.* 1462
Details: *c.* 1462, held by a Lancastrian garrison.[68]

Knaresborough, Yorkshire

Date range: 1462
Details: October 1462, held by a Yorkist garrison serving under the instructions of John Neville, Lord Montagu.[69]

Langley, Northumberland

Date range: 1463–4
Details: Winter 1463/4–May 1464, held by a Lancastrian garrison.[70]

Ludlow, Shropshire

Date range: 1460
Details: 1460, held by a Lancastrian garrison led by Edmund Delamere.[71]

Naworth, Cumberland

Date range: 1462
Details: July 1462, held by a Lancastrian garrison led by Sir Humphrey Dacre.[72]

Newcastle upon Tyne, Northumberland

Date range: 1461–4
Details: 1461–4, held by a Yorkist garrison led by Thomas, Lord Lumley. From 29 September 1461–13 January 1462 this consisted of a force of 120 men.[73]

Norham, Norhamshire

Date range: 1461–4
Details: 1461–winter 1463/4, held by a Yorkist garrison led by Robert, Lord Ogle.[74] Winter of 1463/4–summer of 1464, held by a Lancastrian garrison.[75]

Pembroke, Pembrokeshire

Date range: 1461–2, 1471
Details: Until 30 September 1461, held by a Lancastrian garrison led by Sir John Skydmore, until his surrender of the castle on 30 September 1461.[76] 30 September 1461–3 October 1462, held by a Yorkist garrison of forty-seven men led by John ap Howell ap Jankyn.[77] Summer 1471, held by a Lancastrian garrison led by Jasper Tudor.[78]

Pencelli, the lordship of Brecon

Date range: 1460
Details: From the late spring or summer of 1460, held by a Lancastrian garrison.[79]

Penrith, Cumberland

Date range: 1460
Details: Late 1460, held by a Lancastrian garrison under the command of John, Lord Clifford.[80]

Pontefract, Yorkshire

Date range: 1460, 1464, 1471, 1483, 1485
Details: Late 1460, held by a Lancastrian garrison under the command of Henry Percy, earl of Northumberland.[81] 1464, held by a Yorkist garrison of twenty men led by Walter Calverley, esquire, constable of the castle, for six weeks.[82] 1471, held by a Yorkist garrison led by Sir James Harrington.[83] 1483, held by a Yorkist garrison of thirty men led by Sir John Neville.[84] 1485, held by a Tudor garrison led by John Enyngham.[85]

Portchester, Hampshire

Date range: 1457
Details: 1457, held by a garrison led by Sir John Lisle and Sir Henry Bruyn.[86]

Powderham, Devon

Date range: 1455
Details: Winter 1455, held by a garrison led by the owner of the castle, Sir Philip Courtenay.[87]

Prudhoe, Northumberland

Date range: 1463
Details: 1463, held by a Yorkist garrison led by its constable William Burgh.[88]

Radnor, the lordship of Radnor

Date range: 1460
Details: From the late spring or summer of 1460, held by a Lancastrian garrison.[89]

Rhuddlan, Flintshire

Date range: 1455–68
Details: 1455–61, held by a Lancastrian garrison of six men.[90] 1461–8, held by a Yorkist garrison of six men.[91]

Rochester, Kent

Date range: 1471
Details: Summer 1471, held by a Yorkist garrison of forty horsemen and sixty footmen for thirty days led by Thomas Seyntleger.[92]

Roxburgh, Roxburghshire

Date range: 1455–60
Details: Roxburgh was held by a permanent garrison until the capture and destruction of the castle by the Scots in the late summer of 1460.[93]

St Michael's Mount, Cornwall

Date range: 1473–4
Details: Late October/November 1473–15 February 1474, held by a Lancastrian garrison of 80–400 men, led by John de Vere, earl of Oxford.[94]

Sandal, Yorkshire

Date range: 1460
Details: 1460, held by a Yorkist garrison led by Edmund Fitzwilliam.[95]

Sheriff Hutton, Yorkshire

Date range: 1486
Details: 1486, held by a Tudor garrison led by John Dawney.[96]

Skipton, Yorkshire

Date range: 1461, 1464
Details: Until May 1461, held by a Lancastrian garrison until its capture by Yorkists in May 1461.[97] Winter of 1463/4–late spring 1464, held by a Lancastrian garrison until its capture by the Yorkists in late spring 1464.[98]

Tenby, Pembrokeshire

Date range: 1461–2
Details: 1461, held by a Lancastrian garrison until the autumn of 1461. It is unclear when the Yorkists gained control of the castle and if it was besieged.[99] 10 December 1461–2 April 1462, held by a Yorkist garrison led by John ap Glo Thomas. This originally consisted of twenty men, which was reduced to twelve on 25 December. The garrison was temporarily reinforced by a contingent of thirty-six men from Pembroke Castle led by John ap Howell ap Jankyn in the late spring or summer of 1462.[100]

Thorpe Waterville, Northamptonshire

Date range: 1461
Details: Until early April 1461, held by a Lancastrian garrison.[101] 1461, held by a Yorkist garrison of thirteen men commanded by John, Lord Wenlock.[102]

Tower of London

Date range: 1460–1, 1470–1

Details: 1460, held by a Lancastrian garrison led by Thomas, Lord Scales, and Robert, Lord Hungerford.[103] 1461, held by a Yorkist garrison supplied by the civic authorities of London.[104] 1470, held by a Yorkist garrison led by John Tiptoft, earl of Worcester, until 3 October when they surrendered custody to a contingent of Londoners. Two days later, the latter were replaced by the forces of Richard Neville, earl of Warwick.[105] May 1471, held by a Yorkist garrison led by Anthony Woodville, Earl Rivers, and Henry Bourchier, earl of Essex.[106]

Tynemouth, Northumberland

Date range: 1461–2

Details: 2 May 1461–11 January 1462, held by a Yorkist garrison led by Sir George Lumley. This originally consisted of a force of forty men, which was reduced to twenty-four men from 13 September onwards.[107]

Wallingford, Berkshire

Date range: 1461

Details: 1461, held by a Yorkist garrison led by Sir Robert Harcourt.[108]

Wark, Northumberland

Date range: 1460

Details: 1460, held by an English garrison prior to its capture by a Scottish army.[109]

Wigmore, the lordship of Wigmore

Date range: 1460

Details: From the late spring or summer of 1460, held by a Lancastrian garrison.[110]

Wisbech, Isle of Ely

Date range: 1461

Details: Early 1461, held by a Yorkist garrison serving under the instructions of William Grey, bishop of Ely.[111]

Wressle, Yorkshire

Date range: 1460

Details: Late 1460, held by a Lancastrian garrison under the command of Henry Percy, earl of Northumberland.[112]

List of Abbreviations

A Brief Latin Chronicle – James Gairdner, ed., *Three Fifteenth Century Chronicles* (London: Printed for the Camden Society, 1880), pp. 164–85.

A Short English Chronicle – James Gairdner, ed., *Three Fifteenth Century Chronicles* (London: Printed for the Camden Society, 1880), pp. 1–80.

An English Chronicle – John Sylvester Davies, ed., *An English Chronicle of the Reigns of Richard II, Henry IV, Henry V, and Henry VI, written before the Year 1471* (London: Camden Society, 1856).

Annales – Joseph Stevenson, ed., *Letters and Papers Illustrative of the Wars of the English in France during the Reign of Henry the Sixth, King of England, volume 2, part 2* (London: Longman, Green, Longman, and Roberts, 1864).

Arrivall – John Bruce, ed., *Historie of the Arrivall of Edward IV. In England and the Finall Recouerye of His Kingdomes From Henry VI A.D. M.CCCC.LXXI.* (London: Printed for the Camden Society by J.B. Nichols and Son, 1838).

Bale's Chronicle – Ralph Flenley, ed., *Six Town Chronicles of England* (Oxford: At the Clarendon Press, 1911), pp. 114–52.

Benet's Chronicle – Alison Hanham, ed., *John Benet's Chronicle, 1399–1462: An English Translation with New Introduction* (Basingstoke: Palgrave Macmillan, 2016).

BIA – Borthwick Institute for Archives.

BL – The British Library.

Brief Notes – James Gairdner, ed., *Three Fifteenth Century Chronicles* (London: Printed for the Camden Society, 1880), pp. 148–63.

CA – College of Arms.

CCR – Calendar of the Close Rolls (HMSO, 1949–53).

Chronicles of London – Charles Lethbridge Kingsford, ed., *Chronicles of London* (Oxford: At the Clarendon Press, 1905).

CPR – Calendar of the Patent Rolls (HMSO, 1901–14).

Crowland – Nicholas Pronay and John Cox, eds, *The Crowland Chronicle Continuations: 1459–1486* (London: Alan Sutton Publishing for Richard III and Yorkist History Trust, 1986).

CSPV – Rawdon Brown, ed., *Calendar of State Papers and Manuscripts, Relating to English Affairs, Existing in the Archives and Collections of Venice, and in Other Libraries of Northern Italy. Vol. I. 1202–1509* (London: Longman, Green, Longman, Roberts, and Green, 1864).

DUL – Durham University Library.

Fabyan – Henry Ellis, ed., *The New Chronicles of England and France* (London: Printed for F. C. and J. Rivington etc., 1811).

Gough – Ralph Flenley, ed., *Six Town Chronicles of England* (Oxford: At the Clarendon Press, 1911), pp. 153–65.

Great Chronicle – A.H. Thomas and I.D. Thornley, eds, *The Great Chronicle of London* (London: Alan Sutton, 1983).

Gregory's Chronicle – James Gairdner, ed., *The Historical Collections of a Citizen of London in the Fifteenth Century* (London: Printed for the Camden Society, 1876), pp. 57–239.

Hardyng – Henry Ellis, ed., *The Chronicle of Iohn Hardyng* (London: Printed for F.C. and J. Rivington etc., 1812).

Hearne's Fragment – J.A. Giles, ed., *The Chronicles of the White Rose of York* (London: James Bohn, 1845), p. 5–34.

Letters and Papers – Joseph Stevenson, ed., *Letters and Papers Illustrative of the Wars of the English in France during the Reign of Henry the Sixth, King of England, volume 2, part 2* (London: Longman, Green, Longman, and Roberts, 1864).

LMA – London Metropolitan Archives.

Mancini – C.A.J. Armstrong, ed., *The Usurpation of Richard the Third* (London: Oxford University Press, 1936).

NLW – National Library of Wales.

NRO – Northamptonshire Record Office.

PL, I – James Gairdner, ed., *The Paston Letters A.D. 1422–1509*, Volume I (London: 1872).

PL, III – James Gairdner, ed., *The Paston Letters A.D. 1422–1509*, Volume III (London: Chatto & Windus, 1904).

PL, IV – James Gairdner, ed., *The Paston Letters A.D. 1422–1509*, Volume IV (London: Chatto & Windus, 1904).

PL, V – James Gairdner, ed., *The Paston Letters A.D. 1422–1509*, Volume V (London: Chatto & Windus, 1904).

PL, VI – James Gairdner, ed., *The Paston Letters A.D. 1422–1509*, Volume VI (London: Chatto & Windus, 1904).

SRO – Shropshire Record Office.

STRO – Stafford Record Office.

Tanner – Ralph Flenley, ed., *Six Town Chronicles of England* (Oxford: At the Clarendon Press, 1911), pp. 166–83.

TNA – The National Archives.

Vergil – Henry Ellis, ed., *Three Books of Polydore Vergil's English History, Comprising the Reigns of Henry VI., Edward IV., and Richard III.* (London: Printed for the Camden Society, 1844).

Warkworth – James Orchard Halliwell, ed., *A Chronicle of the First Thirteen Years of the Reign of King Edward the Fourth, by John Warkworth, D.D. Master of the St Peter's College, Cambridge* (London: Camden Society, 1839).

Waurin – William Hardy, ed., *Recueil des Croniques et Anchiennes Istories de la Grant Bretaigne, a Present Nomme Engleterre Par Jehan de Waurin*, Volume V (London: Printed for Her Majesty's Stationery Office, 1891).

Whethamstede – H.T. Riley, ed., *Registra Quorundam Abbatum Monasterii S. Albani, Qui Sæculo XVmo. Floruere. Vol I. Registrum Abbatiae Johannis Whethamstede, Abbatis Monasterii Sancti Albani, Iterum Susceptae; Robert Blakeney, Capellano, Quondam Adscriptum* (London: Longman & Co., 1872).

WSRA – Wiltshire and Swindon Record Office.

Notes

Introduction

1. CA, L. 15, ff. 32r–33v.
2. For a few examples of books on the Wars of the Roses see, David Santiuste, *Edward IV and the Wars of the Roses* (Barnsley: Pen & Sword Military, 2010); Michael Hicks, *The Wars of the Roses* (London: Yale University Press, 2012); J.L. Laynesmith, *Cecily Duchess of York* (London: Bloomsbury Academic, 2017).
3. For examples see, N.J.G. Pounds, *The Medieval Castle in England and Wales: A Social and Political History* (Cambridge: Cambridge University Press, 1990), p. 250; M.W. Thompson, *The Decline of the Castle* (Cambridge: Cambridge University Press, 1987), pp. 33–5; Anthony Emery, 'The Development of Raglan Castle and Keeps in Late Medieval England', *Archaeological Journal*, 132 (1975), pp. 151–86 (p. 182).
4. For a discussion of the chronicles of the period see, Antonia Gransden, *Historical Writing in England. Volume 2, c. 1307 to the Early Sixteenth Century* (London: Routledge and Kegan Paul, 1982), pp. 249–307.
5. For an introduction to these sources see, A.L. Brown, *The Governance of Late Medieval England 1272–1461* (London: Edward Arnold, 1989).

Chapter One: The History of the Castle

1. Dan Spencer, *The Castle at War in Medieval England and Wales* (Stroud: Amberley Publishing, 2018), pp. 12–38.
2. Ibid.
3. Ibid., pp. 33–6, 41–5, 48–9.
4. Ibid., pp. 27–8, 38, 47, 82–3.
5. John Goodall, *The English Castle, 1066–1650* (New Haven: Yale University Press, 2011), pp. 191–2.
6. Ibid., pp. 212–27; Alastair Oswald and Jeremy Ashbee, *Dunstanburgh Castle* (London: English Heritage, 2016), pp. 5–12.
7. Rick Turner, *Caerphilly Castle* (Cardiff: Cadw, 2016), p. 49.
8. John R. Kenyon, *Kidwelly Castle* (Cardiff: Cadw, 2017), pp. 25–32.
9. Goodall, *The English Castle*, pp. 321–2.
10. Ibid., pp. 348–56.
11. C.M. Woolgar, *The Great Household in Late Medieval England* (London: Yale University Press, 1999), pp. 46–82.
12. Sidney Painter, 'Castle-Guard', *The American Historical Review*, 40 (1935), pp. 450–9.
13. John S. Moore, 'Anglo-Norman Garrisons', *Anglo-Norman Studies*, 22 (1999), pp. 205–59.
14. Seymour Phillips, *Edward II* (London: Yale University Press, 2011), pp. 397–8.

15. See, J.G. Bellamy, *The Law of Treason in England in the Later Middle Ages* (Cambridge: Cambridge University Press, 1970).

16. For the Anglo-Scottish wars of Edward I see, Michael Prestwich, *Edward I* (London: Yale University Press, 1997), pp. 469–555.

17. S.B. Chrimes, 'Some Letters of John of Lancaster as Warden of the East Marches Towards Scotland', *Speculum*, 14 (1939), pp. 3–27; R.A. Griffiths, *The Reign of Henry VI* (Stroud: Sutton Publishing Limited, 2004), pp. 404–5.

18. TNA, E 101/42/40.

19. *CPR 1446–52*, p. 508.

20. See, David Grummitt, *The Calais Garrison: War and Military Service in England, 1436–1558* (Woodbridge: Boydell Press, 2008).

21. TNA, SC 6/1224/1; SC 6/1217/1.

22. Dan Spencer, 'Royal Castles and Coastal Defence in the Late Fourteenth Century', *Nottingham Medieval Studies*, 61 (2017), pp. 147–70 (p. 153).

23. *CPR 1452–61*, p. 141.

24. *CPR 1446–52*, pp. 331, 336.

25. H.M. Colvin, *The History of the King's Works*, Volume 2 (London: HMSO, 1963), pp. 629–41.

26. STRO, D 641/1/2/336; TNA, E 101/54/17.

27. P.D.A. Harvey, *Manorial Records* (London: British Records Association, 1999), pp. 1–3; O.H. Creighton, *Castles and Landscapes: Power, Community and Fortification in Medieval England* (London: Equinox Publishing Ltd, 2002), pp. 89–91, 177–93.

28. *CPR 1452–61*, p. 64.

29. Colvin, *The History of the King's Works*, Volume 2, pp. 706–29; N.J.G. Pounds, *The Medieval Castle in England and Wales: A Social and Political History* (Cambridge: Cambridge University Press, 1990), pp. 101, 108, 111; T.F. Tout, 'Firearms in England in the Fourteenth Century', *The English Historical Review*, 26 (1911), pp. 666–702.

30. H.C. Maxwell Lyte, *A History of Dunster and of the Families of Mohun & Luttrell* (London: The St Catherine Press Ltd, 1909), pp. 94–100.

31. These examples are all taken from the inventory for 1448. MC, FP 43, ff. 4v–5, 8–11.

32. *CPR 1452–61*, p. 37.

33. *CPR 1461–67*, p. 210.

34. *CPR 1452–61*, p. 240.

35. *CPR 1452–61*, p. 470.

36. *CPR 1405–8*, p. 355.

37. Colvin, *The History of the King's Works*, Volume 2, p. 829.

38. Anne Curry, 'Montagu, Thomas [Thomas de Montacute], fourth earl of Salisbury (1388–1428)', *Oxford Dictionary of National Biography* [https://doi.org/10.1093/ref:odnb/18999, accessed 27 December 2018].

39. Colvin, *The History of the King's Works*, Volume 2, pp. 642–3, 657–8, 667, 681–93, 692–3, 738–9, 768–9, 776–83, 837–8, 844–5, 847–9, 853–4.

40. J.R.S. Phillips, 'Edward II [Edward of Caernarfon] (1284–1327)', *Oxford Dictionary of National Biography* [https://doi.org/10.1093/ref:odnb/8518, accessed 27 December 2018].

41. R.A. Griffiths, 'Edward [Edward of Westminster], Prince of Wales', *Oxford Dictionary of National Biography* [https://doi.org/10.1093/ref:odnb/8524, accessed 27 December 2018].

42. Griffiths, *The Reign of Henry VI*, pp. 259–60; *CPR 1446–52*, p. 559; Colvin, *The History of the King's Works*, Volume 2, pp. 628, 680, 768, 781, 849.

43. A.L. Brown, *The Governance of Late Medieval England 1272–1461* (London: Edward Arnold, 1989), p. 177.

44. Michael Hicks, *The Wars of the Roses* (London: Yale University Press, 2012), p. 42.

45. John Watts, 'Richard of York, third duke of York (1411–1460)', *Oxford Dictionary of National Biography* [https://doi.org/10.1093/ref:odnb/23503, accessed 6 December 2018].

46. Anthony Tuck, 'Neville, Ralph, first earl of Westmorland (*c.* 1364–1425)', *Oxford Dictionary of National Biography* [www.oxforddnb.com/view/10.1093/, accessed 6 December 2018]; A.J. Pollard, 'Neville, Richard, fifth earl of Salisbury (1400–1460)', *Oxford Dictionary of National Biography* [https://doi.org/10.1093/ref:odnb/19954/, accessed 6 December 2018].

47. A.J. Pollard, 'Neville, Ralph, second earl of Westmorland (b. in or before 1407, d. 1484)', *Oxford Dictionary of National Biography* [https://doi.org/10.1093/ref:odnb/19952/, accessed 6 December 2018].

48. A.J. Pollard, 'Neville, Richard, sixteenth earl of Warwick and sixth earl of Salisbury [called the Kingmaker] (1428–1471)', *Oxford Dictionary of National Biography* [https://doi.org/10.1093/ref:odnb/19955/, accessed 6 December 2018].

49. R.A. Griffiths, 'Percy, Henry, second earl of Northumberland (1394–1455)', *Oxford Dictionary of National Biography* [http://www.oxforddnb.com/view/article/183, accessed 6 December 2018].

50. Henry Summerson, 'Clifford, Thomas, eighth Baron Clifford (1414–1455)', *Oxford Dictionary of National Biography* [https://doi.org/10.1093/ref:odnb/5663, accessed 6 December 2018].

51. Carole Rawcliffe, 'Stafford, Humphrey, first duke of Buckingham (1402–1460)', *Oxford Dictionary of National Biography* [https://doi.org/10.1093/ref:odnb/26207, accessed 6 December 2018].

52. Martin Cherry, 'Courtenay, Thomas, thirteenth earl of Devon (1414–1458)', *Oxford Dictionary of National Biography* [https://doi.org/10.1093/ref:odnb/50218, accessed 6 December 2018].

53. Colin Richmond, 'Mowbray, John, third duke of Norfolk (1415–1461)', *Oxford Dictionary of National Biography* [https://doi.org/10.1093/ref:odnb/19454, accessed 27 December 2018]; James Ross, *John de Vere, Thirteenth Earl of Oxford (1442–1513): 'The Foremost Man of the Kingdom'* (Woodbridge: Boydell, 2011), pp. 92–3.

54. Goodall, *The English Castle*, pp. 86, 104, 134–5, 263–5, 309–10, 275–6, 314–17.

Chapter Two: Lancaster and York

1. Roger Virgoe, 'The Death of William De La Pole, Duke of Suffolk', *Bulletin of the John Rylands Library*, 47 (1965), pp. 489–502; R.A. Griffiths, *The Reign of King Henry VI: The Exercise of Royal Authority, 1422–1461* (London: Benn, 1981), pp. 286–8, 676–84.

2. Griffiths, *The Reign of King Henry VI*, pp. 11–22; C.T. Allmand, *Henry V* (New Haven: Yale University Press, 1997), pp. 61–184.

3. Michael Hicks, *The Wars of the Roses* (London: Yale University Press, 2012), pp. 56–9; Griffiths, *The Reign of King Henry VI*, pp. 178–205, 459–99.

4. Griffiths, *The Reign of King Henry VI*, pp. 509–33.

5. For Portchester Castle see, TNA, E 28/80, no. 46, and for the Carisbrooke petition see SC 8/28, no. 1353. Coastal defence measures are discussed by Griffiths, *The Reign of King Henry VI*, pp. 423–33.

6. Griffiths, *The Reign of King Henry VI*, pp. 107–21, 376–94; Hicks, *The Wars of the Roses*, pp. 49–55.

7. Griffiths, *The Reign of King Henry VI*, pp. 610–14, 635–40; *An English Chronicle*, pp. 65–6; *Gregory's Chronicle*, pp. 190–1; *Great Chronicle*, pp. 181–3.

8. Accounts of how the rebels entered London differ, with *An English Chronicle* stating that this occurred due to the favour of some of the inhabitants, whereas *Gregory's Chronicle* claims that this only occurred after some fighting took place. *An English Chronicle*, p. 66; *Gregory's Chronicle*, p. 191.

9. Griffiths, *The Reign of King Henry VI*, pp. 614–17; *An English Chronicle*, pp. 66–8; *Gregory's Chronicle*, pp. 191–4; *Great Chronicle*, pp. 183–5; TNA, E 404/66, no. 202.

10. Griffiths, *The Reign of King Henry VI*, pp. 344–5, 361–2, 686–8.

11. Ibid., pp. 642, 645–7, 690–1; *CPR 1446–52*, p. 388.

12. *Annales*, p. 770; R.L. Storey, *The End of the House of Lancaster* (Gloucester: Alan Sutton Publishing, 1986), pp. 84–92; Griffiths, *The Reign of King Henry VI*, pp. 574–7.

13. Storey, *The End of the House of Lancaster*, pp. 93–104; Griffiths, *The Reign of King Henry VI*, pp. 693–700; Hicks, *The Wars of the Roses*, pp. 100–5; *CPR 1446–52*, p. 537; *CPR 1452–61*, pp. 23–4.

14. Hicks, *The Wars of the Roses*, pp. 103–6; Griffiths, *The Reign of King Henry VI*, pp. 698–700, 715–26; *CPR 1452–61*, pp. 18–19.

15. Storey, *The End of the House of Lancaster*, pp. 126–32; Griffiths, *The Reign of King Henry VI*, pp. 736–7.

16. Original text 'personnes of riotous and evyl disposicon'. For the attempt to seize Lancaster Castle and the source of the quote see, TNA, DL 37/23. T.B. Pugh, 'Richard, Duke of York, and the Rebellion of Henry Holand, Duke of Exeter, in May 1454', *Historical Research*, 63 (1990), pp. 248–62; Storey, *The End of the House of Lancaster*, pp. 142–9; Griffiths, *The Reign of King Henry VI*, pp. 737–8.

17. Griffiths, *The Reign of King Henry VI*, pp. 738–43; Storey, *The End of the House of Lancaster*, pp. 159–61; TNA, DL 37/23.

18. C.A.J. Armstrong, 'Politics and the Battle of St. Albans, 1455', *Historical Research*, 33:87 (1960), pp. 1–72; Anthony Goodman, *The Wars of the Roses* (London: Routledge & Kegan Paul, 1991), pp. 22–5; Griffiths, *The Reign of King Henry VI*, pp. 741–6.

19. For the report concerning the armed men of York, Warwick and Salisbury see, *PL*, I, pp. 345–6. Ibid., pp. 335–6, 344–5; Griffiths, *The Reign of King Henry VI*, pp. 746–8; Hicks, *The Wars of the Roses*, pp. 112–13.

20. G.H. Radford, 'The Fight at Clyst in 1455', *Report and Transactions for the Devonshire Association*, 44 (1912), pp. 252–7; Storey, *The End of the House of Lancaster*, pp. 165–9; Hicks, *The Wars of the Roses*, pp. 115–16; *PL*, I, pp. 350–2; Griffiths, *The Reign of King Henry VI*, p. 753.

21. This quote is from Radford, 'The Fight at Clyst in 1455', p. 257.

22. Ibid., pp. 257–60; Storey, *The End of the House of Lancaster*, pp. 169–71; John Goodall, *The English Castle, 1066–1650* (New Haven: Yale University Press, 2011), p. 321.

23. Radford, 'The Fight at Clyst in 1455', pp. 261–2; Hicks, *The Wars of the Roses*, p. 116; Griffiths, *The Reign of King Henry VI*, pp. 746–57; Storey, *The End of the House of Lancaster*, pp. 171–5.

24. Original text 'man of a hot, firie and cholerrick spiritt' and 'craftie, ambitiouse beyond measure', quoted from R.A. Griffiths, *Sir Rhys ap Thomas and his Family: A Study in the Wars of the Roses and Early Tudor Politics* (Cardiff: University of Wales Press, 1993), p. 161.

25. Original text 'at were gretely in Wales', quoted from *PL, I*, pp. 392–3. For the petition see, William Rees, ed., *Calendar of Ancient Petitions relating to Wales* (Cardiff: University of Wales Press, 1975), pp. 184–6.

26. Griffiths, *Sir Rhys ap Thomas and his Family*, pp. 12–24; Griffiths, *The Reign of King Henry VI*, p. 779; *CPR 1452–61*, pp. 24–5.

27. Original text 'saith he is noo monis mon but only youres', quoted from T.B. Pugh, 'The magnates, knights and gentry', in *Fifteenth-century England, 1399–1509*, ed. S.B. Chrimes, C.D. Ross and R.A. Griffiths (Manchester: Manchester University Press, 1972), pp. 86–128 (p. 92).

28. A. Herbert, 'Public Order and Private Violence in Herefordshire, 1413–61' (Unpublished MA thesis, Swansea, 1978), p. 250; H.M. Colvin, *The History of the King's Works*, Volume 2 (London: HMSO, 1963), pp. 600–1; Griffiths, *The Reign of King Henry VI*, p. 780; R.A. Griffiths, 'Herbert, William, first earl of Pembroke (*c.* 1423–1469)', *Oxford Dictionary of National Biography* [https://doi.org/10.1093/ref:odnb/13053, accessed 6 March 2019].

29. Herbert, 'Public Order and Private Violence in Herefordshire', pp. 246, 250–1; Griffiths, *The Reign of King Henry VI*, p. 780; TNA, SC 6/1224/1; H.M. Colvin, *The History of the King's Works*, Volume 1 (London: HMSO, 1963), pp. 299–308; *CPR 1452–61*, p. 340.

30. Griffiths, *The Reign of King Henry VI*, p. 815; *CPR 1452–61*, pp. 371, 390–2, 394, 405–6, 415; TNA, E 159/234, brevia directa baronibus, Trinity, rot. 15; C 81/774, no. 10448.

31. Quoted from *CPR 1452–61*, p. 413; Ibid., pp. 402–3, 406–10; Griffiths, *The Reign of King Henry VI*, pp. 805, 815; Hicks, *The Wars of the Roses*, p. 130.

32. G.L. Harriss, 'The Struggle for Calais: An Aspect of the Rivalry between Lancaster and York', *The English Historical Review*, 75 (1960), pp. 30–53 (pp. 40–8); Griffiths, *The Reign of King Henry VI*, pp. 808–10; *PL, I*, pp. 428–9.

Chapter Three: Civil War

1. R.A. Griffiths, *The Reign of King Henry VI: The Exercise of Royal Authority, 1422–1461* (London: Benn, 1981), pp. 805–8; Michael Hicks, *The Wars of the Roses* (London: Yale University Press, 2012), pp. 137–9.

2. Quoted from A.J. Pollard, *North-eastern England during the Wars of the Roses* (Oxford: Clarendon Press, 1990), pp. 269–70; John Weaver, *Middleham Castle* (London: English Heritage, 2013), pp. 5–20, 26–7.

3. Anne Curry and Rosemary Horrox, eds, *The Parliament Rolls of Medieval England, 1275–1504: XII Henry VI. 1447–1460* (London: The Boydell Press, 2012), p. 458; Griffiths, *The Reign of King Henry VI*, p. 817; Hicks, *The Wars of the Roses*, pp. 139–41; *PL, I*, p. 438.

4. *Gregory's Chronicle*, p. 204; *An English Chronicle*, p. 80; *Benet's Chronicle*, pp. 45–6; Curry and Horrox, eds, *The Parliament Rolls of Medieval England, XII*, p. 458; TNA, SC 6/779/8; C 81/777, no. 10704.

5. Original text 'bare walles', quoted from *An English Chronicle*, p. 83. *Fabyan*, p. 635; *Gregory's Chronicle*, pp. 205–7; *CPR 1452–61*, pp. 586–7; Curry and Horrox, *The Parliament Rolls of Medieval England, XII*, pp. 458–61; TNA, C 81/777, no. 10714.

6. Griffiths, *The Reign of King Henry VI*, pp. 822, 827, 854; G.L. Harriss, 'The Struggle for Calais: An Aspect of the Rivalry between Lancaster and York', *The English Historical Review*, 75 (1960), pp. 30–53 (p. 48); *Gregory's Chronicle*, p. 205; *Crowland*, p. 111.

7. Quoted from Curry and Horrox, *The Parliament Rolls of Medieval England, XII*, pp. 460–1.

8. Griffiths, *The Reign of King Henry VI*, pp. 823–6; Hicks, *The Wars of the Roses*, pp. 146–7.

9. Quoted from C.S. Knighton, ed., *Calendar of Inquisitions Miscellaneous Preserved in the Public Record Office, Volume VIII, 1422–1485* (Woodbridge: Boydell, 2003), pp. 158–60. Griffiths, *The Reign of King Henry VI*, pp. 825–7; *Waurin*, p. 277; *CPR 1452–61*, pp. 534, 537, 546–7.

10. *CPR 1452–61*, pp. 565–6, 576; NRO, W(A) box 1/parcel XI/no. 3; TNA, C 81/1376, no. 9.

11. R.R. Davies, *The Age of Conquest Wales 1063–1415* (Oxford: Oxford University Press, 1991), p. 363; John Goodall, *The English Castle, 1066–1650* (New Haven: Yale University Press, 2011), p. 223.

12. *CPR 1452–61*, p. 534.

13. Original text 'of power ... to subdue any castell or place that woll rebel', TNA, E 404/71/3, no. 43. For the three bombards see, E 364/90, rot. D; Dan Spencer, 'The Lancastrian Armament Programme of the 1450s and the Development of Field Guns', *The Ricardian*, 25 (2015), pp. 61–70; Dan Spencer, *Royal and Urban Gunpowder Weapons in Late Medieval England* (Boydell & Brewer, 2019), pp. 30, 33.

14. *CPR 1452–61*, pp. 550, 564–5, 606; TNA, C 81/1376, no. 9; C 49/32, no. 12A.

15. *CPR 1452–61*, pp. 562, 574, 578, 602, 605.

16. Original text 'the saufgarde of theym and for the defence of robberyes and for the trakyng of theves', TNA, C 81/1476, no. 30.

17. Original text 'knaes son' and 'not his parte to have syche langage of Lords, beyng of the Kyngs blood' quoted from *PL, III*, pp. 204–5; *CPR 1452–61*, pp. 555–6; Anthony Goodman, *The Wars of the Roses* (London: Routledge & Kegan Paul, 1991), p. 30; *Letters and Papers*, p. 512.

18. The size of Exeter's fleet and his cowardice in failing to confront Warwick is given in *Benet's Chronicle*, p. 46. Whereas for the claim that his fleet lacked supplies see, *An English Chronicle*, p. 85. *Letters and Papers*, pp. 513–16; *Annales*, p. 772; Goodman, *The Wars of the Roses*, p. 30; TNA, C 81/778, no. 10819.

19. Quoted from *CPR 1452–61*, p. 566; Ibid., pp. 527, 557–61, 563–4, 602–4, 609, 611.

20. *Benet's Chronicle*, p. 46; Richard K. Morris, *Kenilworth Castle* (London: English Heritage, 2012), pp. 42–5.

21. *CPR 1452–61*, p. 561; Cora L. Scofield, *The Life and Reign of Edward the Fourth: King of England and of France and Lord of Ireland*, Volume one (Stroud: Fonthill Media Limited, 2016), pp. 64–77; Griffiths, *The Reign of King Henry VI*, p. 859; *An English Chronicle*, pp. 85–6.

22. Original text 'rewle and gouernaunce', quoted from *An English Chronicle*, p. 95. For the claim that Scales sought to become captain of the city see *A Short English Chronicle*, p. 73.

23. Caroline M. Barron, 'London and the Crown 1451–61', in *The Crown and Local Communities in England and France in the Fifteenth Century*, ed. by J.R.L. Highfield (Gloucester: Alan Sutton, 1981), pp. 88–109 (p. 96); Reginald R. Sharpe, *London and the Kingdom*, Volume one (London: Longmans & Co., 1894), pp. 256–8.

24. *An English Chronicle*, pp. 94–5; *A Short English Chronicle*, pp. 73–4; Scofield, *The Life and Reign of Edward the Fourth*, Volume one, pp. 79–81.

25. *An English Chronicle*, pp. 95–6; *Benet's Chronicle*, p. 47; TNA, C 81/778, no. 10876; H.M. Colvin, *The History of the King's Works*, Volume 2 (London: HMSO, 1963), pp. 706–29.

26. *An English Chronicle*, pp. 95–6; *A Short English Chronicle*, p. 73; *Benet's Chronicle*, p. 47; *Annales*, p. 773; Sharpe, *London and the Kingdom*, Volume 1, p. 259.

27. *An English Chronicle*, p. 96; *A Short English Chronicle*, p. 74; TNA, C 81/784, no. 267; Scofield, *The Life and Reign of Edward the Fourth*, Volume one, pp. 81, 91.

28. Original text 'in all placis of London was grete watche for doute of tresoun', quoted from *A Short English Chronicle*, p. 74. Details of William Barton's and Thomas Brown's actions are recorded in a later court case, TNA, KB 27/800, m. 9; E 163/8/10. The undated exchange of letters is preserved in the journal of the common council, LMA, COL/CC/01/01/007. This has been printed in full in Reginald R. Sharpe, *London and the Kingdom*, Volume 3 (London: Longmans, Green & Co., 1895), pp. 384–5. Scofield, *The Life and Reign of Edward the Fourth*, Volume one, pp. 89–91.

29. Original text 'the erle of Warrewyk shalle nat come to the kynges presence, and yef he come he shalle dye', quoted from *An English Chronicle*, p. 96. Ibid., pp. 95–8; *Whethamstede*, pp. 373–4. George Poulson, ed., *Beverlac; or the Antiquities and History of the Town of Beverley, in the County of York, and of the Provostry and Collegiate Establishment of St. John's; with a Minute Description of the Present Minster and the Church of St. Mary*, Volume one (Beverley: Printed for George Scaum, 1829), p. 227.

30. Original text 'dyspoyly nakyd as a worme', quoted from *Gregory's Chronicle*, p. 211. *An English Chronicle*, p. 98; *A Short English Chronicle*, p. 75; *Annales*, p. 773; TNA, C 81/778, no. 10876; Scofield, *The Life and Reign of Edward the Fourth*, Volume one, pp. 92–3.

31. The most detailed account of this episode is provided by *Gregory's Chronicle*, pp. 207–9. The account of Margaret's residence at Eccleshall Castle prior to the Battle of Northampton and the theft of her goods by John Cleger is provided by the author of the *Annales*, p. 773. The value of her stolen goods is provided by the author of *An English Chronicle*, pp. 98–9.

32. *An English Chronicle*, p. 99; *Benet's Chronicle*, p. 48; Griffiths, *The Reign of King Henry VI*, pp. 409–10, 753–4, 866; Colvin, *The History of the King's Works*, Volume 2, pp. 818–21; Knighton, *Calendar of Inquisitions Miscellaneous*, pp. 155–6; Scofield, *The Life and Reign of Edward the Fourth*, Volume one, pp. 99–100; Thomas Thomson, ed., *The Auchinleck Chronicle* (Edinburgh: Printed for Private Circulation, 1819), pp. 57–8.

33. Hicks, *The Wars of the Roses*, pp. 159–60; For Conwy Castle see, TNA, SC 6/1217/3. For Carreg Cennen and Kidwelly see, DL 29/596/9558; DL 29/584/9249.

34. Harris Nicolas, ed., *Proceedings and Ordinances of the Privy Council of England*, Volume six (London: Record Commission, 1837), pp. 302–4.

35. Original text 'grete hurte and inconvenience' and 'pryncipall doers and stirrers', ibid., pp. 304–5; *CPR 1452–61*, p. 610.

36. For Pontefract see, Colvin, *The History of the King's Works*, Volume 2, pp. 781–3; for Wressle see, Goodall, *The English Castle*, p. 330; *CPR 1452–61*, p. 428; R.A. Griffiths, 'Local Rivalries and National Politics: The Percies, the Nevilles, and the Duke of Exeter, 1452–55', *Speculum*, 43 (1968), pp. 589–632 (pp. 593–4).

37. Original text 'straunge commission' and 'to punych them by the fawtes to the Kyngs lawys', *PL, III*, pp. 233–4. Curry and Horrox, *The Parliament Rolls of Medieval England XII*, pp. 516–32.

38. Quoted from the printed text, *CPR 1452–61*, p. 649. Ibid., pp. 650–2, 659. For the ownership of Penrith Castle see, Anthony Tuck, 'Neville, Ralph, first earl of Westmorland (*c.* 1364–1425)', *Oxford Dictionary of National Biography* [www.oxforddnb.com/view/10.1093/, accessed 6 December 2018].

39. Original text 'grete strength and myght', TNA, C 49/32, no. 8.

40. *Annales*, p. 774.

41. Original text 'Owtt of prison & owt of hys enuymys hondys upon payn of forfetor of lyffe & lyme'. This relates to a commission said to have been issued to the town of Beverley, which is mentioned in a petition from the reign of Edward IV. No specific date is stated for when the commission was issued but it took place prior to the Battle of Wakefield on 30 December. TNA, C 1/27, no. 435.

42. Quoted text from DUL, CCB B/1/9. The municipal documents of the town of Beverley in Yorkshire records that messengers were sent to Neville at Raby Castle on 23 October and 13 December, with messengers sent to Northumberland at York on 13 December and other unspecified days in the same month, Poulson, *Beverlac*, pp. 231–3. *Annales*, p. 774.

43. *Gregory's Chronicle*, pp. 209–10; *Annales*, pp. 774–5; Michael K. Jones, 'Beaufort, Henry, second duke of Somerset (1436–1464)', *Oxford Dictionary of National Biography* [https://doi.org/10.1093/ref:odnb/1860, accessed 22 April 2019].

44. Original text 'Charge and labour to ride into the parties of the seid realme of Englond and Wales … to represse, subdue and appese them', quoted from Curry and Horrox, *The Parliament Rolls of Medieval England, XII*, p. 531. The first session of Parliament was said to have been prorogued on 29 November, therefore the bill would have been passed before this date, *Benet's Chronicle*, p. 49. For his intention to recruit men en route see, *Bale's Chronicle*, p. 152.

45. Original text 'take vpon theyme the rule governaunce and defens of the kyngys Castell' and 'haue entre and rule of the said Castell', quoted from E.W.W. Veale, ed., *The Great Red Book of Bristol*, Volume 1 (Bristol: Bristol Record Society, 1933), p. 137; *CPR 1452–61*, pp. 632–3. March spent Christmas at Shrewsbury according to the author of the *Annales*, p. 775, whereas he was at Gloucester according to *A Short English Chronicle*, p. 76.

46. *Annales*, p. 775; *An English Chronicle*, p. 106; *Benet's Chronicle*, p. 49; *Bale's Chronicle*, p. 152; *Whethamstede*, p. 381; TNA, E 404/71/5, no. 38; *CPR 1452–61*, pp. 653–4. For the description of Sandal Castle see, Goodall, *The English Castle*, p. 183.

47. *Bale's Chronicle* attributes the Yorkist defeat to the treachery of their opponents who broke a truce to attack them, *Bale's Chronicle*, p. 152. *Annales*, p. 775; *Fabyan*, p. 638; *Great Chronicle*, p. 193; *Waurin*, pp. 324–6; *Benet's Chronicle*, p. 49; *An English Chronicle*, pp. 106–7; *Brief Notes*, p. 154; *Whethamstede*, pp. 381–3; *Tanner*, p. 167; *CSPV*, p. 95. For Sandal Castle see, TNA, DL 29/560/8899.

48. Original text 'pepill in the northe robbe and styll, and ben apoyntyd to pill all thys cwntre, and gyffe a way menys goods and lufflods in all the sowthe cwntre', quoted from *PL, III*, p. 250. Thomson, *The Auchinleck Chronicle*, p. 59. For the council meeting held at York see, Michael Hicks, 'A Minute of the Lancastrian Council at York, 20 January 1461', *Northern History* (1999), pp. 214–21; *Annales*, p. 775. For the plundering carried out by the Lancastrian army see, *Brief Notes*, pp. 154–5; *Benet's Chronicle*, p. 49; *PL, III*, p. 250; *A Short English Chronicle*, p. 76; *Whethamstede*, pp. 388–90, 394, 399–401; Poulson, *Beverlac*, p. 234.

49. Original text 'mysruled and outerageous people in the north parties ... entending aswell the destrucćon of ... oure trewe subgitts' quoted from Nicolas, *Proceedings and Ordinances of the Privy Council of England*, pp. 307–10. *CPR 1452–61*, pp. 657–9; Barron, 'London and the Crown 1451–61', p. 98; *PL, III*, pp. 265–6; *Brief Notes*, p. 155.

50. Original text 'wyckedly ... went to the contrary parte of the northe' and 'trewe lordis', quoted from *A Short English Chronicle*, p. 76. *Benet's Chronicle*, pp. 49–50; *Gregory's Chronicle*, pp. 211–14; Friedrich W.D. Brie, ed., *The Brut or The Chronicles of England* (London: Kegan Paul, 1906), pp. 531–2; *Great Chronicle*, p. 194; *Fabyan*, p. 638; *An English Chronicle*, pp. 107–9; *Whethamstede*, pp. 390–6; *Tanner*, p. 167; *Brief Notes*, pp. 154–5; Barron, 'London and the Crown 1451–61', pp. 98, 108, n. 82; Hannes Kleineke, 'Robert Bale's Chronicle and the Second Battle of St. Albans', *Historical Research*, 87 (2014), pp. 744–50 (pp. 749–50); *CSPV*, p. 101.

51. *An English Chronicle*, p. 110; *Great Chronicle*, p. 193; *A Short English Chronicle*, pp. 76–7; *Annales*, pp. 775–6; *Fabyan*, pp. 638–40; *Gough*, pp. 161–2; Barron, 'London and the Crown 1451–61', pp. 98–9.

52. Original text 'both the newe kynge and the olde were fulle besyd to make hyr party strong', quoted from *Gregory's Chronicle*, pp. 216–17. For other accounts of the Battle of Towton see, *Waurin*, pp. 335–42; *CSPV*, pp. 99–108; *Hearne's Fragment*, pp. 8–10; *Benet's Chronicle*, p. 50; *A Short English Chronicle*, p. 77; *Annales*, pp. 777–8. For Edward's preparations for the campaign see, *CCR 1461–68*, pp. 54–6. Also see, David Santiuste, *Edward IV and the Wars of the Roses* (Barnsley: Pen & Sword Military, 2010), pp. 49–62; Goodman, *The Wars of the Roses*, pp. 51–2.

Chapter Four: Securing the Realm

1. Original text 'divers ... grete rebels' and 'sayd to be in secrete places', quoted from TNA, C 81/1488, no. 212. For the siege of Thorpe Waterville also see, *CPR 1461–67*, p. 28; PSO 1/23, no. 1209; *PL, III*, p. 267. For the ownership of the castle see, Michael M.N. Stansfield, 'The Holland Family, Dukes of Exeter, Earls of Kent and Hunting-don, 1352–1475' (Unpublished DPhil thesis, University of Oxford, 1987), p. 248. For the aftermath of Towton, see Stansfield, 'The Holland Family', p. 166; *Gregory's Chronicle*, p. 217; *A Short English Chronicle*, p. 77; *Benet's Chronicle*, p. 50.

2. For the seizure of castles see, *CPR 1452–61*, p. 34. For garrisons at Wallingford and Kenilworth, see TNA, DL 37/30. For Corfe see, *CPR 1461–67*, p. 31; E 404/71/1, no. 77. For Buckenham Castle see, *CPR 1461–67*, p. 67. For the siege of Hammes Castle see, DL 37/31.

3. *CPR 1452–61*, pp. 390, 637–8.

4. *CPR 1461–67*, pp. 37–8, 96; TNA, E 404/72/1, no. 30. For the discussion of the defences and early history of Carisbrooke see, Christopher Young, *Carisbrooke Castle*

(London: English Heritage, 2013); H.M. Colvin, *The History of the King's Works*, Volume 2 (London: HMSO, 1963), pp. 591–5. For the shipment of weaponry sent to the castle in 1450 see, E 404/66, no. 216. For the French attack on Jersey see, Cora L. Scofield, *The Life and Reign of Edward the Fourth: King of England and of France and Lord of Ireland*, Volume one (Stroud: Fonthill Media Limited, 2016), p. 179.

5. Scofield, *The Life and Reign of Edward the Fourth*, Volume one, pp. 174–84; *PL*, *III*, p. 269; *Benet's Chronicle*, pp. 50–1; TNA, E 404/72/1, no. 14.

6. Original text 'great dishonor and rebuke', 'other our kins-men and frinds, within short time to ayenge', 'well-willed', 'our especiall trust is in you', and 'faithful dilligence for the safeguard of hit', quoted from John Williams, *Ancient and Modern Denbigh: A Descriptive History of the Castle, Borough, and Liberties* (Denbigh: Printed and Published by J. Williams, Vale Street, 1856), pp. 86–7.

7. For Tenby see, E. Laws, 'Notes on the Fortifications of Mediaeval Tenby', *Archaeologia Cambrensis*, 51 (1896), pp. 177–92. For Pembroke see, John Goodall, *The English Castle, 1066–1650* (New Haven: Yale University Press, 2011), pp. 163, 208. For the letter from the Milanese ambassador see, Allen B. Hinds, ed., *Calendar of State Papers and Manuscripts, Existing in the Archives and Collections of Milan. Vol I* (London: HMSO, 1912), pp. 93, 101.

8. Michael J. Bennett, 'Stanley, Sir William (*c.* 1435–1495)', *Oxford Dictionary of National Biography* [https://doi.org/10.1093/ref:odnb/26282, accessed 9 May 2019]; TNA, SC 6/779/10. For his authorisation to grant pardons to rebels see, SC 8/29, no. 1435A.

9. *CPR 1461–67*, pp. 36–8, 98–9; TNA, DL 37/30; E.W.W. Veale, ed., *The Great Red Book of Bristol*, Volume 1 (Bristol: Bristol Record Society, 1933), pp. 137–8. For a description of Chirk see, Goodall, *The English Castle*, pp. 222–3. For the siege see, SC 6/779/10.

10. *CPR 1461–67*, pp. 43, 99–100.

11. Original text 'divers many other gentilmen' and 'clense the countreye afore us', quoted from Henry Ellis, ed., *Original Letters Illustrative of English History; Including Numerous Royal Letters From Autographs in the British Museum, And One or Two Other Collections*, Volume I, second edition (London: Printed for Harding, Triphook and Lepard, 1825), pp. 15–16.

12. Original text 'beyng vitailled, manned and appareld for longe tyme after', quoted from TNA, SC 8/29, no. 1435B. SC 8/29, no. 1435A; Rosemary Horrox, ed., *The Parliament Rolls of Medieval England 1275–1504, volume XIII, Edward IV 1461–1470* (London: The Boydell Press, 2005), p. 47; Rosemary Horrox, ed., *The Parliament Rolls of Medieval England 1275–1504, volume XIV, Edward IV 1472–1483* (London: The Boydell Press, 2005), pp. 65–8. For John Skydmore's service as a commissioner of peace for Herefordshire in the reign of Henry VI see, *CPR 1452–61*, p. 666.

13. Original text 'moost part of gentilmen and men of worship ar comen yn to the Kyng', quoted from *PL*, *III*, p. 312.

14. Quoted from the modernised English text from Horrox, *The Parliament Rolls of Medieval England 1275–1504, volume XIII*, p. 46. For the suggestion that Jasper and Exeter afterwards went to Scotland see, R.S. Thomas, 'Tudor, Jasper [Jasper of Hatfield], duke of Bedford (*c.* 1431–1495)', *Oxford Dictionary of National Biography* [https://doi.org/10.1093/ref:odnb/27796, accessed 9 May 2019]; Michael Hicks, 'Holland, Henry, second duke of Exeter', *Oxford Dictionary of National Biography* [https://doi.org/10.1093/ref:odnb/50223, accessed 9 May 2019].

15. For the history of Rhuddlan see, H.M. Colvin, *The History of the King's Works*, Volume 1 (London: HMSO, 1963), pp. 318–27. For the garrison and constable of the castle prior to 1461 see, TNA, SC 6/779/7. For the siege see, SC 6/779/10. Gunpowder is recorded as having been expended at the siege in a later set of chamberlain accounts for 1463–4, SC 6/780/2. For garrisons being installed in castles in December see, SC 6/1217/4.

16. For the defence of Pembroke and Tenby see, NLW, Badminton 1564. For William Herbert remaining at Pembroke until at least 14 October see, TNA, C 81/1488, no. 220. For the possible identification of William Herbert, esquire, as the half-brother of Lord Herbert see, G.H.R. Kent, 'The Estates of the Herbert Family in the Mid-Fifteenth Century' (Unpublished doctoral thesis, Keele University, 1973), p. 41.

17. Original text 'grete nombre' quoted from TNA, SC 6/1224/7. For the garrison at Carmarthen see, SC 6/1224/6. For a description of Carreg Cennen see, Colvin, *The History of the King's Works*, Volume 2, p. 602. For the Gruffydd family see, R.A. Griffiths, *Sir Rhys ap Thomas and his Family: A Study in the Wars of the Roses and Early Tudor Politics* (Cardiff: University of Wales Press, 1993), pp. 24–8.

18. Original text 'of such strengthe that all the misgoverned men of that cuntre there entendid to have enhited the same castell & to have lyved by robberye and spoylyng oure people', 'stode divided in two parties like to have growen to grete myschef & manslaghter', and 'grete power and multitude of people' quoted from TNA, SC 6/1224/7. For the capture and slighting of Carreg Cennen see, ibid. Also see, Barry Lewis, ed., *Guto'r Glyn.net*, no. 21, 'In praise of William Herbert of Raglan, first earl of Pembroke, after the capture of Harlech castle, 1468' [http://www.gutorglyn.net/gutorglyn/poem/?poem-selection=021&first-line=022, accessed 14 December 2019]. For Sir Richard Herbert see, Kent, 'The Estates of the Herbert Family in the Mid-Fifteenth Century', p. 39.

19. Horrox, *The Parliament Rolls of Medieval England 1275–1504, volume XIII*, p. 45; *PL, III*, p. 271.

20. Quotations from James Orchard Halliwell, ed., *Letters of the Kings of England*, Volume I (London: Henry Colburn, 1848), pp. 123–5. Horrox, *The Parliament Rolls of Medieval England 1275–1504, volume XIII*, p. 45.

21. For the garrison at Newcastle see, George Poulson, ed., *Beverlac; or the Antiquities and History of the Town of Beverley, in the County of York, and of the Provostry and Collegiate Establishment of St. John's; with a Minute Description of the Present Minster and the Church of St. Mary*, Volume one (Beverley: Printed for George Scaum, 1829), pp. 240–1. For the garrison at Tynemouth see, TNA, E 404/72/4, no. 44. For the Lumleys see, Keith Dockray, 'Lumley, George, third Baron Lumley (d. 1507)', *Oxford Dictionary of National Biography* [https://doi.org/10.1093/ref:odnb/17175, accessed 16 May 2019].

22. A.J. Pollard, *North-eastern England during the Wars of the Roses* (Oxford: Clarendon Press, 1990), p. 298. For Sir Roger Ogle's commission see, *CPR 1461–1467*, p. 29.

23. *CPR 1461–67*, pp. 30–1, 576–7. Hinds, *Calendar of State Papers and Manuscripts*, pp. 101–2. For the siege of Skipton see, TNA, DL 29/481/7760. For a description of Skipton and its strategic location see, O.H. Creighton, *Castles and Landscapes. Power Community and Fortification in Medieval England* (London: Equinox Publishing Ltd, 2002), p. 40; T.D. Whitaker, *The History and Antiquities of the Deanery of Craven in the County of York* (London: J. Nichols and Son, 1812), p. 322.

24. For the Lancastrian-Scottish attack on Carlisle and the quotation see Horrox, *The Parliament Rolls of Medieval England 1275–1504, volume XIII*, p. 45. For the report on the lifting of the siege see, *PL, III*, pp. 276–7. For Richard Salkeld's role in the defence of Carlisle see, *CPR 1467–77*, p. 25. For the damage inflicted on the city see, ibid., pp. 82, 87. For the damage to the walls of Carlisle see, Michael R. McCarthy, *Carlisle Castle: A Survey and Documentary History* (London: English Heritage, 1990), p. 161. For a description of Carlisle Castle see, Henry Summerson, *Carlisle Castle* (London: English Heritage, 2017). For Warwick's indenture with a gunner at Carlisle on 24 June see, TNA, E 326/6402.

25. Quoted from Horrox, *The Parliament Rolls of Medieval England 1275–1504, volume XIII*, p. 45.

26. Quoted from TNA, C 81/1377, no. 3. For the letter from the prior of Durham see, James Raine, ed., *The Priory of Hexham*, Volume one (Durham: Andrews, 1864), appendix, p. ci. For the imprisonment of Humphrey Neville see, Horrox, *The Parliament Rolls of Medieval England 1275–1504, volume XIII*, p. 123.

27. For the appointments given to Warwick and Ogle see, *CPR 1461–67*, pp. 79, 87. For the soldiers sent by Coventry see, Mary Dormer, ed., *The Coventry Leet Book, or, Mayor's Register, Containing the Records of the City Court Leet or View of Frankpledge, A.D. 1420–1555, with Divers Other Matters* (Oxford: Oxford University Press, 1907–13), pp. 317–19. For the garrison at Alnwick see, *CPR 1461–67*, p. 79. For the garrison at Cockermouth see, TNA, SC 6/1121/11. For the garrison and military supplies at Newcastle see, E 403/824, mm. 3, 6; E 404/72/1, nos. 35, 85–7; DL 37/32. For Tynemouth see, E 404/72/4, no. 44. For the commissions of array see, *CPR 1461–7*, pp. 561–2, 569, 575.

28. Original text 'Rule of hys sowdyours', quoted from *Annales*, pp. 779–80; *Great Chronicle*, pp. 198–9. Another account states that Alnwick was surrendered on 31 July, *Gough*, p. 163. For the description of Naworth see, Anthony Emery, *Greater Medieval Houses of England and Wales, 1300–1500, Volume I: Northern England* (Cambridge: Cambridge University Press, 1996), p. 233. For a description of Alnwick see, Goodall, *The English Castle*, pp. 138, 242–4, 266–7.

29. For the arrests of Lancastrian sympathisers and commissions of oyer and terminer see, *CPR 1461–67*, pp. 101–2, 132–3. For the Oxford conspiracy see, *Annales*, pp. 778–9; *A Short English Chronicle*, p. 78; *Benet's Chronicle*, p. 51; *Gregory's Chronicle*, p. 218; *Great Chronicle*, p. 198; Scofield, *The Life and Reign of Edward the Fourth*, Volume one, pp. 231–3. For coastal defence measures and Hasting see, *CPR 1461–67*, pp. 100–1, 132, 280; TNA, E 404/72/2, nos. 29, 44.

30. *PL, III*, pp. 306–7; *Waurin*, p. 431; Scofield, *The Life and Reign of Edward the Fourth*, Volume one, pp. 246–7, 250–5.

31. Original text 'the moste party of alle Northumberlond', quoted from *Warkworth*, pp. 1–3. Robert Davies, ed., *Extracts from the Municipal Records of the City of York during the Reigns of Edward IV. Edward V. And Richard III* (London: J.B. Nichols & Son, 1843), pp. 20–1; *CPR 1461–67*, p. 132. For the campaign see, *Waurin*, p. 431; *Gregory's Chronicle*, p. 218; *Annales*, p. 780. For the garrison at Knaresborough see, TNA, DL 29/481/7761.

32. For the peers and knights in Edward's army see, *Brief Notes*, pp. 157–8. For the Yorkist preparations see, TNA, E 404/72/2, no. 46; E 403/827A, mm. 3, 8–11; *CPR 1461–67*,

p. 231. For the flight of Margaret and skirmish on Holy Island see, *Great Chronicle*, pp. 199–201; *Gregory's Chronicle*, pp. 218–19; *Waurin*, p. 433; *Brief Notes*, p. 156.

33. For the illness of the king see, *Great Chronicle*, p. 200; *Fabyan*, p. 653. For the account of the sieges from the letter see, *PL, IV*, pp. 59–61. For compensation paid to Alnwick Abbey see, TNA, E 403/827A, m. 15.

34. For the various contingents in the Yorkist army see, TNA, DL 37/32; Davies, *Extracts from the Municipal Records of the City of York*, pp. 22–3; Anne Crawford, ed., *The Household Books of John Howard, Duke of Norfolk, 1462–1471, 1481–1483* (Stroud: Sutton for Richard III & Yorkist History Trust, 1992), I, 181–4. For the estimation as to the size of the Yorkist army and Lancastrian garrisons see, *Brief Notes*, pp. 158–9. For the artillery see, E 403/827A, mm. 11–12. For a description of Dunstanburgh see, Alastair Oswald and Jeremy Ashbee, *Dunstanburgh Castle* (London: English Heritage, 2016).

35. For the surrender of the castles see, *Annales*, p. 780. For Edward's first letter, with the dates of the surrender of Bamburgh and Dunstanburgh, see, Halliwell, *Letters of the Kings of England*, pp. 130–1. For his second letter see, BIA, YDA/2/20, f. 341r.

36. Original text 'comyne one boldy, thei myghte have takyne and distressit alle the lordes and comeners' and 'hade lye ther so longe in the felde, and were greved with colde and rayne, that thei hade no coreage to feght', quoted from *Warkworth*, pp. 2–3. *Annales*, pp. 780–1; *Fabyan*, p. 653; *Great Chronicle*, pp. 199–201.

37. For the pardon to Sir Ralph Percy see, Horrox, *The Parliament Rolls of Medieval England 1275–1504, volume XIII*, pp. 122–3. For the pardon to the garrison of Dunstanburgh see, *CPR 1461–67*, p. 262. For the entrusting of the two castles to Ralph Percy and his subsequent treachery see, *Gregory's Chronicle*, pp. 219–20.

38. For Sir Ralph Grey's service at the siege of Naworth, his subsequent alienation and his capture of Sir John Astley see, *Annales*, pp. 779, 781–2. For the appointment of Sir John Astley as captain and Sir Ralph Grey as constable of Alnwick, together with the latter's treachery see, *Gregory's Chronicle*, p. 220. For Sir John Astley's previous service to Edward IV see, *CPR 1461–67*, pp. 10, 190. For subsequent funds allocated for his ransom see, *CPR 1461–67*, pp. 359, 379. For his prowess at Smithfield in 1442 see, Friedrich W.D. Brie, ed., *The Brut or The Chronicles of England* (London: Kegan Paul, 1906), p. 482. For the French report see, L.M.E. Dupont, ed., *Anchiennes Cronicques d'Engleterre par Jehan de Wavrin*, Volume 3 (Paris: Librarie de la Société de L'Histoire de France, 1873), pp. 159–61.

39. For the Yorkist garrison at Norham see, TNA, SC 6/780/2; SC 6/780/4. For the Scottish siege see, *Gregory's Chronicle*, pp. 220–1. For a description of Norham see, Goodall, *The English Castle*, pp. 134–5, 347.

40. Original text 'with his trutours and rebelles have entred this lande wt grete puissance entendyng to do … all the hurt and damage that thay can ymagine' quoted from BIA, YDA/2/20, f. 341v. For Hastings letter and an account of the siege see, Scofield, *The Life and Reign of Edward the Fourth*, Volume one, pp. 293–4, 300. For the English raid into Scotland also see, George Burnett, ed., *The Exchequer Rolls of Scotland. Vol. VII. A.D. 1460–1469* (Edinburgh: HM General Register House, 1884), p. 495. For the siege and flight of Margaret and Brézé see, *Gregory's Chronicle*, pp. 220–1.

41. Original text 'oure viage ayenst our enemyes of Scotland to procede ayeniste their accustomed pride' quoted from WSRA, G 25/1/21, f. 67r.

42. Original text 'ordaynyd a grete navy and a grete armye … alle was loste and in vayne, and cam too noo purpose', quoted from *Gregory's Chronicle*, p. 221. For military preparations see, TNA, E 404/72/3, nos. 75–6; E 403/831, m. 12.

43. Original text 'Kyngys garde', 'fals Duke' and 'kepte hyt surely alle that wyntyr' quoted from *Gregory's Chronicle*, pp. 221, 2233. Ibid., pp. 219, 221–3. For this episode also see, Horrox, *The Parliament Rolls of Medieval England 1275–1504, volume XIII*, p. 122; *Fabyan*, p. 653. For the household men sent to Newcastle see, TNA, E 404/72/4, nos. 78–9.

44. Original text 'at his propre charges and costes at his owne perill to the use of the said Duke onlesse that such casualte falle by infortune of were that it shall passe his might and power so to doo', quoted from NYRO, ZRL 1/28. For the letter of protection see, Charles Spencer Perceval, 'Notes on a Selection of Ancient Charters, Letters, and Other Documents from the Muniment Room of Sir John Lawson, of Brough Hall, near Catterick, in Richmondshire, Baronet', *Archaeologia*, 47 (1882), pp. 179–204 (p. 190). For Burgh's constableship of Prudhoe and Clarence's ownership see, *CPR 1461–67*, pp. 143, 212–13. For Lancastrians who made their way to Northumberland see, Horrox, *The Parliament Rolls of Medieval England 1275–1504, volume XIII*, pp. 122–3; Scofield, *The Life and Reign of Edward the Fourth*, Volume one, pp. 309, 313.

45. Original text 'greate charges and costs … in resistyng and subdyng of our traictours enuemyes and rebells', quoted from TNA, E 159/242, brevia directa baronibus, Pascha, rot. 6d. For the capture of castles by the Lancastrians see, *A Brief Latin Chronicle*, pp. 178–9.

46. Original text 'at suche tyme as the castell of Skipton in Craven was taken by our traytors' quoted from TNA, DL 37/33. For the survey of Naworth see, C.S. Knighton, ed., *Calendar of Inquisitions Miscellaneous Preserved in the Public Record Office, Volume VIII, 1422–1485* (Woodbridge: Boydell, 2003), p. 210. For the garrison at Durham see, *CPR 1461–67*, p. 328.

47. For negotiations with Scotland see, Scofield, *The Life and Reign of Edward the Fourth*, Volume one, pp. 328–9. For accounts of the battles and executions see, *Gregory's Chronicle*, pp. 223–6; *Waurin*, pp. 440–1; *Annales*, p. 782. For items abandoned by Henry and another account of the executions of Lancastrian prisoners see, *A Brief Latin Chronicle*, p. 179. For Henry's bycocket see, *Chronicles of London*, p. 178; *Fabyan*, p. 654.

48. Original text 'bryng in to oure obeissaunce oure castells kepte by oure traytours and rebelles', quoted from WSRA, G 25/1/21, f. 70v. For Edward's arrival at Pontefract on 22 May see, Scofield, *The Life and Reign of Edward the Fourth*, Volume one, p. 334. For Henry's bycocket and its presentation to Edward see, *Chronicles of London*, p. 178. For the siege of Skipton Castle see, TNA, SC 6/780/2; SC 6/780/4.

49. For the surrender of the Tower of Hexham and the castles of Langley and Bywell see, *A Brief Latin Chronicle*, p. 179. For the authorisation given to Warwick and Montagu see, *CPR 1461–67*, pp. 342–3. For Lancastrians taking refuge in Bamburgh after Hexham see, *Annales*, p. 782. Colvin, *The History of the King's Works*, Volume 2, pp. 554–8.

50. Original text 'if ye deliver not this juelle the whiche the king our most dradde soverain lord … specially desirethe to have it hoole, unbroken, with ordennaunce. If ye suffre any greet gunne laid unto the wal & be shote & preuidice the wal it shall cost yowe the chiftens hede and so proceeding for evy gunne shet to the leest hedy of any personne

wt in the said place' quoted from CA, L. 15, ff. 32r–33v. For other accounts of the siege see, *Annales*, p. 782; *Gregory's Chronicle*, p. 227; *A Short English Chronicle*, p. 79; *Fabyan*, p. 654.

51. For accounts of Henry's capture and captivity see *Warkworth*, p. 5; *Annales*, p. 785; *A Short English Chronicle*, p. 80; *Gregory's Chronicle*, pp. 232–3. For the reward given to Sir James Harrington see, *CPR 1461–67*, pp. 460–1. Note that Waddington Hall is now in the county of Lancashire having formerly been part of the West Riding of Yorkshire.

52. *Warkworth*, p. 3.

53. Horrox, *The Parliament Rolls of Medieval England 1275–1504, volume XIII*, pp. 61–2.

54. The number of soldiers serving in these garrisons had varied throughout the 1450s. For example, twenty soldiers were allocated for the castle and five soldiers for the town of Beaumaris in 1452–3, which had decreased to six men for the castle alone by 1458–9, TNA, SC 6/1217/1; SC 6/1217/3. For the garrisoning of these castles in the 1450s and 1460s see, SC 6/1224/1–9; SC 6/1225/1–2; SC 6/1217/1–6; DL 29/636/10339.

55. For the activities of the northern rebels and the authorisation given to Mowbray see, *PL, IV*, pp. 95–6. For the military operations carried out by Howard see, Crawford, *The Household Books of John Howard*, I, 160–1, 232–4. Mowbray and Howard appear to have returned to East Anglia in the summer as they were given a commission on 4 June to investigate treasons in Norfolk and Suffolk, *CPR 1461–67*, p. 348. For Hamner's presence in the Harlech garrison see, Horrox, *The Parliament Rolls of Medieval England 1275–1504, volume XIII*, pp. 61–2.

56. Quotations from Horrox, *The Parliament Rolls of Medieval England 1275–1504, volume XIII*, pp. 124–5. For the renewed calls for the garrison of Harlech to surrender see, Ibid.

57. Original text 'certayne commissions', quoted from TNA, E 404/73/3, nos. 73A-B. For artillery sent for the expedition see, ibid. For the military activities of Shrewsbury see, *The Manuscripts of Shrewsbury and Coventry Corporations, Historical Manuscript Commission Fifteenth Report, Appendix, Part X* (London: Printed for HMSO, by Eyre and Spottiswoode, 1899), p. 30. For Ludlow see, SRO, XLB/8/1/14, f. 30. For the letter dated 6 November reporting that Tiptoft had travelled to Denbigh see, Thomas Stapleton, ed., *Plumpton Correspondence* (London: Printed for the Camden Society, 1839), p. 17.

58. For Jasper and Louis XI see, R.S. Thomas, 'Tudor, Jasper [Jasper of Hatfield], duke of Bedford (*c.* 1431–1495)', *Oxford Dictionary of National Biography* [https://doi.org/10.1093/ref:odnb/27796, accessed 10 June 2019]. For the ships provided to him see, Scofield, *The Life and Reign of Edward the Fourth*, Volume one, p. 458. For the claim that Jasper held sessions in the name of Henry VI see, *Gregory's Chronicle*, p. 237. For William Stanley's response and the garrison at Chester Castle see, TNA, SC 6/780/7.

59. For the commission of array see *CPR 1461–67*, p. 103. For the size of Herbert's army see *Annales*, p. 791. For the financing of Herbert's army and for the ordnance company see, TNA, E 404/74/1, nos. 67–8, 90, 129. My thanks to Dr Adam Chapman for bringing these documents to my attention.

60. Original text 'lovyd Kyng Harry' and 'so stronge that men sayde that hyt was inpossybylle unto any man to gete hyt' quoted from *Gregory's Chronicle*, p. 237. For the most detailed account of this campaign and siege see, *Annales*, p. 791. Also see, Barry Lewis,

204 Notes for pp. 98–102

ed., *Guto'r Glyn.net*, no. 21, 'In praise of William Herbert of Raglan, first earl of Pembroke, after the capture of Harlech castle, 1468' [http://www.gutorglyn.net/gutorglyn/poem/?poem-selection=021&first-line=022, accessed 14 December 2019]. For the death of Philip Vaghan see, John H. Harvey, ed., *William Worcestre Itineraries: Edited from the Unique MS. Corpus Christi College Cambridge, 210* (Oxford: At the Clarendon Press, 1969), p. 205. Also see, *Great Chronicle*, pp. 206–7; J.J. Smith, ed., *Abbreviata Cronica 1377–1469* (Cambridge: Publications of the Cambridge Antiquarian Soc., I, 1840), pp. 11–12. For the recovery of Jersey see, Scofield, *The Life and Reign of Edward the Fourth*, Volume one, pp. 478–80.

Chapter Five: The Wheel of Fortune

1. Charles Ross, *Edward IV* (London: Eyre Methuen, 1974), pp. 64, 68–70; Michael Hicks, *The Wars of the Roses* (London: Yale University Press, 2012), pp. 171–2.

2. Quoted from Ross, *Edward IV*, p. 63, n. 2. Ibid., pp. 70–1; Michael Hicks, *Warwick the Kingmaker* (Oxford: Blackwell Publisher Ltd, 1998), pp. 220–34; Hicks, *The Wars of the Roses*, pp. 186–7; *CPR 1461–67*, pp. 45, 186, 189, 215, 422, 434–5; TNA, DL 29/481/7760; DL 29/525/8373.

3. Ross, *Edward IV*, pp. 71–2; *CPR 1461–67*, pp. 340–1, 484; *CPR 1467–77*, p. 91.

4. J.L. Laynesmith, *Cecily Duchess of York* (London: Bloomsbury Academic, 2017), pp. 86–7; Michael Hicks, *False, False, Fleeting, Perjur'd Clarence: George, Duke of Clarence, 1449–78* (Gloucester: Alan Sutton, 1980), pp. 170–3, 180–3; Charles Ross, *Richard III* (London: Yale University Press, 1999), pp. 9–10; *CPR 1461–67*, pp. 131–2, 197, 212–13, 226–7, 327, 331, 454–5; *CPR 1467–77*, pp. 88–9, 139.

5. Michael Hicks, 'Elizabeth [née Elizabeth Woodville] (*c.* 1437–1492)', *Oxford Dictionary of National Biography* [https://doi.org/10.1093/ref:odnb/8634, accessed 17 June 2019]; Ross, *Edward IV*, pp. 95–6; *CPR 1461–67*, pp. 430, 445, 480–2, 535; *CPR 1467–77*, p. 41.

6. Quoted from Ross, *Edward IV*, p. 76. Ibid., pp. 75–7. R.A. Griffiths, 'Herbert, William, first earl of Pembroke (*c.* 1423–1469)', *Oxford Dictionary of National Biography* [https://doi.org/10.1093/ref:odnb/13053, accessed 14 June 2019]; *CPR 1461–67*, pp. 43, 114, 119, 268, 286, 366–7, 425–6, 526–7; TNA, SC 6/1224/5; DL 29/616/9881.

7. Quoted from Ross, *Edward IV*, p. 76. Ibid., pp. 75–7; Griffiths, 'Herbert, William, first earl of Pembroke (*c.* 1423–1469)'; G.H.R. Kent, 'The Estates of the Herbert Family in the Mid-Fifteenth Century' (Unpublished doctoral thesis, Keele University, 1973), pp. 392–420; *CPR 1461–67*, pp. 271, 352; *CPR 1467–77*, pp. 22, 41, 113; TNA, SC 6/1224/5; SC 6/1224/7.

8. Ross, *Edward IV*, pp. 73–5, 78–9. For grants given to Hastings see, *CPR 1461–67*, pp. 352–4; *CPR 1467–77*, pp. 22–3, 26–7. For Stafford see, *CPR 1461–67*, pp. 120, 129, 323, 360, 438–9; *CPR 1467–77*, pp. 22–3. For Donne see, *CPR 1461–67*, pp. 40, 111, 430–1; TNA, DL 29/574/9083; SC 6/1224/5. For Alvred Cornburgh and John Wode see, *CPR 1461–67*, p. 357–8, 447.

9. Quoted from David Williams, *The History of Monmouthshire* (London: Printed by H. Baldwin, 1746), p. 133. For a description of Raglan and its history see, John R. Kenyon, *Raglan Castle* (Cardiff: Cadw, 2003); John Goodall, *The English Castle, 1066–1650* (New Haven: Yale University Press, 2011), pp. 368–9.

10. Quoted from H.M. Colvin, *The History of the King's Works*, Volume 2 (London: HMSO, 1963), p. 680. For works at Bristol, the Tower of London and Fotheringhay see, TNA, E 364/104, rot. B-dorse.

11. Quoted from *Hearne's Fragment*, p. 23. Ross, *Edward IV*, p. 71; A.J. Pollard, 'Neville, Richard, sixteenth earl of Warwick and sixth earl of Salisbury [called the Kingmaker] (1428–1471)', *Oxford Dictionary of National Biography* [https://doi.org/10.1093/ref:odnb/19955, accessed 20 June 2019].

12. Original text 'after that rose grete discencyone evere more and more betwene the Kyng and hym', and 'to hyme in fee as many knyghtys, squyers, and gentylmenne as he myght, to be stronge', quoted from *Warkworth*, pp. 3–4. Ross, *Edward IV*, pp. 84–92, 110.

13. For the account of the capture of the messenger see, *Annales*, p. 788. Note that this account states that the captive was sent to the earl at Middleham Castle, whereas a warrant for issue records that two men, who almost certainly included the same individual, were sent to Sheriff Hutton see, TNA, E 404/74/1. For Warwick's anger at the Burgundian alliance see, *Crowland*, p. 115. Also see, Ross, *Edward IV*, pp. 104–16.

14. Original text 'one batayle aftere another, and moche troble and grett losse of goodes amonge the comone peple', quoted from *Warkworth*, p. 12. Pollard, 'Neville, Richard, sixteenth earl of Warwick and sixth earl of Salisbury'; Ross, *Edward IV*, pp. 124–5.

15. Original text 'Kyng oure soveregne lordys true subgettes of diverse partyes of this his realme of Engelond', 'as gret lyvelode and possessions as evyr had kyng of Engelond', and 'above theire disertis and degrees', quoted from *Warkworth*, pp. 46, 48. Ibid., pp. 46–51. For the Yorkshire rebellions see, K.R. Dockray, 'The Yorkshire Rebellions of 1469', *The Ricardian*, 6 (1983), pp. 246–57. For Sir John Conyer see, Rosemary Horrox, 'Conyers Family (per. *c.* 1375–*c.* 1525)', *Oxford Dictionary of National Biography* [https://doi.org/10.1093/ref:odnb/52783, accessed 24 June 2019].

16. Ross, *Edward IV*, pp. 128–32. For the letter to Coventry see, Mary Dormer, ed., *The Coventry Leet Book, or, Mayor's Register, Containing the Records of the City Court Leet or View of Frankpledge, A.D. 1420–1555, with Divers Other Matters* (Oxford: Oxford University Press, 1907–13), pp. 342–3. For the Battle of Edgecote see, *Hearne's Fragment*, pp. 24–5; *Warkworth*, p. 7; *Hardyng*, p. 442; *A Brief Latin Chronicle*, p. 183.

17. Quoted from *Crowland*, p. 117. For Humphrey's rebellion see, ibid. For the king's imprisonment at the castles of Warwick and Middleham see, *Hardyng*, pp. 442–3; *Warkworth*, p. 7. For these events in general see, Cora L. Scofield, *The Life and Reign of Edward the Fourth: King of England and of France and Lord of Ireland*, Volume one (Stroud: Fonthill Media Limited, 2016), pp. 499–504; Ross, *Edward IV*, pp. 133–5.

18. For the offices given to Gloucester see, *CPR 1467–77*, pp. 178–80, 185. For his commission to besiege the castles and to try the rebels see, ibid., pp. 181, 185. Scofield, *The Life and Reign of Edward the Fourth*, Volume one, pp. 504–6.

19. For a description of Caister see, Goodall, *The English Castle*, pp. 351–2; C.M. Woolgar, *The Great Household in Late Medieval England* (London: Yale University Press, 1999), pp. 63–7. G.L. Harriss, 'Fastolf, Sir John (1380–1459)', *Oxford Dictionary of National Biography* [https://doi.org/10.1093/ref:odnb/9199, accessed 24 June 2019]; Colin Richmond, 'Paston Family (per. *c.* 1420–1504)', *Oxford Dictionary of National Biography* [http://www.oxforddnb.com/view/article/52791, accessed 24 June 2019]; Helen Castor, 'Paston, John (I) (1421–1466)', *Oxford Dictionary of National Biography* [https://doi.org/10.1093/ref:odnb/21511, accessed 24 June 2019].

20. Original text 'provyd men, and connyng in the werr, and in fetys of armys', quoted from *PL, IV*, p. 306. For the third duke's temporary occupation of Caister see, *PL, III*, p. 286. For assaults made against servants of the Pastons see, *PL, V*, p. 30. For John Paston see, Richmond, 'Paston Family (per. *c.* 1420–1504)'.

21. For the garrison at Caister and the quote see, John H. Harvey, ed., *William Worcestre Itineraries: Edited from the Unique MS. Corpus Christi College Cambridge, 210* (Oxford: At the Clarendon Press, 1969), p. 191. For inventories of arms and armour at Caister see, MCO, FP 77; Norman Davis, ed., *Paston Letters and Papers of the Fifteenth Century*, Part 1, The Early English Text Society (Oxford: Oxford University Press, 2004), pp. 112—13. For the inventory of guns at Caister see, Davis, *Paston Letters and Papers of the Fifteenth Century*, p. 434.

22. Original text 'feythfull frende of owrs' and 'endifferent men to kepe the place', quoted from *PL, IV*, pp. 36–7. For the size of Norfolk's army and the siege see, Harvey, *William Worcestre Itineraries*, pp. 189, 191.

23. Original text 'reklesnese … whych shold be half impossybell in my mynd that thay shold myssuse so mech stuff' and 'yf thay myght in any wyse kepe it and save ther lyves', quoted from *PL, V*, pp. 41–4.

24. Original text 'your brother and his felesshep stand in grete joperte at Cayster', 'sore brokyn with gonnes of the toder parte' and 'grettest rebuke to you that ever came to any jentilman, for every man in this countre marvaylleth gretly that ye suffre them to be so longe in so gret joperte with ought help or other remedy', quoted from *PL, V*, pp. 45–7.

25. Original text 'on lyve and mery', quoted from *PL, V*, pp. 47–9.

26. Original text 'lak of vetayl, gonepowdyr, menys herts, lak of suerte of rescwe' quoted from *PL, V*, pp. 56–7. For the letters see, ibid., pp. 53–6. For the bombardment of Caister see, Harvey, *William Worcestre Itineraries*, p. 191.

27. P. Holland, 'The Lincolnshire Rebellion of March 1470', *The English Historical Review*, 103 (1988), pp. 849–69; John Gough Nichols, ed., *Chronicle of the Rebellion in Lincolnshire, 1470* (Printed for the Camden Society, 1847), pp. 5–11.

28. Original text 'partiners and chef provocars', quoted from Nichols, *Chronicle of the Rebellion in Lincolnshire*, p. 11. Ibid., pp. 11–18, 21–3; *PL, V*, pp. 70–1; *Hearne's Fragment*, p. 26; *Crowland*, p. 121; *Great Chronicle*, pp. 209–10; *Warkworth*, pp. 8–9.

29. For the seizure of their estates see, *CPR 1467–77*, pp. 218–19. For royal orders to seize Carlisle see, TNA, E 159/248, brevia directa baronibus, Trinity, rot. 3d. For William Parr's appointment see, PSO 1/34, no. 1782A; *CPR 1467–77*, p. 209. For Parr's defection to Edward see, Nichols, *Chronicle of the Rebellion in Lincolnshire*, pp. 14–16. For Gloucester's appointment see, R.L. Storey, 'The Wardens of the Marches of England towards Scotland, 1377–1489', *The English Historical Review*, 72 (1957), pp. 593–615 (p. 607).

30. For Warwick's alliance with the Lancastrian exiles see, Scofield, *The Life and Reign of Edward the Fourth*, Volume one, pp. 523–30; Henry Ellis, ed., *Original Letters Illustrative of English History; Including Numerous Royal Letters From Autographs in the British Museum, And One or Two Other Collections*, Volume I, second series (London: Printed for Harding and Lepard, 1827), pp. 132–9. For FitzHugh's rebellion see, *Chronicles of London*, p. 181; *Hearne's Fragment*, pp. 28–9; *CPR 1467–77*, pp. 214–16. For Edward's defensive measures see, *CPR 1467–77*, p. 221; TNA, E 159/252, brevia directa

baronibus, Hillary, rot. 1. Scofield, *The Life and Reign of Edward the Fourth*, Volume one, pp. 523, 526.

31. Original text 'pyes neste to mayntene his astate withe', quoted from *Warkworth*, pp. 10–11. *Crowland*, pp. 121–3.

32. Original text 'for the suerte of oure moost dere beloved wif the Quene oure childryn and other oure welbeloved subgetts thamie beyng within the same for theire comfort and defense', quoted from TNA, E 159/252, brevia directa baronibus, Hillary, rot. 1. For the defensive measures undertaken by the Londoners see, LMA, COL/CC/01/01/ 007, f. 222r; Charles Welch, *History of the Tower Bridge* (London: Smith, Elder and Co., 1894), p. 262. For Tiptoft's presence in the Tower see, PSO 1/34, no. 1777. For the flight of the queen see, *Great Chronicle*, p. 211; *Chronicles of London*, p. 182.

33. Original text 'nozt so clenly kepte as schuld seme suche a Prynce', quoted from *Warkworth*, p. 11. For the events concerning the Tower see, Reginald R. Sharpe, *London and the Kingdom*, Volume three (London: Longmans, Green & Co., 1895), pp. 386–7; Reginald R. Sharpe, *London and the Kingdom*, Volume one (London: Longmans & Co., 1894), p. 269. For Henry's release from the Tower also see, *Chronicles of London*, p. 182; *Crowland*, p. 123; *Great Chronicle*, p. 212.

34. Original text 'Bowcher of England', quoted from *Great Chronicle*, p. 212. For his cruelty in 1470 see, *Warkworth*, p. 9. For his trial and execution also see, *Chronicles of London*, p. 182; *Warkworth*, p. 13; Benjamin G. Kohl, 'Tiptoft [Tibetot], John, first earl of Worcester', *Oxford Dictionary of National Biography* [https://doi.org/10.1093/ ref:odnb/27471, accessed 7 July 2019].

35. Quoted from Scofield, *The Life and Reign of Edward the Fourth*, Volume one, p. 543, n. 1. Ibid., pp. 542–6; *Crowland*, p. 123.

36. The most detailed account of this campaign is provided by the *Arrivall*, pp. 1–9. For the claim that Edward had 300 Flemish handgunners see, *Warkworth*, p. 13. Ibid., pp. 13–14; Hannes Kleineke, 'Gerhard von Wesel's Newsletter from England, 17 April 1471', *The Ricardian*, 16 (2006), pp. 66–83 (p. 77); *Crowland*, pp. 122–3; *Great Chronicle*, pp. 214–15.

37. Original text 'more lyker a play then the shewyng of a prynce to wynne mennys hertys', quoted from *Great Chronicle*, p. 215. Kleineke, 'Gerhard von Wesel's Newsletter from England', pp. 77–80; *Arrivall*, pp. 9–17; *Warkworth*, pp. 14–15.

38. Kleineke, 'Gerhard von Wesel's Newsletter from England', pp. 80–7; *Warkworth*, pp. 16–17; *Arrivall*, pp. 17–21; *Crowland*, pp. 124–5; L.M.E. Dupont, ed., *Anchiennes Cronicques d'Engleterre par Jehan de Wavrin*, Volume 3 (Paris: Librarie de la Société de L'Histoire de France, 1873), pp. 124–8. Also see, David Santiuste, *Edward IV and the Wars of the Roses* (Barnsley: Pen & Sword Military, 2010), pp. 116–20; Anthony Goodman, *The Wars of the Roses* (London: Routledge & Kegan Paul, 1991), pp. 76–9.

39. The recipient of Courtenay's letter is not specified. Original text 'mooste werly and fensibill a ray', quoted from BL, Add MS 41140, f. 169. For the campaign and Battle of Tewkesbury see, *Arrivall*, pp. 22–31; *Crowland*, pp. 126–7; *Warkworth*, pp. 17–19; Dupont, *Anchiennes Cronicques d'Engleterre par Jehan de Wavrin*, pp. 132–40. For Beauchamp's position as constable of Gloucester Castle see, *CPR 1467–77*, pp. 183, 315. Also see, Santiuste, *Edward IV and the Wars of the Roses*, pp. 127–38; Goodman, *The Wars of the Roses*, pp. 81–2.

40. *Arrivall*, pp. 31–3; Dupont, *Anchiennes Cronicques d'Engleterre par Jehan de Wavrin*, p. 140.

41. Original text 'disposyd to have helped to have suche mischiefe wroght than to defend it' and 'put theyr hands in riche mens coffres', quoted from *Arrivall*, p. 34.

42. Original text 'Capteyn and leder of oure liege lorde king Henrys people in Kent', 'disceyved by simple seynges and fayned tales', 'accepte and obey the kyng', and 'grete victories', quoted from Sharpe, *London and the Kingdom*, Volume three, pp. 387–91.

43. Quoted from Welch, *History of the Tower Bridge*, pp. 262–3. Bruce Watson, 'Medieval London Bridge and its Role in the Defence of the Realm', *Transactions of the London and Middlesex Archaeological Society*, 50 (1999), pp. 17–22 (pp. 18–19); Sharpe, *London and the Kingdom*, Volume three, p. 391; LMA, COL/CC/01/01/08, ff. 7, 26r.

44. TNA, E 403/844, mm. 5–7.

45. Quoted from Welch, *History of the Tower Bridge*, p. 262. For damage to the bridge and the beer houses see, ibid., pp. 262–3; Sharpe, *London and the Kingdom*, Volume three, p. 391. For the rebels leaving their ships at St Katharine's and their concerns about being trapped between the king's army and London see, *Arrivall*, pp. 34–5. For the barges sent by Anthony Woodville see, TNA, E 403/844, m. 5.

46. Original text 'made so sharp shott agaynst them, that they durst not abyde in eny place alonge the watarsyde, and so were driven from theyr owne ordinaunce', quoted from *Arrivall*, p. 36. For the siege also see, Sharpe, *London and the Kingdom*, Volume three, pp. 391–2; *Warkworth*, p. 19; *Hardyng*, pp. 459–60; *Chronicles of London*, p. 185; *Vergil*, p. 154; Dupont, *Anchiennes Cronicques d'Engleterre par Jehan de Wavrin*, pp. 143–4.

47. Original text 'mighty shott of hand Gunnys & sharp shott of arowis which did more scathe to the portcolyous and to the stoon werk of the Gate then to any Enemyes on eythir syde', quoted from *Great Chronicle*, p. 219.

48. *Great Chronicle*, pp. 219–20; *Arrivall*, pp. 36–7; *Crowland*, p. 129.

49. *Arrivall*, p. 38; *Warkworth*, pp. 20–1. For Henry's funeral arrangements see, TNA, E 403/844, mm. 7–8; *Great Chronicle*, p. 220; *Crowland*, pp. 130–1.

50. Original text 'Such as were Rych were hangid by the purys, and the othir that were nedy were hangid by the nekkis' quoted from *Great Chronicle*, p. 221. For Fauconberg's garrisoning of Sandwich and surrender see, *Arrivall*, pp. 38–9. For the royal garrisons at Sandwich and Rochester see, TNA, E 403/844, m. 4. For the second quote see, *Crowland*, pp. 128–9. For the punishment meted out to rebels in Kent also see, Ross, *Edward IV*, pp. 182–3; *Warkworth*, pp. 21–2.

51. Original text 'lamentyng greatly both his owne chaunce, & also the euell fortune that kinge Hery had' and 'some train or guile', quoted from *Hardyng*, p. 460. Also see, *Vergil*, pp. 154–5. For the expenses of William Herbert see, TNA, E 403/844, m. 5.

52. Original text 'soe stronglie beseeg'd the said castle ... that they were driven to this hard choice, eyther to perish through famine, or else to putt themselves into such handes from whom they could expect for little mercie or favour', quoted from R.A. Griffiths, *Sir Rhys ap Thomas and his Family: A Study in the Wars of the Roses and Early Tudor Politics* (Cardiff: University of Wales Press, 1993), p. 179. *Vergil*, pp. 154–5; *Hardyng*, p. 460; S.B. Chrimes, *Henry VII* (London: Yale University Press, 1999), pp. 15–18.

Chapter Six: The Yorkist Supremacy

1. Original text 'grete rums' of the landing of oure rebel and trator John late Erl of Oxenford' and 'sit stie and be quiet', quoted from BL, Add Ch 56425. For Oxford's departure from Dieppe and failure in Essex see, *PL*, *V*, pp. 184, 188–9. S.J. Gunn,

'Vere, John de, thirteenth earl of Oxford (1442–1513)', *Oxford Dictionary of National Biography* [https://doi.org/10.1093/ref:odnb/28214, accessed 31 July 2019].

2. Original text, 'xx^ti menne may kepe it ageyne alle the world', quoted from *Warkworth*, p. 26. For his companions see, *CPR 1467–77*, p. 418. For the claim that Oxford's force comprised eighty men see, John H. Harvey, ed., *William Worcestre Itineraries: Edited from the Unique MS. Corpus Christi College Cambridge, 210* (Oxford: At the Clarendon Press, 1969), p. 103. *Warkworth* instead claims that he had 400 men, p. 26.

3. Original text 'hade riyhte good chere of the comons' and 'scheff reulere of Cornwayle', quoted from *Warkworth*, p. 26. For Bodrugan's conduct of the siege see, ibid., pp. 26–7. For the instructions issued on 27 October see, *CPR 1467–77*, pp. 399–400.

4. Original text 'his owne menne wulde have brought hym oute', quoted from *Warkworth*, p. 27. For the Yorkist forces allocated for the siege see, TNA, E 101/71/5, nos. 15–16; E 405/57, mm. 1, 5–7; E 405/58, m. 5; *CPR 1467–77*, pp. 399, 412. Worcester improbably claims that the besiegers were 11,000-strong, Harvey, *William Worcestre Itineraries*, p. 103. For Oxford suing for pardon and the provisions in the castle see, *PL, V*, p. 203. For the latter also see, *Warkworth*, p. 27.

5. *CPR 1467–77*, p. 241; *CCR 1468–1476*, p. 315; Rosemary Horrox, 'Harrington Family (per. c. 1300–1512)', *Oxford Dictionary of National Biography* [https://doi.org/10.1093/ref:odnb/54525, accessed 20 October 2019].

6. For William and John Parr see, *CPR 1467–77*, p. 264. For castle constableships see, ibid., pp. 310, 331.

7. Charles Ross, *Richard III* (London: Yale University Press, 1999), pp. 24–6, p. 31, n. 30; *CPR 1467–77*, pp. 260, 297, 483, 556–7, 560; *CPR 1476–85*, p. 90.

8. Charles Ross, *Edward IV* (London: Eyre Methuen, 1974), pp. 187–91, 239–45; *CPR 1461–67*, pp. 457–8; Michael Hicks, 'George, duke of Clarence (1449–1478)', *Oxford Dictionary of National Biography* [https://doi.org/10.1093/ref:odnb/10542, accessed 31 July 2019].

9. Ross, *Edward IV*, pp. 193–6; *CPR 1467–77*, p. 429; TNA, PSO 1/46, no. 2386.

10. For Prince Edward residing at Ludlow see, Ross, *Edward IV*, pp. 196–7. For the ordinances and the quotes see, James Orchard Halliwell, ed., *Letters of the Kings of England*, Volume I (London: Henry Colburn, 1848), pp. 136–44.

11. For Edward's investment in magnificent display see, Ross, *Edward IV*, pp. 257–64. For his stay with Gruuthuse see, Livia Visser-Fuchs, 'Brugge, Lodewijk van [Louis de Bruges; Lodewijk van Gruuthuse], earl of Winchester (c. 1427–1492)', *Oxford Dictionary of National Biography* [https://doi.org/10.1093/ref:odnb/92540, accessed 5 August 2019]. For the account of Gruuthuse's visit see, Charles Lethbridge Kingsford, ed., *English Historical Literature in the Fifteenth Century* (New York: Burt Franklin, 1913), pp. 385–8.

12. Original text 'or lady masse', 'melodyousely songe', 'lytell Parke', and 'of the quenes owen ordinaunce', quoted from Kingsford, *English Historical Literature in the Fifteenth Century*, pp. 386–7.

13. Quoted from *Crowland*, pp. 138–9. For the 1475 campaign and pension see, Ross, *Edward IV*, pp. 205–38.

14. Original text 'Edward the 4. Began a right sumptuous pece of stone work, of the which he clerely finichid one excellent goodly toure of 3. hightes yn building, and brought up the other part likewise from the foundation with stone and mervelus fair cumpacid windows', quoted from Lucy Toulmin Smith, ed., *The Itinerary of John Leland in or*

about the Years 1535–1543 Parts I to III (London: George Bell and Sons, 1907), pp. 95–6. For the accounts of works see, TNA, E 159/257, recorda, Hilary, rots. 32–35d; E 101/478/15. Also see, H.M. Colvin, *The History of the King's Works*, Volume 2 (London: HMSO, 1963), pp. 764–5.

15. For Windsor see, Ross, *Edward IV*, pp. 274–6; John Goodall, *The English Castle, 1066–1650* (New Haven: Yale University Press, 2011), pp. 379–80; Colvin, *The History of the King's Works*, Volume 2, pp. 884–8. For the Tower of London see, Michael Hutchinson, 'Edward IV's Bulwark: Excavations at Tower Hill, London, 1985', *Transactions of the London and Middlesex Archaeological Society*, 47 (1996), 103–44; Colvin, *The History of the King's Works*, Volume 2, p. 729.

16. Original text 'progresse', 'dongeon', 'wt all diligence', 'Rownde Towre', and 'old kechyn', quoted from TNA, DL 5/1, ff. 90r-94v.

17. Original text 'the towre new begonne which is fallen downe', 'kings pleasure therin bee knowen', 'elles wol falle downe and breke' and 'feble that it may nat longe stande', quoted from ibid., ff. 101, 108.

18. For the career of Hastings see, Rosemary Horrox, 'Hastings, William, first Baron Hastings (*c.* 1430–1483)', *Oxford Dictionary of National Biography* [https://doi.org/ 10.1093/ref:odnb/12588, accessed 8 August 2019]. For the licence to crenellate see, H.C. Maxwell Lyte, ed., *Calendar of Charter Rolls*, Volume six (London: HMSO, 1927), p. 242.

19. John Goodall, *Ashby de la Zouch Castle and Kirby Muxloe Castle* (London: English Heritage, 2011), pp. 3–13, 29–31; Goodall, *The English Castle*, pp. 375–7.

20. For the accounts of works and the quotes see, A.H. Thompson, 'The Building Accounts of Kirby Muxloe Castle', *Transactions of the Leicestershire Architectural and Archaeological Society*, 11 (1913–20), pp. 193–345. For the building of the castle also see, Goodall, *Ashby de la Zouch Castle and Kirby Muxloe Castle*, pp. 18–32; Goodall, *The English Castle*, pp. 377–8.

21. Goodall, *The English Castle*, pp. 377–8.

22. Original text 'make ayeinst the said Scottes rigorous and cruel werre', quoted from Joseph Bain, ed., *Calendar of Documents Relating to Scotland. Volume 4, A.D. 1357–1509. Addenda–1221–1435* (Edinburgh: HM General Register House, 1888), p. 413. For the Anglo-Scottish marriage alliance in 1474 and resumption of war in 1480 see Ross, *Edward IV*, pp. 212–13, 278–9. For the burning of Bamburgh see, John Pinkerton, *The History of Scotland from the Accession of the House of Stuart to that of Mary*, Volume one (London: Printed for C. Dilly, in the Poultry, 1797), p. 503.

23. Original text 'all such personnes as ye may make in there most defensible arrey', quoted from Thomas Stapleton, ed., *Plumpton Correspondence* (London: Printed for the Camden Society, 1839), p. 40. For military preparations see, *CPR 1476–85*, pp. 205, 213–14. For Gloucester's raid see, Ross, *Edward IV*, p. 279.

24. Quoted from *CSPV*, pp. 142–3. For military preparations see Cora L. Scofield, *The Life and Reign of Edward the Fourth: King of England and of France and Lord of Ireland*, Volume two (London: Longmans, Green, 1923), pp. 305, 316; Michael Hicks, *Richard III. The Self-Made King* (London: Yale University Press, 2019), pp. 205–8; *CPR 1476–85*, pp. 240–1, 249–50, 264, 282, 288. For the English raid on eastern Scotland and Scottish raiding see, John Lesley, *The History of Scotland, From the Death of King James I* (Edinburgh: Bannatyne Club, 1830), pp. 44–5. For naval operations also see,

C.F. Richmond, 'English Naval Power in the Fifteenth Century', *History*, 52 (1967), pp. 1–15 (p. 10). For shortages of food see, *CPR 1476–85*, p. 254.

25. For the size of the English army see, Scofield, *The Life and Reign of Edward the Fourth*, Volume two, p. 344. For the Scottish defences at Berwick see, K.M. Brown, ed., '1482/3/44', *The Records of the Parliaments of Scotland to 1707*, 1482/3/44. [https://www.rps.ac.uk/search.php?action=fetch_index_frame&fn=jamesiii_trans&id=3689&-query=Edward+iv&type=trans&variants=Edward&google=Edward, accessed 11 Aug. 2019]. For an account of the campaign, see a letter from Edward IV to the Pope, *CSPV*, pp. 145–6. Also see, Hicks, *Richard III*, pp. 209–24.

26. Quoted from *CSPV*, p. 146. For the siege of Berwick see, Lesley, *The History of Scotland*, pp. 49–50. For damage to the fortifications see, Colvin, *The History of the King's Works*, Volume 2, pp. 570–1.

27. Quoted from *Crowland*, pp. 146–9. For the siege of Berwick also see, *Vergil*, p. 170.

Chapter Seven: The Final Struggle

1. *Crowland*, pp. 150–5; *Mancini*, pp. 59, 85–9; Charles Ross, *Richard III* (London: Yale University Press, 1999), pp. 65–9.

2. *Mancini*, pp. 90–101; *Crowland*, pp. 154–7; Ross, *Richard III*, pp. 69–74.

3. *Mancini*, pp. 102–3; *Crowland*, pp. 156–9; *CPR 1476–85*, pp. 349–50; TNA, SC 6/1288/3; Ross, *Richard III*, p. 77.

4. Quoted from Angelo Raine, ed., *York Civic Records*, Volume one (Wakefield: Printed for the Society, 1939), pp. 73–4; *Mancini*, pp. 108–11; *Great Chronicle*, p. 231; *Crowland*, pp. 158–9; *Chronicles of London*, p. 190; *Vergil*, pp. 179–82.

5. Quoted from *Mancini*, pp. 112–13; *Crowland*, pp. 158–9; *Great Chronicle*, p. 231; *Vergil*, p. 178.

6. *Crowland*, pp. 159–61; *Mancini*, pp. 114–21; *Vergil*, pp. 182–7; *Great Chronicle*, p. 231; *Chronicles of London*, pp. 190–1. For John Neville's constableship of Pontefract and garrison see, TNA, DL 29/526/8391.

7. *Crowland*, pp. 162–3; *Vergil*, pp. 192–7; *Chronicles of London*, p. 191; Ross, *Richard III*, pp. 105–15, 196; S.B. Chrimes, *Henry VII* (London: Yale University Press, 1999), pp. 22–4.

8. Original text 'a sore and hard dealing man' and 'to the feild against ther wills, and withowt any lust to fight for him, rather by rigorus commandement than for money', quoted from *Vergil*, p. 199. For the measures taken by Howard see, Anne Crawford, ed., *The Household Books of John Howard, Duke of Norfolk, 1462–1471, 1481–1483* (Stroud: Sutton for Richard III & Yorkist History Trust, 1992), II, pp. 468–71. For the poor weather conditions see, Lucy Toulmin Smith, ed., *The Maire of Bristowe is Kalendar* (London: Printed for the Camden Society, 1972), p. 46; R.A. Griffiths, *Sir Rhys ap Thomas and his Family: A Study in the Wars of the Roses and Early Tudor Politics* (Cardiff: University of Wales Press, 1993), p. 205.

9. Quoted from *Crowland*, pp. 164–5; *Vergil*, pp. 199–201; *Chronicles of London*, pp. 191–2; Griffiths, *Sir Rhys ap Thomas and his Family*, pp. 205–6; *Great Chronicle*, pp. 234–5; T.B. Pugh, *The Marcher Lordships of South Wales, 1415–1536* (Cardiff: University of Wales Press, 1963), pp. 240–1.

10. For the architecture of Bodiam see, John Goodall, *The English Castle, 1066–1650* (New Haven: Yale University Press, 2011), pp. 314–17. For the order to lay siege to

the castle see, *CPR 1476–85*, p. 370. For the 1483 rebellion also see, Michael Hicks, *Richard III. The Self-Made King* (London: Yale University Press, 2019), pp. 293–305.

11. Quoted from *Crowland*, pp. 172–3. Ross, *Richard III*, p. 118. For the grant of Plympton Castle see, *CPR 1476–85*, p. 531. For Barnstaple and Torrington see, *CPR 1476–85*, p. 429. For Exeter, *CPR 1476–85*, p. 502. For Carisbrooke see, *CPR 1476–85*, p. 410. For Southampton see, *CPR 1476–85*, p. 412.

12. For the constables and garrisons of castles in north Wales see, TNA, SC 6/1217/7; SC 6/782/10; Rosemary Horrox and P.W. Hammond, eds, *British Library Harleian Manuscript 433. Vol. 1, Register of Grants for the Reigns of Edward V and Richard III* (Gloucester: A. Sutton for the Richard III Society, 1979), pp. 104, 155. For south Wales see, *CPR 1476–85*, p. 414; Ross, *Richard III*, p. 158.

13. Ross, *Richard III*, pp. 196–200; Chrimes, *Henry VII*, pp. 28–30; *Vergil*, pp. 203–8. For English attacks on Breton shipping see, *CPR 1476–85*, pp. 402, 426, 465.

14. Original text 'ravisshyd with joy' and 'great nobilytie and knowledge in the warres', quoted from *Vergil*. For the siege also see, ibid., pp. 212–13; *Hardyng*, pp. 538–9; TNA, E 101/198/13, ff. 91r–92v. For the death of Prince Edward see, *Crowland*, pp. 170–1.

15. Original text 'to be redy in there most defensible arraye', quoted from *PL, VI*, pp. 81–4. For his naval preparations and courier system see *Crowland*, pp. 172–7. Also see, Ross, *Richard III*, pp. 203–9.

16. Ross, *Richard III*, pp. 200–2, 210–12; Chrimes, *Henry VII*, pp. 36–44; *Vergil*, pp. 215–18. For the surrender of Shrewsbury see, William Campbell, ed., *Materials for a History of the Reign of Henry VII*, Volume one (London: Longman & Co., 1873), p. 156. Financial accounts for castles in southern Wales, such as for Pembroke and Carmarthen, do not survive for this period. Yet, as these places were often garrisoned during times of crisis during the reigns of Henry VI and Edward IV, it is probable that they were defended at this time. For the garrisons of the castles of north Wales see, TNA, SC 6/1217/7.

17. Original text 'killyd fyghting manfully in the thickkest presse of his enemyes', quoted from *Vergil*, p. 224. For the campaign and battle also see, ibid., pp. 218–27; *Crowland*, pp. 178–83; *Great Chronicle*, pp. 237–8; *Chronicles of London*, p. 193; Anthony Goodman, *The Wars of the Roses* (London: Routledge & Kegan Paul, 1991), pp. 91–5; Chrimes, *Henry VII*, pp. 45–9.

18. Chrimes, *Henry VII*, pp. 50–2, 58–62.

19. Ibid., pp. 54–8; Campbell, *Materials for a History of the Reign of Henry VII*, Volume one, pp. 258–9, 594–5; *CPR 1485–94*, pp. 24, 28–9, 90; H.C. Maxwell Lyte, *A History of Dunster and of the Families of Mohun & Luttrell* (London: The St Catherine Press Ltd, 1909), p. 129.

20. For the acts of attainders against supporters of Richard see, Michael Hicks, *The Wars of the Roses* (London: Yale University Press, 2012), pp. 235–42. For the rebellion of Lovell and Stafford see, C.H. Williams, 'The Rebellion of Humphrey Stafford in 1486', *The English Historical Review*, 43 (1928), pp. 181–9; Denys Hay, ed., *The Anglica Historia of Polydore Vergil, A.D. 1485–1537* (London: Offices of the Royal Historical Society, 1950), pp. 10–11. For the defence of Sheriff Hutton see, TNA, E 159/263, brevia directa baronibus, Pascha, rots. 1–1d. For the defence of Brecon Castle see, BL, Egerton Roll 2192, mm. 4d–5; Griffiths, *Sir Rhys ap Thomas and his Family*, p. 47.

21. Chrimes, *Henry VII*, pp. 72, 76. For Henry's correspondence with York see, Lorraine C. Attreed, ed., *The York House Books 1461–1490. Volume 1* (Stroud: Alan Sutton, 1991), pp. 549, 556, 561–2.

22. Hay, *The Anglica Historia of Polydore Vergil*, pp. 12–23; Thomas Hearne, ed., *Joannis Lelandi Antiquarii de rebus Britannicis Collectanea*, volume four (London: Ben White, 1774), pp. 209–12; Attreed, *The York House Books 1461–1490*, pp. 570–2.

23. Hay, *The Anglica Historia of Polydore Vergil*, pp. 24–5; Hearne, *Joannis Lelandi Antiquarii de rebus Britannicis Collectanea*, pp. 212–15; Attreed, *The York House Books 1461–1490*, p. 573.

Appendix A: Brief Biographies of Key Figures

1. Michael Hicks, 'Neville [Fauconberg], Thomas [called the Bastard of Fauconberg] (d. 1471)', *Oxford Dictionary of National Biography* [https://doi.org/10.1093/ref:odnb/9201, accessed 20 October 2019].

2. Martin Cherry, 'Bonville, William, first Baron Bonville (1392–1461)', *Oxford Dictionary of National Biography* [https://doi.org/10.1093/ref:odnb/50217, accessed 20 October 2019].

3. Linda Clark, 'Bourchier, Henry, first earl of Essex (c. 1408–1483)', *Oxford Dictionary of National Biography* [https://doi.org/10.1093/ref:odnb/2987, accessed 20 October 2019].

4. C.S.L. Davies, 'Stafford, Henry, second duke of Buckingham (1455–1483)', *Oxford Dictionary of National Biography* [https://doi.org/10.1093/ref:odnb/26204, accessed 20 October 2019].

5. Carole Rawcliffe, 'Stafford, Humphrey, first duke of Buckingham (1402–1460)', *Oxford Dictionary of National Biography* [https://doi.org/10.1093/ref:odnb/26207, accessed 20 October 2019].

6. John Watts, 'Butler, James, first earl of Wiltshire and fifth earl of Ormond (1420–1461)', *Oxford Dictionary of National Biography* [https://doi.org/10.1093/ref:odnb/4188, accessed 20 October 2019].

7. I.M.W. Harvey, 'Cade, John [Jack] [alias John Mortimer; called the Captain of Kent] (d. 1450)', *Oxford Dictionary of National Biography* [https://doi.org/10.1093/ref:odnb/4292, accessed 20 October 2019].

8. Christopher Harper-Bill, 'Cecily [Cicely] [née Cecily Neville], duchess of York (1415–1495)', *Oxford Dictionary of National Biography* [https://doi.org/10.1093/ref:odnb/50231, accessed 20 October 2019].

9. Richard Vaughan, *Charles the Bold: the Last Valois Duke of Burgundy* (Woodbridge: Boydell Press, 2002).

10. Michael Hicks, 'George, duke of Clarence (1449–1478)', *Oxford Dictionary of National Biography* [https://doi.org/10.1093/ref:odnb/10542, accessed 20 October 2019].

11. Henry Summerson, 'Clifford, John, ninth Baron Clifford (1435–1461)', *Oxford Dictionary of National Biography* [https://doi.org/10.1093/ref:odnb/5654, accessed 20 October 2019].

12. Henry Summerson, 'Clifford, Thomas, eighth Baron Clifford (1414–1455)', *Oxford Dictionary of National Biography* [https://doi.org/10.1093/ref:odnb/5663, accessed 20 October 2019].

214 Notes for pp. 157–60

13. Martin Cherry, 'Courtenay, Thomas, thirteenth earl of Devon (1414–1458)', *Oxford Dictionary of National Biography* [https://doi.org/10.1093/ref:odnb/50218, accessed 20 October 2019].

14. Ibid.

15. A.C. Reeves, 'Cromwell, Ralph, third Baron Cromwell (1393?–1456)', *Oxford Dictionary of National Biography* [https://doi.org/10.1093/ref:odnb/6767, accessed 20 October 2019].

16. R.A. Griffiths, 'Devereux, Walter, first Baron Ferrers of Chartley (*c.* 1432–1485)', *Oxford Dictionary of National Biography* [https://doi.org/10.1093/ref:odnb/50222, accessed 20 October 2019].

17. R.S. Thomas, 'Tudor, Edmund [Edmund of Hadham], first earl of Richmond (*c.* 1430–1456)', *Oxford Dictionary of National Biography* [https://doi.org/10.1093/ref:odnb/27795, accessed 20 October 2019].

18. Rosemary Horrox, 'Edward IV (1442–1483)', *Oxford Dictionary of National Biography* [https://doi.org/10.1093/ref:odnb/8520, accessed 20 October 2019].

19. R.A. Griffiths, 'Edward [Edward of Westminster], prince of Wales (1453–1471)', *Oxford Dictionary of National Biography* [https://doi.org/10.1093/ref:odnb/8524, accessed 20 October 2019].

20. R.A. Griffiths, 'Percy, Thomas, first Baron Egremont (1422–1460)', *Oxford Dictionary of National Biography* [https://doi.org/10.1093/ref:odnb/50235, accessed 20 October 2019].

21. Michael Hicks, 'Elizabeth [née Elizabeth Woodville] (*c.* 1437–1492)', *Oxford Dictionary of National Biography* [https://doi.org/10.1093/ref:odnb/8634, accessed 20 October 2019].

22. Michael Hicks, 'Holland, Henry, second duke of Exeter (1430–1475)', *Oxford Dictionary of National Biography* [https://doi.org/10.1093/ref:odnb/50223, accessed 20 October 2019].

23. G.L. Harriss, 'Fastolf, Sir John (1380–1459)', *Oxford Dictionary of National Biography* [https://doi.org/10.1093/ref:odnb/9199, accessed 20 October 2019].

24. Rosemary Horrox, 'Grey, Edmund, first earl of Kent (1416–1490)', *Oxford Dictionary of National Biography* [https://doi.org/10.1093/ref:odnb/11529, accessed 20 October 2019].

25. Rosemary Horrox, 'Harrington Family (per. *c.* 1300–1512)', *Oxford Dictionary of National Biography* [https://doi.org/10.1093/ref:odnb/54525, accessed 20 October 2019].

26. Rosemary Horrox, 'Hastings, William, first Baron Hastings (*c.* 1430–1483)', *Oxford Dictionary of National Biography* [https://doi.org/10.1093/ref:odnb/12588, accessed 20 October 2019].

27. R.A. Griffiths, 'Henry VI (1421–1471)', *Oxford Dictionary of National Biography* [https://doi.org/10.1093/ref:odnb/12953, accessed 20 October 2019].

28. S.J. Gunn, 'Henry VII (1457–1509)', *Oxford Dictionary of National Biography* [https://doi.org/10.1093/ref:odnb/12954, accessed 20 October 2019].

29. R.A. Griffiths, 'Herbert, William, first earl of Pembroke (*c.* 1423–1469)', *Oxford Dictionary of National Biography* [https://doi.org/10.1093/ref:odnb/13053, accessed 20 October 2019].

30. Ibid.

31. Anne Crawford, 'Howard, John, first duke of Norfolk (d. 1485)', *Oxford Dictionary of National Biography* [https://doi.org/10.1093/ref:odnb/13921, accessed 20 October 2019].

32. Michael Hicks, 'Hungerford, Robert, third Baron Hungerford and Baron Moleyns (*c.* 1423–1464)', *Oxford Dictionary of National Biography* [https://doi.org/10.1093/ref:odnb/14178, accessed 20 October 2019].

33. Norman Macdougall, 'James III (1452–1488)', *Oxford Dictionary of National Biography* [https://doi.org/10.1093/ref:odnb/14589, accessed 20 October 2019].

34. R.S. Thomas, 'Tudor, Jasper [Jasper of Hatfield], duke of Bedford (*c.* 1431–1495)', *Oxford Dictionary of National Biography* [https://doi.org/10.1093/ref:odnb/27796, accessed 20 October 2019].

35. Paul Murray Kendall, *Louis XI. 'The Universal Spider'* (London: Allen & Unwin, 1971).

36. Diana E.S. Dunn, 'Margaret [Margaret of Anjou] (1415–1461)', *Oxford Dictionary of National Biography* [https://doi.org/10.1093/ref:odnb/19454, accessed 20 October 2019].

37. Rosemary Horrox, 'Neville, John, Marquess Montagu (*c.* 1431–1471)', *Oxford Dictionary of National Biography* [https://doi.org/10.1093/ref:odnb/19946, accessed 20 October 2019].

38. Colin Richmond, 'Mowbray, John, third duke of Norfolk (1415–1461)', *Oxford Dictionary of National Biography* [https://doi.org/10.1093/ref:odnb/19454, accessed 20 October 2019].

39. Colin Richmond, 'Mowbray, John, fourth duke of Norfolk (1444–1476)', *Oxford Dictionary of National Biography* [https://doi.org/10.1093/ref:odnb/19455, accessed 20 October 2019].

40. Michael Hicks, 'Neville, George (1432–1476)', *Oxford Dictionary of National Biography* [https://doi.org/10.1093/ref:odnb/19934, accessed 20 October 2019].

41. A.J. Pollard, 'Neville, Sir Humphrey (*c.* 1439–1469)', *Oxford Dictionary of National Biography* [https://doi.org/10.1093/ref:odnb/19944, accessed 20 October 2019].

42. R.A. Griffiths, 'Percy, Henry, second earl of Northumberland (1394–1455)', *Oxford Dictionary of National Biography* [https://doi.org/10.1093/ref:odnb/21933, accessed 20 October 2019].

43. R.A. Griffiths, 'Percy, Henry, third earl of Northumberland (1421–1461)', *Oxford Dictionary of National Biography* [https://doi.org/10.1093/ref:odnb/21934, accessed 20 October 2019].

44. Steven G. Ellis, 'Percy, Henry, fourth earl of Northumberland (*c.* 1449–1489)', *Oxford Dictionary of National Biography* [https://doi.org/10.1093/ref:odnb/21935, accessed 20 October 2019].

45. P.W. Hammond, 'Percy, Sir Ralph (1425–1464)', *Oxford Dictionary of National Biography* [https://doi.org/10.1093/ref:odnb/21951, accessed 20 October 2019].

46. Rosemary Horrox, 'Richard III (1452–1485)', *Oxford Dictionary of National Biography* [https://doi.org/10.1093/ref:odnb/23500, accessed 20 October 2019].

47. A.J. Pollard, 'Neville, Richard, fifth earl of Salisbury (1400–1460)', *Oxford Dictionary of National Biography* [https://doi.org/10.1093/ref:odnb/19954, accessed 20 October 2019].

48. Helen Castor, 'Scales, Thomas, seventh Baron Scales (1399?–1460)', *Oxford Dictionary of National Biography* [https://doi.org/10.1093/ref:odnb/24776, accessed 20 October 2019].

49. Colin Richmond, 'Beaufort, Edmund, first duke of Somerset (*c.* 1406–1455)', *Oxford Dictionary of National Biography* [https://doi.org/10.1093/ref:odnb/1855, accessed 20 October 2019].

50. Michael K. Jones, 'Beaufort, Edmund, styled third duke of Somerset', *Oxford Dictionary of National Biography* [https://doi.org/10.1093/ref:odnb/1856, accessed 20 October 2019].

51. Michael K. Jones, 'Beaufort, Henry, second duke of Somerset (1436–1464)', *Oxford Dictionary of National Biography* [https://doi.org/10.1093/ref:odnb/1860, accessed 20 October 2019].

52. Michael Hicks, 'Stafford, Humphrey, earl of Devon (*c.* 1439–1469)', *Oxford Dictionary of National Biography* [https://doi.org/10.1093/ref:odnb/26208, accessed 20 October 2019].

53. Michael J. Bennett, 'Stanley, Thomas, first earl of Derby (*c.* 1433–1504)', *Oxford Dictionary of National Biography* [https://doi.org/10.1093/ref:odnb/26279, accessed 20 October 2019].

54. Michael J. Bennett, 'Stanley, Sir William (*c.* 1435–1495)', *Oxford Dictionary of National Biography* [https://doi.org/10.1093/ref:odnb/26282, accessed 20 October 2019].

55. John Watts, 'Pole, William de la, first duke of Suffolk (1396–1450)', *Oxford Dictionary of National Biography* [https://doi.org/10.1093/ref:odnb/22461, accessed 20 October 2019].

56. Roger Virgoe, 'Tailboys, Sir William (*c.* 1416–1464)', *Oxford Dictionary of National Biography* [https://doi.org/10.1093/ref:odnb/26949, accessed 20 October 2019].

57. Benjamin G. Kohl, 'Tiptoft [Tibetot], John, first earl of Worcester (1427–1470)', *Oxford Dictionary of National Biography* [https://doi.org/10.1093/ref:odnb/27471, accessed 20 October 2019].

58. R.A. Griffiths, 'Tudor, Owen [Owain ap Maredudd ap Tudur] (*c.* 1400–1461)', *Oxford Dictionary of National Biography* [https://doi.org/10.1093/ref:odnb/27797, accessed 20 October 2019].

59. R.A. Griffiths, 'Vaughan family (per. *c.* 1400–*c.* 1504)', *Oxford Dictionary of National Biography* [https://doi.org/10.1093/ref:odnb/48656, accessed 20 October 2019].

60. A.J. Pollard, 'Neville, Richard, sixteenth earl of Warwick and sixth earl of Salisbury [called the Kingmaker] (1428–1471)', *Oxford Dictionary of National Biography* [https://doi.org/10.1093/ref:odnb/19955, accessed 20 October 2019].

61. A.J. Pollard, 'Neville, Ralph, second earl of Westmorland (b. in or before 1407, d. 1484)', *Oxford Dictionary of National Biography* [https://doi.org/10.1093/ref:odnb/19952, accessed 20 October 2019].

62. Michael Hicks, 'Woodville [Wydeville], Anthony, second Earl Rivers (*c.* 1440–1483)', *Oxford Dictionary of National Biography* [https://doi.org/10.1093/ref:odnb/29937, accessed 20 October 2019].

63. Michael Hicks, 'Woodville [Wydeville], Richard, first Earl Rivers (d. 1469)', *Oxford Dictionary of National Biography* [https://doi.org/10.1093/ref:odnb/29939, accessed 20 October 2019].

64. John Watts, 'Richard of York, third duke of York (1411–1460)', *Oxford Dictionary of National Biography* [https://doi.org/10.1093/ref:odnb/23503, accessed 20 October 2019].

Appendix B: Recorded and Possible Sieges, 1455–87

1. A. Herbert, 'Public Order and Private Violence in Herefordshire, 1413–61' (Unpublished MA thesis, Swansea, 1978), p. 250.
2. *Annales*, pp. 779–80; *Great Chronicle*, pp. 198–9; *Gough*, p. 163.
3. *Annales*, p. 780.
4. *Brief Notes*, pp. 158–9; *Annales*, pp. 780–1; *Warkworth*, pp. 2–3; *Fabyan*, p. 653; *Great Chronicle*, pp. 199–201.
5. *CPR 1461–7*, p. 79.
6. Ibid. *Annales*, pp. 779–80; *Great Chronicle*, pp. 198–9; *Gough*, p. 163.
7. *Annales*, pp. 781–2; *Gregory's Chronicle*, p. 220.
8. *Brief Notes*, pp. 158–9; *Annales*, p. 780; James Orchard Halliwell, ed., *Letters of the Kings of England*, Volume I (London: Henry Colburn, 1848), pp. 130–1.
9. CA, L. 15, ff. 32r–33v; *Annales*, p. 782; *Gregory's Chronicle*, p. 227; *A Short English Chronicle*, p. 79; *Fabyan*, p. 654.
10. *Warkworth*, pp. 1–3.
11. R.A. Griffiths, *The Reign of King Henry VI: The Exercise of Royal Authority, 1422–1461* (London: Benn, 1981), pp. 753–4; *CPR 1452–61*, p. 356.
12. *CSPV*, pp. 145–6; John Lesley, *The History of Scotland, From the Death of King James I* (Edinburgh: Bannatyne Club, 1830), pp. 49–50; K.M. Brown, ed., '1482/3/44', *The Records of the Parliaments of Scotland to 1707*, 1482/3/44. [https://www.rps.ac.uk/search.php?action=fetch_index_frame&fn=jamesiii_trans&id=3689&query=Edward+iv&type=trans&variants=Edward&google=Edward, accessed 11 August 2019].
13. *CPR 1476–85*, p. 370.
14. John H. Harvey, ed., *William Worcestre Itineraries: Edited from the Unique MS. Corpus Christi College Cambridge, 210* (Oxford: At the Clarendon Press, 1969), pp. 189, 191; *PL*, *IV*, pp. 36–7, 41–9, 56–7.
15. *CPR 1467–77*, p. 181.
16. *CPR 1461–7*, pp. 37–8, 96; TNA, E 404/72/1, no. 30.
17. *CPR 1467–77*, p. 25.
18. Ibid. Rosemary Horrox, ed., *The Parliament Rolls of Medieval England 1275–1504*, *volume XIII, Edward IV 1461–1470* (London: The Boydell Press, 2005), p. 45.
19. TNA, E 159/248, brevia directa baronibus, Trinity, rot. 3d.
20. Herbert, 'Public Order and Private Violence in Herefordshire, 1413–61', p. 250.
21. William Rees, ed., *Calendar of Ancient Petitions relating to Wales* (Cardiff: University of Wales Press, 1975), pp. 184–6.
22. *PL*, *I*, pp. 392–3; R.A. Griffiths, *Sir Rhys ap Thomas and his Family: A Study in the Wars of the Roses and Early Tudor Politics* (Cardiff: University of Wales Press, 1993), pp. 12–24; Griffiths, *The Reign of King Henry V*, p. 779.
23. *CPR 1467–77*, p. 181.
24. TNA, SC 6/779/10.
25. TNA, C 1/46, no. 48.
26. *CPR 1452–61*, pp. 550, 564–5, 606; TNA, C 81/1376, no. 9; C 49/32, no. 12A.
27. *Brief Notes*, pp. 158–9; *Annales*, p. 780; Halliwell, *Letters of the Kings of England*, Volume I, pp. 130–1; *CPR 1461–67*, p. 262.
28. *Warkworth*, pp. 1–3.
29. *Annales*, p. 791; *Gregory's Chronicle*, p. 237.

30. *CPR 1467–77*, p. 241.
31. Hannes Kleineke, 'Gerhard von Wesel's Newsletter from England', *The Ricardian*, 16 (2006), pp. 66–83 (pp. 77–80).
32. *CPR 1467–77*, p. 181.
33. *Annales*, pp. 779–80.
34. Ibid.
35. *Gregory's Chronicle*, pp. 220–1; Cora L. Scofield, *The Life and Reign of Edward the Fourth: King of England and of France and Lord of Ireland*, Volume one (Stroud: Fonthill Media Limited, 2016), pp. 293–4, 300.
36. *A Brief Latin Chronicle*, pp. 178–9.
37. Griffiths, *Sir Rhys ap Thomas and his Family*, p. 179; *Vergil*, pp. 154–5; *Hardyng*, p. 460.
38. G.H. Radford, 'The Fight at Clyst in 1455', *Report and Transactions for the Devonshire Association*, 44 (1912), pp. 252–7; R.L. Storey, *The End of the House of Lancaster* (Gloucester: Alan Sutton Publishing, 1986), pp. 165–9; Michael Hicks, *The Wars of the Roses* (London: Yale University Press, 2012), pp. 115–16.
39. TNA, SC 6/779/10.
40. Griffiths, *The Reign of King Henry VI*, p. 812.
41. *An English Chronicle*, p. 99; *Benet's Chronicle*, p. 48; Thomas Thomson, ed., *The Auchinleck Chronicle* (Edinburgh: Printed for Private Circulation, 1819), pp. 57–8.
42. *Warkworth*, pp. 26–7; Harvey, *William Worcestre Itineraries*, p. 103; TNA, E 101/71/5, nos. 15–16; E 405/57, mm. 1, 5–7; E 405/58, m. 5; *CPR 1467–77*, pp. 399–400, 412; *PL, V*, p. 203.
43. TNA, DL 29/481/7760.
44. *A Brief Latin Chronicle*, pp. 178–9; TNA, DL 37/33.
45. TNA, SC 6/780/2; SC 6/780/4.
46. TNA, C 81/1488, no. 212; PSO 1/23, no. 1209; *CPR 1461–67*, p. 28; *PL, III*, p. 267.
47. *An English Chronicle*, pp. 95–8; *A Short English Chronicle*, pp. 73–4; *Benet's Chronicle*, p. 47; *Annales*, p. 773; *Gregory's Chronicle*, p. 211.
48. Kleineke, 'Gerhard von Wesel's Newsletter from England', pp. 77–80.
49. *Arrivall*, pp. 31–8; *Warkworth*, p. 19; *Hardyng*, pp. 459–60; *Chronicles of London*, p. 185; Charles Welch, *History of the Tower Bridge* (London: Smith, Elder and Co., 1894), pp. 262–3; TNA, E 403/844, mm. 5–7; LMA, COL/CC/01/01/08, ff. 7, 26r; Reginald R. Sharpe, *London and the Kingdom*, Volume three (London: Longmans, Green & Co., 1895), pp. 387–91.
50. Thomson, *The Auchinleck Chronicle*, pp. 57–8.
51. Kleineke, 'Gerhard von Wesel's Newsletter from England', pp. 77–80.
52. *Warkworth*, pp. 1–3.
53. *PL, IV*, pp. 59–61.

Appendix C: Recorded Garrisons, 1455–87

1. TNA, SC 6/1224/1–9; SC 6/1225/1–8; SC 6/1226/1–9.
2. *CPR 1461–7*, p. 79.
3. *Annales*, pp. 779–80; *Great Chronicle*, pp. 198–9; *Gough*, p. 163.
4. *Annales*, p. 780.
5. *Brief Notes*, pp. 158–9; *Annales*, pp. 780–1; *Warkworth*, pp. 2–3; *Fabyan*, p. 653; *Great Chronicle*, pp. 199–201.
6. *Annales*, pp. 781–2; *Gregory's Chronicle*, p. 220.

7. CA, L. 15, f. 32r.
8. TNA, SC 8/28, no. 1380A
9. *Brief Notes*, pp. 158–9; *Annales*, p. 780; James Orchard Halliwell, ed., *Letters of the Kings of England*, Volume I (London: Henry Colburn, 1848), pp. 130–1.
10. *Gregory's Chronicle*, p. 220.
11. *Annales*, pp. 781–2; *Gregory's Chronicle*, p. 220.
12. TNA, SC 6/1217/2–7; DL 29/636/10339–40; DL 29/636/10342–3; Rosemary Horrox and P.W. Hammond, eds, *British Library Harleian Manuscript 433. Vol. 1, Register of Grants for the Reigns of Edward V and Richard III* (Gloucester: A. Sutton for the Richard III Society, 1979), pp. 96, 239.
13. R.A. Griffiths, *The Reign of King Henry VI: The Exercise of Royal Authority, 1422–1461* (London: Benn, 1981), pp. 403, 753–4, 811–13.
14. *PL, III*, p. 271; *CSPV*, pp. 145–6; K.M. Brown, ed., '1482/3/44', *The Records of the Parliaments of Scotland to 1707*, 1482/3/44. [https://www.rps.ac.uk/search.php? action=fetch_index_frame&fn=jamesiii_trans&id=3689&query=Edward+iv&type= trans&variants=Edward&google=Edward, accessed 11 August 2019].
15. Charles Ross, *Richard III* (London: Yale University Press, 1999), p. 78; S.B. Chrimes, *Henry VII* (London: Yale University Press, 1999), p. 56.
16. *CPR 1476–85*, p. 370.
17. BL, Egerton Roll 2192, mm. 4d–5; R.A. Griffiths, *Sir Rhys ap Thomas and his Family: A Study in the Wars of the Roses and Early Tudor Politics* (Cardiff: University of Wales Press, 1993), p. 47.
18. E.W.W. Veale, ed., *The Great Red Book of Bristol*, Volume 1 (Bristol: Bristol Record Society, 1933), p. 137.
19. *CPR 1461–67*, p. 67.
20. *A Brief Latin Chronicle*, p. 179.
21. TNA, SC 6/1217/2–7; DL 29/636/10339–40; DL 29/636/10342–3.
22. John H. Harvey, ed., *William Worcestre Itineraries: Edited from the Unique MS. Corpus Christi College Cambridge, 210* (Oxford: At the Clarendon Press, 1969), p. 191.
23. William Rees, ed., *Calendar of Ancient Petitions relating to Wales* (Cardiff: University of Wales Press, 1975), pp. 184–6.
24. *CPR 1467–77*, p. 181.
25. TNA, E 404/68, no. 82; E 159/234, brevia directa baronibus, Trinity, rot. 15; E 404/72/1, no. 30.
26. TNA, E 159/242 brevia directa baronibus, Trinity, rots. 8-d.
27. Michael R. McCarthy, *Carlisle Castle: A Survey and Documentary History* (London: English Heritage, 1990), pp. 160–2.
28. Rees, *Calendar of Ancient Petitions relating to Wales*, pp. 184–6.
29. *PL, I*, pp. 392–3; R.A. Griffiths, *Sir Rhys ap Thomas and his Family: A Study in the Wars of the Roses and Early Tudor Politics* (Cardiff: University of Wales Press, 1993), pp. 12–24; Griffiths, *The Reign of King Henry V*, p. 779.
30. Herbert, 'Public Order and Private Violence in Herefordshire, 1413–61', p. 250.
31. TNA, SC 6/1224/6.
32. *CPR 1467–77*, p. 181.
33. Rees, *Calendar of Ancient Petitions relating to Wales*, pp. 184–6.
34. TNA, DL 29/584/9249; DL 29/596/9558.
35. TNA, SC 6/1224/6–7.

36. Ibid.
37. *CPR 1452–61*, p. 287.
38. *PL, III*, pp. 265–6; *CPR 1452–61*, p. 658.
39. TNA, SC 6/780/7.
40. TNA, SC 6/779/10.
41. TNA, C 81/1476, no. 30.
42. TNA, SC 6/1121/11.
43. TNA, SC 6/1217/2–7; DL 29/636/10339–40; DL 29/636/10342–3; C 1/46, no. 48.
44. TNA, E 404/71/1, no. 77.
45. *CPR 1461–67*, p. 232.
46. *CPR 1452–61*, pp. 550, 564–5, 606; TNA, C 81/1376, no. 9; C 49/32, no. 12A.
47. John Williams, *Ancient and Modern Denbigh: A Descriptive History of the Castle, Borough, and Liberties* (Denbigh: Printed and Published by J. Williams, Vale Street, 1856), pp. 86–7.
48. Horrox and Hammond, *British Library Harleian Manuscript 433. Vol. 1*, p. 142.
49. *Brief Notes*, pp. 158–9; *Annales*, p. 780; Halliwell, *Letters of the Kings of England*, Volume I, pp. 130–1; *CPR 1461–67*, p. 262.
50. *Gregory's Chronicle*, p. 220.
51. CA, L. 15, f. 32r.
52. TNA, DL 29/361/5987.
53. DUL, CCB B/1/9.
54. *CPR 1461–67*, p. 328.
55. *CPR 1452–61*, p. 280.
56. *CPR 1467–77*, pp. 183, 315; *Arrivall*, pp. 26–7.
57. TNA, SC 6/1217/2–3.
58. Rosemary Horrox, ed., *The Parliament Rolls of Medieval England 1275–1504, volume XIII, Edward IV 1461–1470* (London: The Boydell Press, 2005), pp. 61–2; *Annales*, p. 791; *Gregory's Chronicle*, p. 237.
59. TNA, SC 6/1217/7; Horrox and Hammond, *British Library Harleian Manuscript 433. Vol. 1*, pp. 104, 155.
60. TNA, DL 29/636/10342–3.
61. *A Brief Latin Chronicle*, p. 179.
62. Anne Crawford, ed., *The Household Books of John Howard, Duke of Norfolk, 1462–1471, 1481–1483* (Stroud: Sutton for Richard III & Yorkist History Trust, 1992), I, pp. 160–1, 232–4.
63. *The Manuscripts of Shrewsbury and Coventry Corporations, Historical Manuscript Commission Fifteenth Report, Appendix, Part X* (London: Printed for HMSO, by Eyre and Spottiswoode, 1899), p. 30.
64. *CPR 1467–77*, p. 241; *CCR 1468–1476*, p. 315.
65. TNA, DL 29/463/7548.
66. Rees, *Calendar of Ancient Petitions relating to Wales*, pp. 184–6.
67. TNA, DL 29/584/9249; DL 29/596/9558.
68. *CPR 1467–77*, p. 181.
69. TNA, DL 29/481/7761.
70. *A Brief Latin Chronicle*, p. 179.
71. *CPR 1452–61*, pp. 586–7.
72. *Annales*, pp. 779–80.

73. TNA, E 403/824, m. 6; DL 37/32; E404/72/4, nos. 78–79.
74. DUL, CCB B/72/7; TNA, SC 6/780/2; SC 6/780/4.
75. *A Brief Latin Chronicle*, pp. 178–9.
76 TNA, SC 8/29, no. 1435B.
77. NLW, Badminton 1564.
78. Griffiths, *Sir Rhys ap Thomas and his Family*, p. 179; *Vergil*, pp. 154–5; *Hardyng*, p. 460.
79. TNA, C 81/1476, no. 30.
80. *CPR 1452–61*, p. 649.
81. TNA, C 49/32, no. 8; *CPR 1452–61*, p. 649.
82. TNA, DL 29/525/8376.
83. TNA, DL 37/47A.
84. TNA, DL 29/526/8391.
85. TNA, DL 29/526/8392.
86. *CPR 1452–61*, p. 405.
87. G.H. Radford, 'The Fight at Clyst in 1455', *Report and Transactions for the Devonshire Association*, 44 (1912), pp. 252–7; R.L. Storey, *The End of the House of Lancaster* (Gloucester: Alan Sutton Publishing, 1986), pp. 165–9; Michael Hicks, *The Wars of the Roses* (London: Yale University Press, 2012), pp. 115–16.
88. NYRO, ZRL 1/28.
89. TNA, C 81/1476, no. 30.
90. TNA, SC 6/779/5–10.
91 .TNA, SC 6/779/10; SC 6/780/2–7.
92. TNA, E 403/844, m. 4.
93. *CPR 1452–61*, pp. 213–14; Thomas Thomson, ed., *The Auchinleck Chronicle* (Edinburgh: Printed for Private Circulation, 1819), pp. 57–8.
94. *Warkworth*, pp. 26–7; Harvey, *William Worcestre*, p. 103; TNA, E 101/71/5, nos. 15–16; E 405/57, mm. 1, 5–7; E 405/58, m. 5; *CPR 1467–77*, pp. 399–400, 412; *PL, V*, p. 203.
95. TNA, DL 29/560/8899.
96. TNA, E 159/263, brevia directa baronibus, Pascha, rots. 1-d.
97. TNA, DL 29/481/7760.
98. TNA, SC 6/780/2; SC 6/780/4.
99. Williams, *Ancient and Modern Denbigh*, pp. 86–7.
100. NLW, Badminton 1564.
101. TNA, C 81/1488, no. 212; PSO 1/23, no. 1209; *CPR 1461–67*, p. 28; *PL, III*, p. 267.
102. TNA, PSO 1/23, no. 1209.
103. *An English Chronicle*, pp. 95–8; *A Short English Chronicle*, pp. 73–4; *Benet's Chronicle*, p. 47; *Annales*, p. 773; *Gregory's Chronicle*, p. 211.
104. Caroline M. Barron, 'London and the Crown 1451–61', in *The Crown and Local Communities in England and France in the Fifteenth Century*, ed. by J.R.L. Highfield (Gloucester: Alan Sutton, 1981), pp. 89–109 (98, 108, n. 82).
105. Reginald R. Sharpe, *London and the Kingdom*, Volume three (London: Longmans, Green & Co., 1895), pp. 386–7; Reginald R. Sharpe, *London and the Kingdom*, Volume one (London: Longmans & Co., 1894), p. 269.
106. *Arrivall*, pp. 31–8; *Warkworth*, p. 19; *Hardyng*, pp. 459–60; *Chronicles of London*, p. 185; Charles Welch, *History of the Tower Bridge* (London: Smith, Elder and Co.,

1894), pp. 262–3; TNA, E 403/844, mm. 5–7; LMA, COL/CC/01/01/08, ff. 7, 26r; Sharpe, *London and the Kingdom*, Volume three, pp. 387–91.

107. TNA, E 404/72/4, no. 44; *CPR 1461–1467*, p. 29; E 403/824, m. 6; E 404/73/1, no. 8.

108. TNA, DL 37/30.

109. Thomson, *The Auchinleck Chronicle*, pp. 57–8.

110. TNA, C 81/1476, no. 30.

111. *Brief Notes*, p. 155.

112. TNA, C49/32, no. 8; *CPR 1452–61*, p. 649.

Bibliography

Unpublished Manuscript Collections

Borthwick Institute for Archives, York
York Diocesan Registry

British Library, London
Additional Manuscripts
Additional Charters
Egerton Manuscripts

College of Arms, London
Heraldic Collections, Pedigrees and Historical Miscellanies

Durham University Library
Books of Great Receipt
Special Collections, Miscellanea on Accounts

London Metropolitan Archives
London Journal Books

Magdalen College, Oxford
Fastolf Papers

National Library of Wales
Badminton Estate Records

Northampton Record Office
Westmorland (Apethorpe)

Shropshire Record Office
Bailiffs' & Chamberlains' Accounts

Stafford Record Office
Records of the Stafford Family

The National Archives, Kew
C 1: Court of Chancery, Six Clerks Office, Early Proceedings, Richard II to Philip and Mary
C 49: Chancery and Exchequer, King's Remembrancer, Parliamentary and Council Proceedings
C 81: Chancery, Warrants for the Great Seal
DL 5: Duchy of Lancaster, Court of Duchy Chamber, Entry Books of Decrees and Orders
DL 29: Accounts of Auditors, Receivers, Feodaries and Ministers

DL 37: Duchy of Lancaster and Palatinate of Lancaster, Chanceries, Enrolments
E 28: Exchequer, Treasury of the Receipt, Council and Privy Seal Records
E 101: King's Remembrancer, Accounts Various
E 159: King's Remembrancer, Memoranda Rolls
E 326: Exchequer, Augmentation Office, Ancient Deeds, Series B
E 364: Exchequer, Pipe Office, Foreign Account Rolls
E 403: Exchequer of Receipt, Issue Rolls
E 404: Exchequer of Receipt, Warrants for Issue
E 405: Exchequer of Receipt, Tellers' Rolls
KB 27: Court of King's Bench: Plea and Crown Sides: Coram Rege Rolls
PSO 1: Privy Seal Office, Signet and other Warrants for the Privy Seal, Series I
SC 6: Special Collections, Ministers Accounts
SC 8: Special Collections, Ancient Petitions

Wiltshire and Salisbury Record Office
City Ledger Book B

Printed Primary Sources

Armstrong, C.A.J., ed., *The Usurpation of Richard the Third* (London: Oxford University Press, 1936)

Attreed, Lorraine C., ed., *The York House Books 1461–1490. Volume 1* (Stroud: Alan Sutton, 1991)

Bain, Joseph, ed., *Calendar of Documents Relating to Scotland. Volume 4, A.D. 1357–1509. Addenda–1221–1435* (Edinburgh: HM General Register House, 1888)

Brie, Friedrich W.D., ed., *The Brut or The Chronicles of England* (London: Kegan Paul, 1906)

Brown, Rawdon, ed., *Calendar of State Papers and Manuscripts, Relating to English Affairs, Existing in the Archives and Collections of Venice, and in Other Libraries of Northern Italy. Vol. I. 1202–1509* (London: Longman, Green, Longman, Roberts, and Green, 1864)

Bruce, John, ed., *Historie of the Arrivall of Edward IV. In England and the Finall Recouerye of His Kingdomes From Henry VI A.D. M.CCCC.LXXI.* (London: Printed for the Camden Society by J.B. Nichols and Son, 1838)

Burnett, George, ed., *The Exchequer Rolls of Scotland. Vol. VII. A.D. 1460–1469* (Edinburgh: HM General Register House, 1884)

Calendar of the Patent Rolls (HMSO, 1901–14)

Calendar of the Close Rolls (London: HMSO, 1949–53)

Campbell, William, ed., *Materials for a History of the Reign of Henry VII*, Volume one (London: Longman & Co., 1873)

Crawford, Anne, ed., *The Household Books of John Howard, Duke of Norfolk, 1462–1471, 1481–1483* (Stroud: Sutton for Richard III & Yorkist History Trust, 1992)

Curry, Anne and Rosemary Horrox, eds, *The Parliament Rolls of Medieval England, 1275–1504: XII Henry VI. 1447–1460* (London: The Boydell Press, 2012)

Davies, John Sylvester, ed., *An English Chronicle of the Reigns of Richard II, Henry IV, Henry V, and Henry VI, written before the Year 1471* (London: Camden Society, 1856)

Davies, Robert, ed., *Extracts from the Municipal Records of the City of York during the Reigns of Edward IV. Edward V. And Richard III* (London: J.B. Nichols & Son, 1843)

Davis, Norman, ed., *Paston Letters and Papers of the Fifteenth Century*, Part 1, The Early English Text Society (Oxford: Oxford University Press, 2004)

Dormer, Mary, ed., *The Coventry Leet Book, or, Mayor's Register, Containing the Records of the City Court Leet or View of Frankpledge, A.D. 1420–1555, with Divers Other Matters* (Oxford: Oxford University Press, 1907–13)

Dupont, L.M.E., ed., *Anchiennes Cronicques d'Engleterre par Jehan de Wavrin*, Volume 3 (Paris: Libraire de la Société de L'Histoire de France, 1873)

Ellis, Henry, ed., *Original Letters Illustrative of English History; Including Numerous Royal Letters From Autographs in the British Museum, And One or Two Other Collections*, Volume I, second series (London: Printed for Harding and Lepard, 1827)

Ellis, Henry, ed., *Original Letters Illustrative of English History; Including Numerous Royal Letters From Autographs in the British Museum, And One or Two Other Collections*, Volume I, second edition (London: Printed for Harding, Triphook, and Lepard, 1825)

Ellis, Henry, ed., *The Chronicle of Iohn Hardyng* (London: Printed for F.C. and J. Rivington etc., 1812)

Ellis, Henry, ed., *The New Chronicles of England and France* (London: Printed for F.C. and J. Rivington etc., 1811)

Ellis, Henry, ed., *Three Books of Polydore Vergil's English History, Comprising the Reigns of Henry VI., Edward IV., and Richard III.* (London: Printed for the Camden Society, 1844)

Flenley, Ralph, ed., *Six Town Chronicles of England* (Oxford: At the Clarendon Press, 1911)

Gairdner, James, ed., *The Historical Collections of a Citizen of London in the Fifteenth Century* (London: Printed for the Camden Society, 1876)

Gairdner, James, ed., *The Paston Letters A.D. 1422–1509*, Volume I (London: 1872)

Gairdner, James, ed., *The Paston Letters A.D. 1422–1509*, Volume III (London: Chatto & Windus, 1904)

Gairdner, James, ed., *The Paston Letters A.D. 1422–1509*, Volume IV (London: Chatto & Windus, 1904)

Gairdner, James, ed., *The Paston Letters A.D. 1422–1509*, Volume V (London: Chatto & Windus, 1904)

Gairdner, James, ed., *The Paston Letters A.D. 1422–1509*, Volume VI (London: Chatto & Windus, 1904)

Gairdner, James, ed., *Three Fifteenth Century Chronicles* (London: Printed for the Camden Society, 1880)

Giles, J.A., ed., *The Chronicles of the White Rose of York* (London: James Bohn, 1845)

Halliwell, James Orchard, ed., *A Chronicle of the First Thirteenth Years of the Reign of King Edward the Fourth, by John Warkworth, D.D. Master of the St Peter's College, Cambridge* (London: Camden Society, 1839)

Halliwell, James Orchard, ed., *Letters of the Kings of England*, Volume I (London: Henry Colburn, 1848)

Hanham, Alison, ed., *John Benet's Chronicle, 1399–1462: An English Translation with New Introduction* (Basingstoke: Palgrave Macmillan, 2016)

Hardy, William, ed., *Recueil des Croniques et Anchiennes Istories de la Grant Bretaigne, a Present Nomme Engleterre Par Jehan de Waurin*, Volume V (London: Printed for Her Majesty's Stationery Office, 1891)

Harvey, John H., ed., *William Worcestre Itineraries: Edited from the Unique MS. Corpus Christi College Cambridge, 210* (Oxford: At the Clarendon Press, 1969)

Hay, Denys, ed., *The Anglica Historia of Polydore Vergil, A.D. 1485–1537* (London: Offices of the Royal Historical Society, 1950)

Hearne, Thomas, ed., *Joannis Lelandi Antiquarii de rebus Britannicis Collectanea*, Volume four (London: Ben White, 1774)

Hinds., Allen B., ed., *Calendar of State Papers and Manuscripts, Existing in the Archives and Collections of Milan. Vol I* (London: HMSO, 1912)

Horrox, Rosemary, ed., *The Parliament Rolls of Medieval England 1275–1504, volume XIII, Edward IV 1461–1470* (London: The Boydell Press, 2005)

Horrox, Rosemary, ed., *The Parliament Rolls of Medieval England 1275–1504, volume XIV, Edward IV 1472–1483* (London: The Boydell Press, 2005)

Horrox, Rosemary, and P.W. Hammond, eds, *British Library Harleian Manuscript 433. Vol. 1, Register of Grants for the Reigns of Edward V and Richard III* (Gloucester: A. Sutton for the Richard III Society, 1979)

Kingsford, Charles Lethbridge, ed., *Chronicles of London* (Oxford: At the Clarendon Press, 1905)

Kingsford, Charles Lethbridge, ed., *English Historical Literature in the Fifteenth Century* (New York: Burt Franklin, 1913)

Knighton, C.S., ed., *Calendar of Inquisitions Miscellaneous Preserved in the Public Record Office, Volume VIII, 1422–1485* (Woodbridge: Boydell, 2003)

Lesley, John, *The History of Scotland, From the Death of King James I* (Edinburgh: Bannatyne Club, 1830)

Lyte, H.C. Maxwell, ed., *Calendar of Charter Rolls*, Volume six (London: HMSO, 1927)

Nichols, John Gough, ed., *Chronicle of the Rebellion in Lincolnshire, 1470* (Printed for the Camden Society, 1847)

Nicolas, Harris, ed., *Proceedings and Ordinances of the Privy Council of England*, Volume six (London: Record Commission, 1837)

Poulson, George, ed., *Beverlac; or the Antiquities and History of the Town of Beverley, in the County of York, and of the Provostry and Collegiate Establishment of St. John's; with a Minute Description of the Present Minster and the Church of St. Mary*, Volume one (Beverley: Printed for George Scaum, 1829)

Pronay, Nicholas, and John Cox, eds, *The Crowland Chronicle Continuations: 1459–1486* (London: Alan Sutton Publishing for Richard III and Yorkist History Trust, 1986)

Raine, Angelo, ed., *York Civic Records*, Volume one (Wakefield: Printed for the Society, 1939)

Raine, James, ed., *The Priory of Hexham*, Volume one (Durham: Andrews, 1864)

Rees, William, ed., *Calendar of Ancient Petitions relating to Wales* (Cardiff: University of Wales Press, 1975)

Riley, H.T., ed., *Registra Quorundam Abbatum Monasterii S. Albani, Qui Sæculo XVmo. Floruere. Vol I. Registrum Abbatiae Johannis Whethamstede, Abbatis Monasterii Sancti Albani, Iterum Susceptae; Robert Blakeney, Capellano, Quondam Adscriptum* (London: Longman & Co., 1872)

Smith, J.J., ed., *Abbreviata Cronica 1377–1469* (Cambridge: Publications of the Cambridge Antiquarian Soc., I, 1840)

Smith, Lucy Toulmin, ed., *The Itinerary of John Leland in or about the Years 1535–1543 Parts I to III* (London: George Bell and Sons, 1907)

Smith, Lucy Toulmin, ed., *The Maire of Bristowe is Kalendar* (London: Printed for the Camden Society, 1972)

Stapleton, Thomas, ed., *Plumpton Correspondence* (London: Printed for the Camden Society, 1839)

Stevenson, Joseph, ed., *Letters and Papers Illustrative of the Wars of the English in France during the Reign of Henry the Sixth, King of England, volume 2, part 2* (London: Longman, Green, Longman, and Roberts, 1864)

The Manuscripts of Shrewsbury and Coventry Corporations, Historical Manuscript Commission Fifteenth Report, Appendix, Part X (London: Printed for HMSO, by Eyre and Spottiswoode, 1899)

Thomas, A.H., and I.D. Thornley, eds, *The Great Chronicle of London* (London: Alan Sutton, 1983)

Thomson, Thomas, ed., *The Auchinleck Chronicle* (Edinburgh: Printed for Private Circulation, 1819)

Veale, E.W.W. ed., *The Great Red Book of Bristol*, Volume 1 (Bristol: Bristol Record Society, 1933)

Secondary Sources

Allmand, C.T., *Henry V* (New Haven: Yale University Press, 1997)

Armstrong, C.A.J., 'Politics and the Battle of St. Albans, 1455', *Historical Research*, 33:87 (1960), pp. 1–72

Barron, Caroline M., 'London and the Crown 1451–61', in *The Crown and Local Communities in England and France in the Fifteenth Century*, ed. by J.R.L. Highfield (Gloucester: Alan Sutton, 1981), pp. 88–109

Bellamy, J.G., *The Law of Treason in England in the Later Middle Ages* (Cambridge: Cambridge University Press, 1970)

Brown, A.L., *The Governance of Late Medieval England 1272–1461* (London: Edward Arnold, 1989)

Chrimes, S.B., *Henry VII* (London: Yale University Press, 1999)

Chrimes, S.B., 'Some Letters of John of Lancaster as Warden of the East Marches Towards Scotland', *Speculum*, 14 (1939), pp. 3–27

Colvin, H.M., *The History of the King's Works*, Volume 1 (London: HMSO, 1963)

Colvin, H.M., *The History of the King's Works*, Volume 2 (London: HMSO, 1963)

Creighton, O.H., *Castles and Landscapes: Power, Community and Fortification in Medieval England* (London: Equinox Publishing Ltd, 2002)

Davies, R.R., *The Age of Conquest Wales 1063–1415* (Oxford: Oxford University Press, 1991)

Dockray, K.R., 'The Yorkshire Rebellions of 1469', *The Ricardian*, 6 (1983), pp. 246–57

Emery, Anthony, *Greater Medieval Houses of England and Wales, 1300–1500, Volume I: Northern England* (Cambridge: Cambridge University Press, 1996)

Emery, Anthony, 'The Development of Raglan Castle and Keeps in Late Medieval England', *Archaeological Journal*, 132 (1975), pp. 151–86

Goodall, John, *Ashby de la Zouch Castle and Kirby Muxloe Castle* (London: English Heritage, 2011)

Goodall, John, *The English Castle, 1066–1650* (New Haven: Yale University Press, 2011)

Goodman, Anthony, *The Wars of the Roses* (London: Routledge & Kegan Paul, 1991)

Gransden, Antonia, *Historical Writing in England. Volume 2, c. 1307 to the Early Sixteenth Century* (London: Routledge & Kegan Paul, 1982)

Griffiths, R.A., 'Local Rivalries and National Politics: The Percies, the Nevilles, and the Duke of Exeter, 1452–55', *Speculum*, 43 (1968), pp. 589–632

Griffiths, R.A., *Sir Rhys ap Thomas and his Family: A Study in the Wars of the Roses and Early Tudor Politics* (Cardiff: University of Wales Press, 1993)

Griffiths, R.A., *The Reign of Henry VI* (Stroud: Sutton Publishing Ltd, 2004)

Griffiths, R.A., *The Reign of King Henry VI: The Exercise of Royal Authority, 1422–1461* (London: Benn, 1981)

Grummitt, David, *The Calais Garrison: War and Military Service in England, 1436–1558* (Woodbridge: Boydell Press, 2008)

Harriss, G.L., 'The Struggle for Calais: An Aspect of the Rivalry between Lancaster and York', *The English Historical Review*, 75 (1960), pp. 30–53

Harvey, P.D.A., *Manorial Records* (London: British Records Association, 1999)

Hicks, Michael, 'A Minute of the Lancastrian Council at York, 20 January 1461', *Northern History* (1999), pp. 214–21

Hicks, Michael, *False, False, Fleeting, Perjur'd Clarence: George, Duke of Clarence, 1449–78* (Gloucester: Alan Sutton, 1980)

Hicks, Michael, *Richard III. The Self-Made King* (London: Yale University Press, 2019)

Hicks, Michael, *The Wars of the Roses* (London: Yale University Press, 2012)

Hicks, Michael, *Warwick the Kingmaker* (Oxford: Blackwell Publisher Ltd, 1998)

Holland, P., 'The Lincolnshire Rebellion of March 1470', *The English Historical Review*, 103 (1988), pp. 849–69

Hutchinson, Michael, 'Edward IV's Bulwark: Excavations at Tower Hill, London, 1985', *Transactions of the London and Middlesex Archaeological Society*, 47 (1996), pp. 103–44

Kendall, Paul Murray, *Louis XI. 'The Universal Spider'* (London: Allen & Unwin, 1971)

Kenyon, John R., *Kidwelly Castle* (Cardiff: Cadw, 2017)

Kenyon, John R., *Raglan Castle* (Cardiff: Cadw, 2003)

Kleineke, Hannes, 'Gerhard von Wesel's Newsletter from England, 17 April 1471', *The Ricardian*, 16 (2006), pp. 66–83

Kleineke, Hannes, 'Robert Bale's Chronicle and the Second Battle of St. Albans', *Historical Research*, 87 (2014), pp. 744–50

Laws, E., 'Notes on the Fortifications of Mediaeval Tenby', *Archaeologia Cambrensis*, 51 (1896), pp. 177–92

Laynesmith, J.L., *Cecily Duchess of York* (London: Bloomsbury Academic, 2017)

Lyte, H.C. Maxwell, *A History of Dunster and of the Families of Mohun & Luttrell* (London: The St Catherine Press Ltd, 1909)

McCarthy, Michael R., *Carlisle Castle: A Survey and Documentary History* (London: English Heritage, 1990)

Moore, John S., 'Anglo-Norman Garrisons', *Anglo-Norman Studies*, 22 (1999), pp. 205–59

Morris, Richard K., *Kenilworth Castle* (London: English Heritage, 2012)

Oswald, Alastair, and Jeremy Ashbee, *Dunstanburgh Castle* (London: English Heritage, 2016)

Painter, Sidney, 'Castle-Guard', *The American Historical Review*, 40 (1935), pp. 450–9

Perceval, Charles Spencer, 'Notes on a Selection of Ancient Charters, Letters, and Other Documents from the Muniment Room of Sir John Lawson, of Brough Hall, near Catterick, in Richmondshire, Baronet', *Archaeologia*, 47 (1882), pp. 179–204

Phillips, Seymour, *Edward II* (London: Yale University Press, 2011)

Pinkerton, John, *The History of Scotland from the Accession of the House of Stuart to that of Mary*, Volume one (London: Printed for C. Dilly, in the Poultry, 1797)

Pollard, A.J., *North-eastern England during the Wars of the Roses* (Oxford: Clarendon Press, 1990)

Pounds, N.J.G., *The Medieval Castle in England and Wales: A Social and Political History* (Cambridge: Cambridge University Press, 1990)

Prestwich, Michael, *Edward I* (London: Yale University Press, 1997)

Pugh, T.B., 'Richard, Duke of York, and the Rebellion of Henry Holand, Duke of Exeter, in May 1454', *Historical Research*, 63 (1990), pp. 248–62

Pugh, T.B., 'The magnates, knights and gentry', in *Fifteenth-century England, 1399–1509*, ed. S.B. Chrimes, C.D. Ross and R.A. Griffiths (Manchester: Manchester University Press, 1972), pp. 86–128

Pugh, T.B., *The Marcher Lordships of South Wales, 1415–1536* (Cardiff: University of Wales Press, 1963)

Radford, G.H., 'The Fight at Clyst in 1455', *Report and Transactions for the Devonshire Association*, 44 (1912), pp. 252–7

Richmond, C.F., 'English Naval Power in the Fifteenth Century', *History*, 52 (1967), pp. 1–15

Ross, Charles, *Edward IV* (London: Eyre Methuen, 1974)

Ross, Charles, *Richard III* (London: Yale University Press, 1999)

Ross, James, *John de Vere, Thirteenth Earl of Oxford (1442–1513): 'The Foremost Man of the Kingdom'* (Woodbridge: Boydell, 2011)

Santiuste, David, *Edward IV and the Wars of the Roses* (Barnsley: Pen & Sword Military, 2010)

Scofield, Cora L., *The Life and Reign of Edward the Fourth: King of England and of France and Lord of Ireland*, Volume one (Stroud: Fonthill Media Ltd, 2016)

Scofield, Cora L., *The Life and Reign of Edward the Fourth: King of England and of France and Lord of Ireland*, Volume two (London: Longmans, Green, 1923)

Sharpe, Reginald R., *London and the Kingdom*, Volume one (London: Longmans & Co., 1894)

Sharpe, Reginald R., *London and the Kingdom*, Volume three (London: Longmans, Green & Co., 1895), pp. 386–7

Spencer, Dan, *Royal and Urban Gunpowder Weapons in Late Medieval England* (Woodbridge: Boydell & Brewer, 2019)

Spencer, Dan, 'Royal Castles and Coastal Defence in the Late Fourteenth Century', *Nottingham Medieval Studies*, 61 (2017), pp. 147–70

Spencer, Dan, *The Castle at War in Medieval England and Wales* (Stroud: Amberley Publishing, 2018)

Spencer, Dan, 'The Lancastrian Armament Programme of the 1450s and the Development of Field Guns', *The Ricardian*, 25 (2015), pp. 61–70

Storey, R.L., *The End of the House of Lancaster* (Gloucester: Alan Sutton Publishing, 1986)

Storey, R.L., 'The Wardens of the Marches of England towards Scotland, 1377–1489', *The English Historical Review*, 72 (1957), pp. 593–615

Summerson, Henry, *Carlisle Castle* (London: English Heritage, 2017)

Thompson, A.H., 'The Building Accounts of Kirby Muxloe Castle', *Transactions of the Leicestershire Architectural and Archaeological Society*, 11 (1913–20), pp. 193–345

Thompson, M.W., *The Decline of the Castle* (Cambridge: Cambridge University Press, 1987)

Tout, T.F., 'Firearms in England in the Fourteenth Century', *The English Historical Review*, 26 (1911), pp. 666–702

Turner, Rick, *Caerphilly Castle* (Cardiff: Cadw, 2016)

Vaughan, Richard, *Charles the Bold: the Last Valois Duke of Burgundy* (Woodbridge: Boydell Press, 2002)

Virgoe, Roger, 'The Death of William De La Pole, Duke of Suffolk', *Bulletin of the John Rylands Library*, 47 (1965), pp. 489–502

Watson, Bruce, 'Medieval London Bridge and its Role in the Defence of the Realm', *Transactions of the London and Middlesex Archaeological Society*, 50 (1999), pp. 17–22

Welch, Charles, *History of the Tower Bridge* (London: Smith, Elder and Co., 1894)

Whitaker, T.D., *The History and Antiquities of the Deanery of Craven in the County of York* (London: J. Nichols and Son, 1812)

Williams, C.H., 'The Rebellion of Humphrey Stafford in 1486', *The English Historical Review*, 43 (1928), pp. 181–9

Williams, David, *The History of Monmouthshire* (London: Printed by H. Baldwin, 1746)

Williams, John, *Ancient and Modern Denbigh: A Descriptive History of the Castle, Borough, and Liberties* (Denbigh: Printed and Published by J. Williams, Vale Street, 1856)

Woolgar, C.M., *The Great Household in Late Medieval England* (London: Yale University Press, 1999)

Young, Christopher, *Carisbrooke Castle* (London: English Heritage, 2013)

Unpublished Theses

Herbert, A., 'Public Order and Private Violence in Herefordshire, 1413–61' (Unpublished MA thesis, University of Swansea, 1978)

Kent, G.H.R., 'The Estates of the Herbert Family in the Mid-Fifteenth Century' (Unpublished doctoral thesis, Keele University, 1973)

Stansfield, Michael M.N., 'The Holland Family, Dukes of Exeter, Earls of Kent and Huntingdon, 1352–1475' (Unpublished DPhil thesis, University of Oxford, 1987)

Electronic Resources

Bennett, Michael J., 'Stanley, Sir William (c. 1435–1495)', *Oxford Dictionary of National Biography* [https://doi.org/10.1093/ref:odnb/26282, accessed 20 October 2019]

Bennett, Michael J., 'Stanley, Thomas, first earl of Derby (c. 1433–1504)', *Oxford Dictionary of National Biography* [https://doi.org/10.1093/ref:odnb/26279, accessed 20 October 2019]

Brown, K.M., ed., '1482/3/44', *The Records of the Parliaments of Scotland to 1707*, 1482/3/44, [https://www.rps.ac.uk/search.php?action=fetch_index_frame&fn=jamesiii_trans&id=3689&query=Edward+iv&type=trans&variants=Edward&google=Edward, accessed 11 August 2019]

Castor, Helen, 'Paston, John (I) (1421–1466)', *Oxford Dictionary of National Biography* [http://www.oxforddnb.com/view/article/215 B11io, accessed 24 June 2019]

Castor, Helen, 'Scales, Thomas, seventh Baron Scales (1399?–1460)', *Oxford Dictionary of National Biography* [https://doi.org/10.1093/ref:odnb/24776, accessed 20 October 2019]

Cherry, Martin, 'Bonville, William, first Baron Bonville (1392–1461)', *Oxford Dictionary of National Biography* [https://doi.org/10.1093/ref:odnb/50217, accessed 20 October 2019]

Cherry, Martin, 'Courtenay, Thomas, thirteenth earl of Devon (1414–1458)', *Oxford Dictionary of National Biography* [https://doi.org/10.1093/ref:odnb/50218, accessed 20 October 2019]

Clark, Linda, 'Bourchier, Henry, first earl of Essex (*c.* 1408–1483)', *Oxford Dictionary of National Biography* [https://doi.org/10.1093/ref:odnb/2987, accessed 20 October 2019]

Crawford, Anne, 'Howard, John, first duke of Norfolk (d. 1485)', *Oxford Dictionary of National Biography* [https://doi.org/10.1093/ref:odnb/13921, accessed 20 October 2019]

Curry, Anne, 'Montagu, Thomas [Thomas de Montacute], fourth earl of Salisbury (1388–1428)', *Oxford Dictionary of National Biography* [https://doi.org/10.1093/ref:odnb/18999, accessed 27 December 2018]

Davies, C.S.L., 'Stafford, Henry, second duke of Buckingham (1455–1483)', *Oxford Dictionary of National Biography* [https://doi.org/10.1093/ref:odnb/26204, accessed 20 October 2019]

Dockray, Keith, 'Lumley, George, third Baron Lumley (d. 1507)', *Oxford Dictionary of National Biography* [https://doi.org/10.1093/ref:odnb/17175, accessed 16 May 2019]

Dunn, Diana E.S., 'Margaret [Margaret of Anjou] (1415–1461)', *Oxford Dictionary of National Biography* [https://doi.org/10.1093/ref:odnb/19454, accessed 20 October 2019]

Ellis, Steven G., 'Percy, Henry, fourth earl of Northumberland (*c.* 1449–1489)', *Oxford Dictionary of National Biography* [https://doi.org/10.1093/ref:odnb/21935, accessed 20 October 2019]

Griffiths, R.A., 'Devereux, Walter, first Baron Ferrers of Chartley (*c.* 1432–1485)', *Oxford Dictionary of National Biography* [https://doi.org/10.1093/ref:odnb/50222, accessed 20 October 2019]

Griffiths, R.A., 'Edward [Edward of Westminster], prince of Wales (1453–1471)', *Oxford Dictionary of National Biography* [https://doi.org/10.1093/ref:odnb/8524, accessed 20 October 2019]

Griffiths, R.A., 'Henry VI (1421–1471)', *Oxford Dictionary of National Biography* [https://doi.org/10.1093/ref:odnb/12953, accessed 20 October 2019]

Griffiths, R.A., 'Herbert, William, first earl of Pembroke (*c.* 1423–1469)', *Oxford Dictionary of National Biography* [https://doi.org/10.1093/ref:odnb/13053, accessed 20 October 2019]

Griffiths, R.A., 'Percy, Henry, second earl of Northumberland (1394–1455)', *Oxford Dictionary of National Biography* [http://www.oxforddnb.com/view/article/183, accessed 20 October 2019]

Griffiths, R.A., 'Percy, Henry, third earl of Northumberland (1421–1461)', *Oxford Dictionary of National Biography* [https://doi.org/10.1093/ref:odnb/21934, accessed 20 October 2019]

Griffiths, R.A., 'Percy, Thomas, first Baron Egremont (1422–1460)', *Oxford Dictionary of National Biography* [https://doi.org/10.1093/ref:odnb/50235, accessed 20 October 2019]

Griffiths, R.A., 'Tudor, Owen [Owain ap Maredudd ap Tudur] (*c.* 1400–1461)', *Oxford Dictionary of National Biography* [https://doi.org/10.1093/ref:odnb/27797, accessed 20 October 2019]

Griffiths, R.A., 'Vaughan family (per. *c.* 1400–*c.* 1504)', *Oxford Dictionary of National Biography* [https://doi.org/10.1093/ref:odnb/48656, accessed 20 October 2019]

Gunn, S.J., 'Henry VII (1457–1509)', *Oxford Dictionary of National Biography* [https://doi.org/10.1093/ref:odnb/12954, accessed 20 October 2019]

Gunn, S.J., 'Vere, John de, thirteenth earl of Oxford (1442–1513)', *Oxford Dictionary of National Biography* [https://doi.org/10.1093/ref:odnb/28214, accessed 31 July 2019]

Hammond, P.W., 'Percy, Sir Ralph (1425–1464)', *Oxford Dictionary of National Biography* [https://doi.org/10.1093/ref:odnb/21951, accessed 20 October 2019]

Harper-Bill, Christopher, 'Cecily [Cicely] [née Cecily Neville], duchess of York (1415–1495)', *Oxford Dictionary of National Biography* [https://doi.org/10.1093/ref:odnb/50231, accessed 20 October 2019]

Harriss, G.L., 'Fastolf, Sir John (1380–1459)', *Oxford Dictionary of National Biography* [https://doi.org/10.1093/ref:odnb/9199, accessed 20 October 2019]

Harvey, I.M.W., 'Cade, John [Jack] [alias John Mortimer; called the Captain of Kent] (d. 1450)', *Oxford Dictionary of National Biography* [https://doi.org/10.1093/ref:odnb/4292, accessed 20 October 2019]

Hicks, Michael, 'Elizabeth [née Elizabeth Woodville] (*c.* 1437–1492)', *Oxford Dictionary of National Biography* [https://doi.org/10.1093/ref:odnb/8634, accessed 20 October 2019]

Hicks, Michael, 'George, duke of Clarence (1449–1478)', *Oxford Dictionary of National Biography* [https://doi.org/10.1093/ref:odnb/10542, accessed 20 October 2019]

Hicks, Michael, 'Holland, Henry, second duke of Exeter (1430–1475)', *Oxford Dictionary of National Biography* [https://doi.org/10.1093/ref:odnb/50223, accessed 20 October 2019]

Hicks, Michael, 'Hungerford, Robert, third Baron Hungerford and Baron Moleyns (*c.* 1423–1464)', *Oxford Dictionary of National Biography* [https://doi.org/10.1093/ref:odnb/14178, accessed 20 October 2019]

Hicks, Michael, 'Neville [Fauconberg], Thomas [called the Bastard of Fauconberg] (d. 1471)', *Oxford Dictionary of National Biography* [https://doi.org/10.1093/ref:odnb/9201, accessed 20 October 2019]

Hicks, Michael, 'Neville, George (1432–1476)', *Oxford Dictionary of National Biography* [https://doi.org/10.1093/ref:odnb/19934, accessed 20 October 2019]

Hicks, Michael, 'Stafford, Humphrey, earl of Devon (*c.* 1439–1469)', *Oxford Dictionary of National Biography* [https://doi.org/10.1093/ref:odnb/26208, accessed 20 October 2019]

Hicks, Michael, 'Woodville [Wydeville], Anthony, second Earl Rivers (*c.* 1440–1483)', *Oxford Dictionary of National Biography* [https://doi.org/10.1093/ref:odnb/29937, accessed 20 October 2019]

Hicks, Michael, 'Woodville [Wydeville], Richard, first Earl Rivers (d. 1469)', *Oxford Dictionary of National Biography* [https://doi.org/10.1093/ref:odnb/29939, accessed 20 October 2019]

Horrox, Rosemary, 'Conyers Family (per. *c.* 1375–*c.* 1525)', *Oxford Dictionary of National Biography* [https://doi.org/10.1093/ref:odnb/52783, accessed 24 June 2019]

Horrox, Rosemary, 'Edward IV (1442–1483)', *Oxford Dictionary of National Biography* [https://doi.org/10.1093/ref:odnb/8520, accessed 20 October 2019]

Horrox, Rosemary, 'Grey, Edmund, first earl of Kent (1416–1490)', *Oxford Dictionary of National Biography* https://doi.org/10.1093/ref:odnb/11529, accessed 20 October 2019]

Horrox, Rosemary, 'Harrington Family (per. *c.* 1300–1512)', *Oxford Dictionary of National Biography* [https://doi.org/10.1093/ref:odnb/54525, accessed 20 October 2019]

Horrox, Rosemary, 'Hastings, William, first Baron Hastings (*c.* 1430–1483)', *Oxford Dictionary of National Biography* [https://doi.org/10.1093/ref:odnb/12588, accessed 20 October 2019]

Horrox, Rosemary, 'Neville, John, Marquess Montagu (*c.* 1431–1471)', *Oxford Dictionary of National Biography* [https://doi.org/10.1093/ref:odnb/19946, accessed 20 October 2019]

Horrox, Rosemary, 'Richard III (1452–1485)', *Oxford Dictionary of National Biography* [https://doi.org/10.1093/ref:odnb/23500, accessed 20 October 2019]

Jones, Michael K., 'Beaufort, Edmund, styled third duke of Somerset', *Oxford Dictionary of National Biography* [https://doi.org/10.1093/ref:odnb/1856, accessed 20 October 2019]

Jones, Michael K., 'Beaufort, Henry, second duke of Somerset (1436–1464)', *Oxford Dictionary of National Biography* [https://doi.org/10.1093/ref:odnb/1860, accessed 20 October 2019]

Kohl, Benjamin G., 'Tiptoft [Tibetot], John, first earl of Worcester (1427–1470)', *Oxford Dictionary of National Biography* [https://doi.org/10.1093/ref:odnb/27471, accessed 20 October 2019]

Lewis, Barry, ed., *Guto'r Glyn.net*, no. 21, 'In praise of William Herbert of Raglan, first earl of Pembroke, after the capture of Harlech castle, 1468' [http://www.gutorglyn.net/gutorglyn/poem/?poem-selection=021&first-line=022, accessed 14 December 2019]

Macdougall, Norman, 'James III (1452–1488)', *Oxford Dictionary of National Biography* [https://doi.org/10.1093/ref:odnb/14589, accessed 20 October 2019]

Phillips, J.R.S., 'Edward II [Edward of Caernarfon] (1284–1327)', *Oxford Dictionary of National Biography* [https://doi.org/10.1093/ref:odnb/8518, accessed 27 December 2018]

Pollard, A.J., 'Neville, Ralph, second earl of Westmorland (b. in or before 1407, d. 1484)', *Oxford Dictionary of National Biography* [https://doi.org/10.1093/ref:odnb/19952/, accessed 20 October 2019]

Pollard, A.J., 'Neville, Richard, fifth earl of Salisbury (1400–1460)', *Oxford Dictionary of National Biography* [https://doi.org/10.1093/ref:odnb/19954/, accessed 20 October 2019]

Pollard, A.J., 'Neville, Richard, sixteenth earl of Warwick and sixth earl of Salisbury [called the Kingmaker] (1428–1471)', *Oxford Dictionary of National Biography* [https://doi.org/10.1093/ref:odnb/19955/, accessed 20 October 2019]

Pollard, A.J., 'Neville, Sir Humphrey (*c.* 1439–1469)', *Oxford Dictionary of National Biography* [https://doi.org/10.1093/ref:odnb/19944, accessed 20 October 2019]

Rawcliffe, Carole, 'Stafford, Humphrey, first duke of Buckingham (1402–1460)', *Oxford Dictionary of National Biography* [https://doi.org/10.1093/ref:odnb/26207, accessed 20 October 2019]

Reeves, A.C., 'Cromwell, Ralph, third Baron Cromwell (1393?–1456)', *Oxford Dictionary of National Biography* [https://doi.org/10.1093/ref:odnb/6767, accessed 20 October 2019]

Richmond, Colin, 'Beaufort, Edmund, first duke of Somerset (c. 1406–1455)', *Oxford Dictionary of National Biography* [https://doi.org/10.1093/ref:odnb/1855, accessed 20 October 2019]

Richmond, Colin, 'Mowbray, John, third duke of Norfolk (1415–1461)', *Oxford Dictionary of National Biography* [https://doi.org/10.1093/ref:odnb/19454, accessed 20 October 2019]

Richmond, Colin, 'Mowbray, John, fourth duke of Norfolk (1444–1476)', *Oxford Dictionary of National Biography* [https://doi.org/10.1093/ref:odnb/19455, accessed 20 October 2019]

Richmond, Colin, 'Paston Family (per. *c.* 1420–1504)', *Oxford Dictionary of National Biography* [http://www.oxforddnb.com/view/article/52791, accessed 24 June 2019]

Summerson, Henry, 'Clifford, John, ninth Baron Clifford (1435–1461)', *Oxford Dictionary of National Biography* [https://doi.org/10.1093/ref:odnb/5654, accessed 20 October 2019]

Summerson, Henry, 'Clifford, Thomas, eighth Baron Clifford (1414–1455)', *Oxford Dictionary of National Biography* [https://doi.org/10.1093/ref:odnb/5663, accessed 20 October 2019]

Thomas, R.S., 'Tudor, Edmund [Edmund of Hadham], first earl of Richmond (*c.* 1430–1456)', *Oxford Dictionary of National Biography* [https://doi.org/10.1093/ref:odnb/27795, accessed 20 October 2019]

Thomas, R.S., 'Tudor, Jasper [Jasper of Hatfield], duke of Bedford (*c.* 1431–1495)', *Oxford Dictionary of National Biography* [https://doi.org/10.1093/ref:odnb/27796, accessed 20 October 2019]

Tuck, Anthony, 'Neville, Ralph, first earl of Westmorland (*c.* 1364–1425)', *Oxford Dictionary of National Biography* [www.oxforddnb.com/view/10.1093/, accessed 6 December 2018]

Virgoe, Roger, 'Tailboys, Sir William (*c.* 1416–1464)', *Oxford Dictionary of National Biography* [https://doi.org/10.1093/ref:odnb/26949, accessed 20 October 2019]

Visser-Fuchs, Livia, 'Brugge, Lodewijk van [Louis de Bruges; Lodewijk van Gruuthuse], earl of Winchester (*c.* 1427–1492)', *Oxford Dictionary of National Biography* [https://doi.org/10.1093/ref:odnb/92540, accessed 5 August 2019]

Watts, John, 'Butler, James, first earl of Wiltshire and fifth earl of Ormond (1420–1461)', *Oxford Dictionary of National Biography* [https://doi.org/10.1093/ref:odnb/4188, accessed 20 October 2019]

Watts, John, 'Pole, William de la, first duke of Suffolk (1396–1450)', *Oxford Dictionary of National Biography* [https://doi.org/10.1093/ref:odnb/22461, accessed 20 October 2019]

Watts, John, 'Richard of York, third duke of York (1411–1460)', *Oxford Dictionary of National Biography* [https://doi.org/10.1093/ref:odnb/23503, accessed 20 October 2019]

Index